# Vedic Tradition
and
# World Religions

Ramakrishnan Srinivasan

Sri Sri Publications Trust

Vedic Tradition and World Religions
Author: Ramakrishnan Srinivasan

1st Edition March 2016
Copyrights Sri Sri Publications Trust, 2016

**Published by:**

Sri Sri Publications Trust
Art of Living International Centre,
21st KM, Kanakapura Road, Udaypura, Bangalore – 560082
Email: info@srisripublications.com

**www.sattvastore.com**
Toll Free 1800-258-8888

© All rights reserved

No part of this book may be reproduced or transmitted in any form or by any means, electronic or mechanical, including photocopying, recording, or any information storage or retrieval system without prior permission in writing from the publisher

ISBN: 978-93-85254-57-4

Layout by: Sri Sri Publications Trust

Printed in India by: Jwalamukhi Mudranalaya Pvt. Ltd., Bangalore
Ph: +91-80-26601064, 26617243

# CONTENTS

| | | |
|---|---|---|
| 1 | Acknowledgements | v |
| 2 | Introduction | 1 |
| 3 | Hindu Tradition | 7 |
| 4 | Buddhism | 21 |
| 5 | The Egyptians | 37 |
| 6 | The Greeks | 45 |
| 7 | The Hebrews | 67 |
| 8 | Zoroastrianism | 75 |
| 9 | Christianity | 81 |
| 10 | Islam | 89 |
| 11 | Chinese Mythology | 103 |
| 12 | Gnosticism | 113 |
| 13 | Paganism | 115 |
| 14 | Some Religious Systems | 125 |
| 15 | Ethics | 137 |
| 16 | Atheist Spirituality | 147 |
| 17 | Ancient Civilizations | 153 |
| 18 | The Problem of Religions | 169 |
| 19 | Intelligent Design vs Creationism | 183 |
| 20 | Creation Myths | 197 |
| 21 | Destruction of Libraries | 201 |
| 22 | Great Discoveries in Archaeology | 211 |
| 23 | Afterword | 225 |

This book is dedicated
to the memory of
Late Arutchelvar Sri N. Mahalingam

# ACKNOWLEDGEMENTS

The research for this work took me more than 3 years and when it was finally completed and entered in the computer, it needed to be studied and corrected by a professor who was also familiar with the subject. My niece, Professor Sita Ramanathan was my natural choice and when I approached her in Pondicherry, she readily accepted my request. She has taken so much time and effort to complete the task that I must express my gratitude to her wholeheartedly. Being a professor of English, she was very valuable in this regard. My profuse thanks go to her.

The next person to be thanked in this regard is my son Srinivasan, who took the trouble of dropping me in the county library every day and picking me up in the evenings the whole of six months that I spent in Virginia for this research.

The most important person I am very much indebted to is the late Arutchelvar Sri N. Mahalingam. After endorsing my earlier research work *Ancient India* for which he had given a lot of research material and discussed the contents from time to time, he asked me what my next book would be about. He then suggested writing on comparative religion for which he offered to buy me air tickets to Europe if required. I said I was going to the US and would do the research there. But before I could show him the final manuscript he passed away suddenly leaving a huge void that cannot be easily filled. My gratitude to him is immeasurable. I dedicate this book to his memory.

To many others who encouraged me in my efforts, it would be difficult to name every person as the list is long. To all these professionals I bow my head in grateful thanks.

# CHAPTER 1
# INTRODUCTION

Religions as we know it started coming up during the last 3000 years. Before this, there was mostly nature worship of the sun and Fertility gods. Fertility of the soil depended on the sun and rain and fertility of humans depended on man. This was represented by the phallus symbol or the Linga and this was the oldest object of worship by human beings worldwide. This phallus worship did not have a name as there were no religions at that point of time and hence there was no need for a name. The Hindus were the first to come up with an ethical principle for life generally known as the Sanatana Dharma or the Eternal Tradition. This survives to this day. The word Dharma has a wide connotation that includes virtue, ethical behaviour, truth, righteous living and so on. The Sanskrit word for it is *rta* or cosmic order. Order implies peaceful living and consideration of all living beings as equal and divine. This then is the original religious teaching that prevailed globally. As we now know, Indians settled everywhere in the world in groups to bring this tradition to all in the world. This has been discussed by the author in his book on Ancient India.

It is thus that civilizations developed worldwide. With civilization, the need for a set of values for the communities was felt and this way culture and morality came to be developed. Morality is a culture based system that varies from region to region and area to area and country to country. Culture is based on thousands of years of customs and mores or rituals practiced by the people at different places. But morality is driven by ethical values that are time honoured. The whole gamut of ethical values is covered by the Hindu Text Statement, that defines the Eternal Tradition or *Sanatana Dharma* - *satyam vada, dharmam chara* or speak the truth and walk the path of dharma or righteousness or virtue. Virtue is that which does not trod upon another person while one is acting individually. That is what we mean by the word dharma. In the Rig Veda, the word *rta* is used to denote this. The exact meaning of this word depends on the context in which we use the word. So, our statement embodies a whole spectrum of value systems within which the human being can function effectively. In fact the ethical value systems we find in the *Manavadharmasastra* or *Manusmrti* covers the entire range of ethical behaviour and this has been the basis of Greek philosophy that has been drawn upon by the different religious systems of the world since the first millennium BCE like Judaism, Christianity, Islam, Taoism, Buddhism etc. This is what we aim to analyse in this book.

Religion itself, like morality, is an area-specific or group-specific set of values but religiousness or spirituality is universal. Judaism talks of one god Yahveh, for whom the Jews were the chosen people. Similarly, Christians aver that it is Jesus, the son of the only father, God, who has given the power to them while others are heretics. Islam says the same thing in respect of Allah the only god. Abraham is cited as the source for all the three religions. It is apparent that all of them cannot be right at the same time. If they agree that there is only one god, it stands to reason that this god could be partial to one group only. All the three gods should be the same. All are the children of one god only and hence it would appear to the rational seeker that this god is the same to all beings without exception and consequently the need for separate religions would seem to be irrational. Many thinkers and philosophers including scientists have studied this aspect though they have given different interpretations to it. Many have studied the nature of consciousness but not the fundamental nature of religions and their exclusivity to specific groups of people. Richard Dawkins has studied this matter in detail and concluded that there is no god and argued forcefully in favour of atheism in his book *God Delusion*. But his approach borders on the fanatical, making atheism another religion. Only great scientists and philosophers like Huxley and Bertrand Russell have preferred agnosticism instead that neither believes nor disbelieves. The word was probably coined by Thomas Huxley but it essentially means that the existence or non-existence of god is immaterial to our lives.

Be that as it may, we have studied these specific issues by analyzing the basic tenets of the major religions and how they have come upon those tenets and tried to compare their systems to find a common denominator or source for them. This study has involved delving into ancient texts in different languages in a historical perspective as also review of different contemporary books on the subject of individual religions. It is necessary to note here, however, that the aim of this study is not against any religion or belief system and the author believes firmly that, religions with their temple worship and rituals do have an important place in the spiritual growth of man. This spiritual development needs to be adopted in three stages as per the Hindu way of life (it is not a religion):

a. The first stage is the religious practice of going to places of worship, rituals, prayers, and so on that helps to condition the mind towards a spiritual outlook. This can be attained by also listening to discourses on the subject and understanding

## Introduction

ourselves. (The Abrahamic religions mentioned above have this idea of 'know thyself' or knowing the essential nature of all living beings).

b. The second stage is in the process of analysis of the understanding derived from the first stage on the essential divinity of all beings and reinforcing our thinking on the same. This stage occurs when we outgrow the first stage.

c. The third stage is the religious praxis or contemplation of the truth about our individual Self or the source of the 'I' in all of us and realizing the same as experience. This stage is difficult and only very few people manage to achieve this.

If we cross the first two stages we may consider ourselves blessed as we would have become truly religious or spiritual and be free from the narrow shackles of religions. This spirituality should be the aim of all people in the world. This automatically makes us ethical and ethically moral or virtuous and culturally advanced. These three stages are well known in Hindu spiritual texts where they are described as *sravana, manana,* and, *nidhidhyasana.* They mean, respectively, thinking (reading and listening), contemplation and, practice. But the fact remains that most people remain in the first stage and fail to outgrow that stage.

Buddha taught the 'Perfection of Wisdom' at Rajgir, India, along with the 'Heart Sutra'. These were discussed in detail by Avalokiteswara and Shariputra in the presence of Buddha. They were commended by Buddha at the end. Essentially it is the philosophy of no-identity enumerated by Nagarjuna in his Madhyamika philosophy of emptiness. This comes nearest to to the philosophy of Vedanta and there is a real convergence of the two. In Vedanta, we find that Brahman is the Universal energy and all else only a manifestation of this energy. This aspect is expressed in Sanskrit as *brahma satyam, Jagan mitya* or Brahman is the only truth and all else is non-existent. That is why the Bhagavata begins and ends with the statement *Satyam param dheemihi* or The Truth (of Brahman) is the subject of supreme contemplation. This means that only Brahman is real and all else is an appearance only. Similarly, the philosophy of no-identity or *sunyavada* also suggests the one reality and all else as emptiness without existing in reality. While Vedanta is much clearer, the latter lends itself to many interpretations and hence may confound the layman.

It is a fact that Buddha was a Hindu Kshatriya, taught by learned Brahmins, and he was clear in his thinking. The pundits taught him Vedanta but his experience with the poor and suffering people made him realize that the Brahminical rituals were at the back of such suffering and it was necessary to reform the society. While these rituals and fire sacrifices may be done by the Brahmins, the common man needs a different approach for his suffering. He then addressed these problems directly by identifying suffering as the main cause and proceeded to build his philosophy. His intentions were not to develop a new religion. His concept of love and compassion naturally followed and since Jesus is said to have spent years in Kashmir learning Indian philosophies, he had borrowed these concepts in his teaching. He also was a reformer and definitely did not want to start a new religion in his name. All these are later developments by the followers of these great teachers. In fact Buddha preferred Pali the common man's Sanskrit for his teachings as he thought this would reach them directly. In all this, one thing is clear; there is nothing great in this human life and having been born, people should aim to be free from the cycle of births. This is the message of Vedanta and consequently the whole purpose of life.

In fact, all religions teach the same principles of non-violence, love, compassion and service to others. Abraham, the Brahmin from Urs, now in Afghanistan, (according to the latest research by Matlock and others), took with him the Vedic teachings of Vedanta when he was hounded out for not following the fire sacrifice of the Brahmins. He took these teachings to Egypt and then to Canaan and taught them to people in the area, who were in the midst of ethnic crises. His followers took him to be a messiah and made his teachings into a dogmatic religion. Thus was born Judaism. The rest, as they say, is history. Even Mohammad never claimed to start a religion. He claimed that he had a series of divine revelations and began teaching them to the turbulent society of that time. Most of the negative value systems like heresy, jihad etc., among some Moslems were later additions by some followers, due to a faulty interpretation of Mohammad's teachings. They all postulate one god but claimed superiority of their gods over that of others. This by itself clearly suggests that none of these were right since there cannot be three powerful 'one god' claimed differently by three different teachers. These arose mainly due to illiteracy and backwardness in their societies as against the advanced Indian civilization. Of course, this point of view will be opposed by many of their followers because each of them would want to impose their religious faith on others with the probable exception of Judaism.

Religions are by themselves divisive and so, unnecessary for human life as has been forcefully argued by Richard Dawkins in his *God Delusion*. But their teachings are relevant as they are basically universal. And so is the concept of god. What humanity needs is an acceptable value system of ethical behaviour with morality conforming to the respective social milieu. Ethics generally leads to moral lives but not necessarily the other way about. The problems faced by the world are economic in nature in which religions have been superimposed. If these religions are absolute as they claim, then why are scores of divisions in each of them? There is absolutely no agreement among them. Everything is a question of interpretation only.

## Introduction

If we take the commonalities in all these religions and establish universal humanist principles applicable to all the peoples of the world, we will have a better world to live in. The number of countries in the world has gone up from about 150, five decades ago to more than two hundred now mainly because of ethnic and religious incompatibilities and religious wars. Sociological and linguistic factors have only added to such divisions. The solution lies in what this author has repeatedly said in his books viz., **keep religions exclusively at the home level and live peacefully outside with all peoples as one family.** Differences would be there but life could be based on a set of common universal values. But this seems to be a dream at present. Materialism and consumerism combined with linguistic chauvinism have contributed to these divisions and they are unlikely to disappear anytime soon. In what follows, we have studied the salient features of different religions of the world for the reader to come to an objective assessment that can hopefully lead to a possible change in the future.

## References:
1. The Vedas- Paramacharya Chandrasekhara Saraswati, Bharatiya Vidya Bhavan.
2. Vedic Tradition- Ramakrishnan Srinivasan, Bharatiya Vidya Bhavan, 2000.
3. Science, Philosophy and Religion- Ramakrishnan Srinivasan, Citadel, Calcutta.
4. The Philosophy of the Upanishads- Paul Deussen, (Translated by Gelden) Oriental Books (reprint).
5. Indian Philosophy- Dr S. Radhakrishnan Vol. I and II, Oxford University Press.
6. Ancient India- Ed. Dr N.Mahalingam, ISIAC

# CHAPTER 2
## THE HINDU TRADITION

There is a general misconception among most Indian and western scholars that Hinduism is a religion but in reality it is only a way of life. It is the oldest ethical tradition in the world going as far back as 10000 BCE or earlier, when there was no religious system and only nature worship followed in most places. That was a time when most of the world was in a primitive stage or barbarism. At that time the great Rishis of India who probably were extra terrestrial, came down from the Tibetan Plateau to civilize or Aryanise the world. They spread their followers to most places in the world with their message of goodwill and the basic principles of ethical life. This became the Eternal Tradition or Sanatana Dharma that apparently was timeless. It stated simply *satyam vada, dharmam chara* as already mentioned. If we look at the inner meaning of this statement it practically covers every aspect of an ethical and moral life. Some of the Rishis of yore had revelations that became the Rig Veda. This Veda had more than hundred thousand hymns that came down to us over the millennia in an uninterrupted oral tradition. In the process, most of the hymns were lost and in the fourth millennium BCE, the sage Vyasa took it upon himself to codify the Rig Veda through four of his disciples and this eventually became the Rig, Yajur (white and black), and Sama Vedas. The Yajur and Sama Vedas contained mostly the hymns of the Rig Veda but were modified for the purpose of ritual sacrifices (Yajur) and musical chanting (Sama). The Atharva Veda was composed later on containing verses on medical, astronomical and other disciplines.

The misconception mentioned above is mainly due to the following:

1. The false theory of Aryan invasion planted by the British to suppress the facts about the ancient Hindus and their civilization. This theory has now been proved to be a hoax by archaeologists and researchers.
2. That Hindu civilization started after 1500 BCE, suggested again by the British though many scholars including Max Muller have retracted their statements later in their lives.
3. The caste system was a product of Hindu religion. In fact there was no caste system at all in ancient times and the scriptures mention the *varnashrama* system that

is based on individual propensities. This classification exists everywhere in the world- teachers, warriors, farmers and traders and lay workmen. This is indeed the system understood in the Hindu tradition- Brahmins, Kshatriyas, Vaisyas and Sudras.

4. That the Upanishads are later than 800 BCE according to the British. Now we know that the major Upanishads are from the last part of the Vedas and are earlier than 3000 BCE.
5. That women cannot be priests or chant the Vedas nor can they achieve immortality according to them. This is quite wrong as many women including wives of Rishis have contributed Vedic Hymns and Upanishadic principles. Maitreyi is an example who also became immortal. Sri Ramana's mother in the last century is another example.

The Vedas as classified by Vyasa have Samhita, Brahmana and Sutra. The Brahmana has Vidhi, Arthavada and Vedanta (Upanishad). Upanishads are attached to the Aranyaka at the end as it is secret knowledge or text only to be imparted to a son or a good pupil. Aranyaka in the Brahmana gives explanations of the rituals and speculations contained in the Brahmana. The Upanishads of the Rig Veda are Aitareya and Kaushitaki; Of the Sama Veda, Chandogya and Kena. The Black Yajur Veda has Taittiriya, Mahanarayana, Kathaka, Svetasvatara, and Maitrayaniya. The White Yajur Veda has Brihadaranyaka and Isa. The Atharva Veda has Mandukya, Jabala, Paingala, and Shavank.

The Upanishads can be classified into five groups- Vedanta, Yoga, Sanyasa, Siva and Vishnu. They are as follows:

1. Vedanta Upanishads: Mundaka, Prasna, Mandukya, Garbha, Pranagnihotra, Pinda, Atma, Sarvopanishadsara, and Garuda.
2. Yoga Upanishads: Brahmavidya, Kshurika, Culika, Nadabindu, Brahmabindu, Amritabindu, Dhyanabindu, Yogatattva and, Hamsa.
3. Sannyasa Upanishads: Brahma, Sannyasa, Aruneya, Kanthasruti, Paramahamsa, Jabala and Asrama.
4. Siva Upanishads: Atharvasivas, Atharvasikha, Nilarudra, Kalagnirudra, and Kaivalya.
5. Vishnu Upanishads: Mahanarayana, atmabodha, Nrsimhapurvatapaniya, Ramapursottarutapaniya and Ramottaratapaniya.

The word Upanishad means 'rahasyam' or secret text (*guhya adesah*, etc). It also means imparting of secret knowledge to a disciple who sits by the teacher's side. *Upa* means by the side.

# The Hindu Tradition

Jesus spoke in parables because the doctrines are easily misunderstood. Pythagoras insists on mystical silence on his students. Heraclitus, Plato, Kant, Schopenhauer, all insisted on the difficulty of grappling with the subject and hence to remain quiet until they are clear. Similarly, the Upanishads refer to secrecy and to teach only to a son or pupil (Aitareya 3.2.6.9. Chandogya 3.11.5, Brihadaranyaka 6:.3.12 and others). Oldenberg refers to the Upanishads *as upasana*, meaning adoration or reverential meditation on Brahman. *Upa + as* is to worship, secret sign, secret import, etc. the Upanishads came down to us by an oral tradition of the Brahmins but the texts themselves trace back frequently to kings (Kshatriyas). In Chandogya 5.11.24, five learned Brahmins request Uddalaka Aruni to instruct them on Atman Vaisvanara. Uddalaka distrusts his capacity and so the six go to the King Asvapati Kaikeya and from him receive instruction after clearing the defective knowledge of the Brahmins. In Brihadaranyaka 2.1, and Kaushitaki 4, the Vedic scholar Gargya Balaki voluntarily expounds to the King Ajatasatru of Kasi twelve erroneous explanations on Brahman. The king, saying it is normally the Brahmins who instruct the kings, then instructs clearly the concept of Brahman to Gargya. In Chandogya 1.8.9 again, two Brahmins are instructed by the king Pravahana Jaivali on the substratum of all things, the *Akasa*. Again in Chandogya 7, Sanatkumara, the God of War, instructs Narada. King Pravahana Jaivali finally instructs Aruni on the transmigration of the Soul.

This aspect can be understood because the concept of Atman is in sharp contrast to Vedic rituals in which Brahmins were adept. Because of this it is presumed that the Kshatriya kings long withheld this teaching from Brahmins. The concept of the Atman gradually traced through the hymns of the Rig and Atharva Vedas was fostered and developed by the Kshatriyas in opposition to the Brahminical rituals and these were expressed as Upanishads and were later developed as the earlier texts in the form of different Upanishads. Brahmins eagerly adopted the doctrine and attached it to the curriculum of schools and this became Vedanta. Soon they laid claims to the new teaching as their exclusive privilege.

Among the extant Upanishads, we have four distinct periods:

1. Ancient Prose Upanishads- Brihadaranyaka, Taittiriya, Aitareya, Kaushitaki, and Kena. Chandogya is later than Brihadaranyaka, Taittiriya is later than Chandogya which talks of three elements, while the former of five elements and three kinds of organisms in Chandogya and four in Aitareya.
2. Material Upanishads- Kathaka, Isa, Svetasvatara, Mundaka, and Mahanarayana.
3. The later prose Upanishads- Prasna, Maitrayaniya, and Mandukya.
4. The later Atharva Upanishads.

5. Mundaka and Prasna were employed by Badarayana and Sankara. There were 45 or 52 Upanishads but the collection of 108 referred in Muktika may have belonged to the South of India. 50 of the 52 were translated into Persian in 1656 CE at the instance of Sultan Mohammad Darashakoh and from Persian to Latin in 1801-2 by Anquetil Duperras. At least five of them are not now extant.

The fundamental conception in the Upanishads is that the universe is Brahman (*sarvam khalividam brahma*) and this Brahman is the atman within all living beings (*esha ma atma antar hrdaye*) or *sa va ayam atma brahma* meaning that truly the Brahman is the Atman (Brih. 4.4.5). Brahman is the cosmic and Atman the psychic principle. This fundamental principle led to the four mahavakyas found in the different Upanishads. The value of this concept is inestimable for humanity as can be seen from its borrowing by Parmenides, Plato, Kant, Schopenhauer, and other later thinkers.

Kant has expressed the idea contained in the Upanishads succinctly- 'The universe is only appearance and not reality' (*ding an sich* or appearance, not the thing in itself). It is the form in which reality presents itself to our consciousness and is independent of it. The concept contained in the Upanishads is in fact the basis for the philosophy of the Greeks from Parmenides, Plato and others followed through in later times by Kant and his successor Schopenhauer. Plato in fact mentions *auto* or Atman in describing his reading of reality. The concept of *maya* or illusion occurs in Svet. Up. 4.10, and it refers to the apparent space and objects contained in it which, according to Kant, are not things in themselves. Yagnavalkya explains in Brih. Up. 2.4.5, that the worldly objects have no value for their own sake but for the sake of the Atman; in fact they exist solely in the Atman. This Atman is the entire universe. He further says 'verily he who has seen, heard, comprehended and known the Self, by him the entire universe is known'. 'Just as from a lump of clay everything that consists of clay is known, the change is a matter of words alone, a mere name, it is in reality only clay' (*vacarambanam vikaro namadeyam*). This is what Parmenides asserts- 'what men regard as real is mere name'. Considering that the Greeks travelled to India and Egypt, it can be presumed that they drew their inspiration from the Upanishads. Kant and others in turn, drew upon the Greeks.

The word dharma has different connotations. It means, spirituality, truth, virtue and so on. But virtue covers most of the other meanings and it is this that the Greeks took up in their philosophy. The word virtue covers practically all aspects of human life in respect of ethics and morality.

# The Hindu Tradition

The basic premises of all religions are:
1. The existence of god.
2. The immortality of the Soul and,
3. The freedom of the will.

These are conceivable only if the universe is mere appearance and not reality (*maya*) and not the Atman. They breakdown completely should this empirical reality be found to constitute the true essence of things:
1. Existence of god will be precluded by the space which is infinite and hence admits of nothing external to itself and nothing within save what is contained in it- matter.
2. Immortality will be precluded by the condition of time, due to which existence has a beginning and an end.
3. Freedom will be precluded by the universal validity of the law of causality (*karma*) since every action has a cause and so the actual moment of action is no longer within our control.

The evident recognition is that all action is worthless since they are simply means to selfish ends and so morally of no use. This is recognized in the New Testament doctrine of the worthlessness of all works, even good ones. The Upanishads altogether reject works. Both make salvation dependent on a complete transformation of a man as a whole. This transformation is the release from all bonds in the empirical reality which has its roots in egotism. Why then do we need a release from existence? (Cp. Beowolf: Life is ephemeral, everything vanishes, light and life together, and 'fate must decide'. The background of pagan philosophy can be perceived in this).

It is due to sin according to the Bible and it is the realm of ignorance according to the Upanishads. The former sees depravity in human nature and the latter, the intellect in man. Bible teaches to 'love thy neighbour as thyself' and the Upanishads teach that 'thy neighbour in truth is thy very self and what separates you is mere illusion'.

Vedanta falls into four main divisions:
1. Theology: Brahman as the first principle of all things.
2. Cosmology: Brahman forming the universe.
3. Psychology: The entrance of the Brahman as the soul into the universe that evolved from him.
4. Eschatology and Ethics: The fate of the soul after death and the manner of life which is therefore required.

He that recognizes both wisdom and ignorance as insufficient and through both thus overpasses death and wins immortality. This is a subtle reference to the need to go beyond the pairs of opposites (*dvandvas*) to realize the Self. That the Rig Veda has subtle reference to this truth could be gleaned from the hymns I.164 x 121, 129 etc. This unity of the universe as the only reality and the rest as appearances is followed up in the Upanishads giving a concrete shape to Vedanta. Both Brahman and Atman denote the first principle of the universe. The Questions posed in the Chand.Up. 5.11.1, *'ko na atma? Kim brahma'?, a*re clearly answered by Sankara by stating that Brahman is the defined (*viseshyam*) and atman as that which defines it (*viseshanam*), the former remaining the limitation imposed on the latter and this way any worship of Brahman as the divinity is condemned.

Indra and the demon Virocana approach Prajapati for instruction. The latter gives three answers:

1. The Self is that which is seen looking into the eye of another, into a brook of water or a mirror that is reflected again in an image- that is the Self, immortal, fearless Brahman.
2. The Self is that which roams about untrammeled in dreams; that is immortal Brahman.
3. When a man is fully wrapped in slumber, reaching a perfect rest, he does not perceive any dream image- that is the Self, the immortal Brahman.

When Indra objects to this as amounting to annihilation, Prajapati clarifies- this cessation of the distinction of subject and object is an entrance to the fullest Light, the Supreme as the knowing subject, unaffected by any change of organs or objects. These are the material, realistic and idealistic standpoints in regard to Brahman respectively.

The Taittiriya Upanishad gives a more detailed position in which the five kosas or sheaths are explained as different Atmans. These are:

Annamayakosa – the Atman dependent on food.
Pranamayakosa - the Atman dependent on vital breath.
Manomayakosa - the Atman dependent on will or mind.
Vijnanamayakosa - the Atman dependent on knowledge.
Anandamayakosa - The Atman in bliss.

In the final bliss, words and thought are not seen, no longer being an object of knowledge. *Akasavat sarvagatacca nityah,* meaning, 'omnipresent like space is eternal', which Newton designated the Sensorium (space) of god and Kant, that god whose sensorium is space, to be the intellect in our Self. Chand.Up. 3.12, 7.9, states- 'This so called Brahman is the space within man, yonder space without man and the space within the heart. That is the perfect, immutable'. Again in 3.13, 7.8, it states- 'His sight is the warmth felt on touch, his hearing is that when the ears are kept closed, there is heard a humming like a crackling sound as a roaring fire'. This is referred to as *vaisvanarah* in the Bhagwad Gita. In effect, Brahman should be sought in the knowing subject i.e., the consciousness (*prajna*) and this is first mentioned in the Vedas where it is equated with *prana*. That is the *satyasya satyam* or only reality. Taitt. Up. 2.7, states:

> Not being was this in the beginning,
> From it being arose,
> Self-fashioned indeed out of itself;
> Therefore is it named well fashioned.
> (cp. Nasadiya Sukta of the Rig Veda).

From the foregoing it should be clear that the highest aim of our endeavour is deliverance from the present existence. Brahmanism, Buddhism and Christianity and not less the philosophy of Schopenhauer (that represents Christianity in its purest form) all agree on this objective.

Brahman as bliss (*ananda*) is clearly explained in the Brih.Up. 2.1.19- when in deep sleep, when one is conscious of nothing, then the veins called *hitah* or beneficial, are acting, 72,000 of which ramify from the heart outwards in the pericardium; into these he glides and reposes, like a king or a great Brahmin, enjoying an excess of bliss, so he also reposes (*atignim anandasya*). Again in 4.4.25, Yagnavalkya says- 'The Atman is not this, not this (*neti, neti*); he is incomprehensible for, he is not comprehended; indestructible, for he is not destroyed; unaffected, unfettered and undisturbed, for, he is not affected, bound or harmed. This Brahman does not grow old or decay, and is immortal, fearless, is Brahman'. It is imperishable (*aksharam*). Plato follows the same argument.

The five elements fire, water, earth, air and, ether find their earliest mention in the Taitt. Up. 2.1- 'from this Atman, in truth, has the ether (space) arisen; from the ether the wind, from the wind the fire, from fire the water and from the water the earth'. These elements correspond with the five organs of knowledge- hearing, touch, sight, taste and, smell.

The 'nous' of the Platonists, the knowing subject, the eternal eye of the universe of Schopenhauer, corresponds to the cosmic intellect as the sustainer of the universe (*Hiranyagarbha, Mahat*). The entire objective universe is possible only in so far as it is sustained by a knowing subject. This subject is manifested in all individuals as the Atman but is by no means identical with them for, the individual subjects pass away but the objective universe continues to exist without them. Space and time are derived from the knowing subject. It is itself, therefore, not in space and does not belong to time, and so empirically non-existent. It only has a metaphysical reality.

The Brahman as the preserver of the universe is like the fire and its sparks that are identical in nature. Brih. Up. 2.1.20 states: 'As the tiny sparks leap forth from the fire, so from this Atman all vital spirits spring forth, all worlds, all gods, all living creatures'. Chand.Up., 8.4.3, has a beautiful verse-'just as he who does not know the hiding place of a treasure of gold does not find it, although he may pass over it again and again, so none of these creatures find the world of Brahman, although they daily enter into it (in deep sleep) for they are constrained by unreality'. 'Those who find this world of Brahman have part in all worlds in a life of freedom'. By this it is meant that such people are not born again being freed from the cycle of births.

'Out of which beings arise, live and at death, into which they enter again, know that to be Brahman' (Taitt. 3.1). we know from science that we can neither create nor destroy matter and can only redistribute it like the ornaments from gold and pottery from clay, so does everything appear from the *Hiranyagarbha* (the Cosmic Egg) and then merge back into it. All this is pure energy according to science and other than energy and its manifestations nothing exists. Anaximander echoes the idea- 'That from which existing things originate, into it they necessarily also disappear'. And Heraclitus- 'All things come forth from fire and return into it'. This idea is carried forward later by the Stoics.

The doctrine of *maya* is reflected in the philosophy of Kant who concludes that the universe as we know it is only appearance and not reality, an idea that has existed in Vedanta for thousands of years. Parmenides too asserts that empirical reality is mere show and for Plato it is mere 'shadows' of the true reality. The origin of this idea in the Upanishads could be traced to the Rig Veda I.164.46- '*ekam sat vipra bahuda vadanti*' or truth is one but called differently by the many and this implies that plurality is only in the mind in the form of mere words and only Unity is real. Brih. 2.4.7.9, says- 'As the notes of a drum, a conch shell, or a lute have no existence in themselves, and can only be received when the instrument that produces them is struck, so all objects and relations of the universe are known by him who knows the Atman. This knowing subject is the sustainer of the universe and is the sole reality; so that with the knowledge of the Atman, everything is known'. The above analysis follows that of Paul Deussen.

# The Hindu Tradition

We will now briefly discuss the Bhagawata which is read and practised by many on a daily basis by doing *parayana* or reading a part of the text. I have followed the analysis of Swami Tapasyananda in this. The Bhagawata was probably composed around the 6th century BCE according to research scholars though it was part of the oral tradition since Veda Vyasa taught it to his disciples in c.4000 BCE. This is one of the eighteen Puranas and we also have eighteen sub-*Puranas*. Vedas in the *Akhyana bhaga* refer to the *Puranas* that have come down to us from the ancient times as part of the oral tradition. The genealogies of great king lines are also to be found in the Puranas in recitals called *Pariplava akhyanas*.

Though the sacrificial rites were the function of Brahmin priests in which Puranas were recited, it gradually got relegated with time to the mixed caste of Sutas. Vyasa, after compiling the original *Puranasamhita*, entrusted it to his Suta disciple Lomaharshana, who made it into six versions and taught them to his six disciples. Three of them made separate *Samhitas* and these together with Lomaharshana's became the source of all Purana literature. By the time of *Apastamba Dharma Sutras* (600-300 BCE), *Puranas* became specialized literature. Apastamba in fact cited three passages from an unspecified Purana and one passage from *Bhavishya Purana*. With the exception of *Markandeya Purana,* all Puranas are sectarian in nature, extolling different gods like Shiva, Vishnu and others that developed into cults. This has been wrongly interpreted by some as rivalry among different cults. Shiva is the passive energy and Shakti is the active aspect of Shiva that has created the universe and sustains it. So Shiva, Vishnu and Brahma are but aspects of the One Brahman. Even in the Vedas, one or other of the gods is exalted but this should be understood as the One Being adored in different names and forms. This is the beauty of the Vedic Tradition in which the One is nothing but Brahman, the Universal Energy or Consciousness, that has manifested as the universe as we see it.

A Purana is supposed to deal with five subjects according to Amarasimha, author of *Amarakosa* (6th century CE). These are:

*Sarga-* Creation of categories of evolution.

*Pratisarga-* Secondary creation in the universe.

*Vamsa-* Genealogies of demons, Manus, Rishis, and Kings.

*Manvantara-* Cosmic cycle ruled over by a Manu or a Patriarch.

*Vamsanucharita-* Accounts of all dynasties.

This was the initial plan. But with time, as it became separate religious literature meant to convey the teachings of the Veda, the concept of Mahapurana evolved and five more topics were added as given in the *Bhagawata* and *Vaivartapurana*. So the ten subjects became as follows:

*Sarga*- Creation.
*Visarga*- Secondary creation.
*Vritti*- Means of sustenance.

*Raksha*- Protection, including incarnations.
*Manvantara*- The epochs of Manu.
*Vamsa*- Genealogy of Royal and priestly lines.
*Vamsanucharita*- History of dynasties.

*Samstha*- Dissolution of four types of the manifested universe. These are:
*Prakrita pralaya*- Dissolution of life.
*Naimittika Pralaya*- Partial dissolution.
*Nitya Pralaya*- Daily dissolution in deep sleep.
*Atyantika Pralaya*- Salvation of man (Nirodha or withdrawal of all Manifestation).
*Hetu*- Purpose of creation.
*Apasraya*- Ultimate support.

The *Brahma Vaivarta Purana* recasts the above ten as follows:
*Srishti* or creation,
*Visrishti*, secondary creation,
*Stithi* or maintenance of the worlds,
*Palana*, protection of life,
*Karma vasana* or latent tendencies of work,
*Manvantara*, Accounts of Manus,
*Pralaya varnana*, dissolution of the worlds,
*Mokshanirupana* or liberation (birthlessness),
*Harikirtana*, discourses on god, and,
*Devakirtana*, discourses on deities.

The *Devi Bhagawata* claims to be the Bhagawata Purana and this relegates Vishnu Bhagawata to upa-purana. But Prof. Hazra puts the former to the 12th century CE and has incorporated the features of the Bhagawata as found in the Matsya, Skandha and Agni Puranas. So the Vishnu Purana is the Super Purana and not the secondary one. Though the Bhagawata took its shape in the 6th century CE, Prof Hazra admits that an earlier version of the text has existed from ancient times but differs from the present as could be gleaned from the Matsya Purana (4th century CE). According to Prof. Siddheswara Bhattacharya, Bhagawata has three phases of development. The earliest form consists of very old material. It was given the shape of Mahapurana in the second phase during the early part of the Current Era and the final phase was given by the Tamil saints (Alwars) in the 6th to 10th centuries.

The Bhagawata was transmitted by the Lord to Brahma and by him to Narada, with permission to elaborate if necessary. It was then revealed to Sanatkumara by Sankarshana and from him to Vidura through Samkhyayana, Parasara and Maitreya (3rd Skandha). In Skandha I, it says Vyasa got it by meditation and spread it through his son Suka. This may be a reference to the three phases of development. That the present Bhagawata is closely connected with the Tamil Saints can be understood from the reference to the Bhakti movement in a passage (X1.5.38-40): 'Men of the Krita and other Ages desired to be born in the Kali Age; for, in Kali are surely born many devotees of Narayana in several parts of the Dravida country through which holy rivers like the Tamraparni, the Kritamala, the Payasvini, and the Cauvery flow'. Also in descriptions of the River Saraswati and its cities Dwarka and others, there is mention of plantain trees and areca palms. These are not found there but in the south only. And in the description of Balarama's pilgrimage, detailed knowledge of cities in the South are given but those in the north, rather casually.

Ramanuja (b. 1017 CE) does not quote from the Bhagawata as he preferred the *Vishnu Purana* following his *Pancharatra Agama* since he does not accept Shiva. But the Bhagawata considers both Shiva and Vishnu as aspects of the One Brahman. *Saktimat* and *Shakti* (Power holder and power) rather than *sariri* and *sarira* (soul and body) are what Bhagawata considers as the relationship between god and the world. But Ramanuja considers the latter view as he was a cult head. In Bhagawata, it is said that the devotees of Shiva are also devotees of Vishnu and vice versa and the two deities are non-different from the Supreme Being the Brahman. The incarnations are the *Saguna Brahman* and the Supreme is the *Nirguna Brahman*. In the 14th chapter of the 12th Skandha, the form of Vishnu is shown as the essence of *sat-chit-ananda* (existence, mind and bliss), and as support of the fourteen spheres of the manifested universe whose parts constitute the limits of His Being. The Bhagawata describes *bhakti* or devotion as the fifth *purusharta* after the four, *dharma*, *artha*, *kama* and *moksha*. Bhakti is itself the transcending *mukti* or liberation. The lower form of *bhakti* is through the three *gunas-sattva*, *rajas* and *tamas*, attributes of *prakriti*. The *tamasic* devotion is through tribal deities with cruel rites and unclean offerings. The *rajasic* devotion is with elaborate offerings and prayers. The *sattvic* devotion is through renunciation and prayer for liberation from *samsara*. In effect the three, show a process of evolution from the lower to the higher levels of devotion for emancipation. The highest form of devotion is however *nirguna*, expressed as self-forgetting love and a sense of oneness with the infinite.

## Vedic Tradition and World Religions

The life span of man in ancient times was immensely greater than in our period. They lived for hundreds of years and this is borne out from the history of South India where the kingship lasted for more than hundred years in the pre-historic period (after 15000 BCE or after the last glacial period) when the Pandyan kings ruled. This gradually came down to about thirty years in the early current era. This would also be borne out if we consider the *vamsavali* or genealogy of those kings in the Puranas. The cyclical nature of life with floods followed by a glacial period with the last glacial period being the 5th according to scientists has been recorded. The period between two glacials gradually reduced over time from tens of thousands of years to about 20000 odd years in the present as they predict the next floods in the foreseeable future.

The Brih. Up. (2.2.1) says that Brahman has two aspects- with form and formless (*murta* and *amurta*) and the Puranas concentrate on the former while Vedanta on the latter. The Taittiriya Samhita of the Rig Veda has this peace invocation:

*Tvamevam pratyaksham brahmasi /*
*Tvamevam pratyaksham brahmavadishyami /*
*Satyam vadishyami /*

(You only are the Brahman; I say that you are truly the Brahman; I am saying the truth).

No discussion on the Hindu Tradition will be complete without reference to the Bhagwad Gita. In this text, we find Arjuna in the battlefield facing his kinsmen and his dilemma as to whether he should fight and kill his own teachers and cousins. Lord Krishna, one of the ten incarnations of God Vishnu is the charioteer of Arjuna. The text in eighteen chapters gives in detail the philosophy of Vedanta and man's duty to be performed at all costs. Some important aspects of Krishna's teaching are given here below.

1. The soul, Atman is a passenger in the body and cannot be slain. After the body falls off, the Soul moves to another body, carrying its *vasanas* or karma. The rituals belong to this world and one should rise above them, and above the dualities of pleasure and pain. The rituals are no more than a small pond amidst a vast flood. We have the right to work but not to desire the fruits of that work. He that withdraws his senses from the world like a tortoise is secure in wisdom.
2. The real enemy to be slain is not the opponent but selfish desire. Desire arises from passion, clouding our vision of the soul like smoke from early morning fires.
3. Krishna teaches us how to act without acting, thus burning karma to ashes. Freedom from fear and anger is a blessing. One who renounces the results of

work, though fully occupied in work, does nothing at all. No karma is attached to him as a baggage to be carried forward to the next life. There should be no sense of ownership and there should be no motive in action.

4. Like a lotus leaf on a pond floating without wetting itself, so the soul sits in the heart of man without being attached to his action and is always in freedom and joy. That is its essential nature. All beings are equal. The soul does not create actions or cause their fruits. Knowledge dispels ignorance in this regard.
5. The mystic whose mind is still and peaceful is like a lamp in a windless place and he is never separated from Brahman. The mind not subdued becomes an enemy. One who sees all beings in him and himself in all beings is a perfect yogi.
6. Goodness, passion and darkness arise out of Brahman. Deluded by the three, we do not change. These are illusions and are hard to overcome. 'Among the good, the distressed, wealth seekers, knowledge seekers and the wise serve Me' (Brahman). After many lives, one gets knowledge and is not born again.
7. The state of mind at death determines our future. He who thinks of the infinite Brahman or God at the time of death merges with the infinite, never to be born again.

The above only gives a bird's eye view of the principles enumerated in the Gita and one needs to study it in detail many times to arrive at the truth.

With this we come to the end in describing the Hindu tradition. However, a question may arise in the minds of the reader- 'Then why do the Hindus worship so many gods and have built thousands of temples over the centuries? The answer is found in the scripture itself. Just as we have the three stages of childhood, family life and old age, so we have three principles of knowledge. These are *sravana, manana* and, *nidhidhyasana* or, learning, contemplation, and practice. In the first stage we acquire the knowledge from the teacher, in the second stage, practise what we have learnt. Then in the third stage, we leave everything to our grown up children and leave for a quiet place in nature for contemplation. The last stage is known as *vanaprastha* or going to the forest. In the first two stages, the individual is in the process of maturing for which the different personal gods and temples of worship serve as aids. In the third stage, we find no need for them as we contemplate on the knowing subject or the 'I' in us.

One could easily perceive the influence of Hindu thought on the Greek scholars and their philosophy as adumbrated in a separate chapter in this book.

## References:

1. The Philosophy of the Upanishads- Paul Deussen, (Translated by Gelden) Oriental Books (reprint).
2. Indian Philosophy- Dr S. Radhakrishnan Vol. I and II, Oxford University Press.
3. Science, Philosophy, and Religion-Ramakrishnan Srinivasan, Citadel.
4. Bhagwad Gita- Ranchor Prime, Barrons.
5. Srimad Bhagawata- Swami Tapasyananda, RK Mission.
6. The Vedas- Paramacharya Sr Chandrasekhara Saraswati, Bharatiya Vidya Bhavan.
7. Vedic Tradithion- Ramakrishnan Srinivasan, Bharatiya Vidya Bhavan, 2000.

# CHAPTER 3
# BUDDHISM

Buddhist philosophy and way of life is based on Hindu philosophy and way without rituals. There is practically no difference in the two as Nagarjuna has clearly observed in his philosophy of non-identity. The basic principles of Buddhist Dhamma are:

- Everyone can achieve enlightenment here and now.
- We need to choose the way that is most suited to our environment and temperament.
- Truth or knowledge is within every one of us and we only need to 'recollect' it by using the way of dharma.

As Manjusri, the Wisdom deity said, 'One instant of total awareness is one instant of perfect freedom and enlightenment'. It is a question of extending this 'one minute' slowly until we are fully enlightened and live a life accordingly with love, without desires, without attachment and without possessions.

We have Zen, Theravadin (Vipassana) and Tibetan Buddhism besides many others. Essentially, we should be free from the thoughts of past, present and future and live a life of service and meditation. Spiritual living implies that we need to be prepared for conscious dying. Dying is a process of living as one gets reborn again and again till one is fully enlightened. Hindus call this *atmajnana* or *brahmajnana* (Self Knowledge or knowledge of Brahman). In the Dhammapada in Pali, Buddha has cited a number of verses from the Mahabharata and other Hindu scriptures literally. The difference is only the language as the latter is in Sanskrit and the former in Pali which is people's Sanskrit. Some of these have been quoted in the book *Vedic Tradition*, by the present author, published by the Bharatiya Vidya Bhavan in their Book University Series in 2000. Living in the present is what Buddhism is all about. Self-awareness is the key. This is difficult but can be attained by proper meditation techniques done over a long period.

Death is something that is connected with the body and not the mind or spirit. When we identify ourselves with the body, sorrow and suffering takes place. Once we stop this identity and let the body live its life of suffering or enjoyment without actively participating in it, death would mean nothing to us. In the Bhagwad Gita, Krishna tells Arjuna that nobody kills and nobody dies since the Atman or Soul is infinite and cannot perish. '*Na mriyate atma, mriyamane sarire*' says Krishna. (The Atman never dies but the body is bound to perish as it is its nature). But this requires experiencing for which spiritual practice is essential.

Self inquiry and meditation are the keys to a spiritual experience. Ramana Maharishi used to tell the seeker to find the source of the 'I' within oneself in order to experience realization. Kabir the mystic said: 'I do not wish to dye my clothes saffron, the colour of holy order; I want to dye my heart with divine love'. So that is the key. Without filling ourselves with love no spiritual practice can be effective. We are all born with infinite love as it is our essential nature. Past karma and death are also born with us. If karma and death are overcome what remains is only love. Once we recognize this infinite love within us waiting to be shared with others, enlightenment dawns. As the Zhosa tribe of Africa say- 'I am because we are'.

Prayer and meditation, being aware, practising Yoga, feeling the breath, smiling, playing and laughing, letting go, forgiving and forgetting, one should walk, exercise, serve with love everything wholeheartedly as part of our own essence, listen, contemplate, be contented, lighten up and expand, celebrate, share, give, walk, or talk gently or softly, surrender, trust and be born anew. Buddha's teaching involves taking refuge in three things:

- Refuge in the Buddha, the Enlightened One.
- Refuge in the Dhamma or his teachings.
- Refuge in the Sangha, the spiritual community.

These are the three jewels (*triratna*) of Buddhism.

Buddhists sing:

*Buddham saranam gacchami.* I take refuge in the Buddha.

*Dhammam saranam gacchami.* I take refuge in the Dhamma.

*Sangham saranam gacchami.* I take refuge in the Sangha.

The three reasons for suffering are: the poison of ignorance, the poison of attachment and the poison of aversion or hate. The Dhamma is an agent of change. *Sutras, Vinayas* and *Abhidhammas* (psychology of the sutras) are the Buddhist canons known as the Tripitaka (three baskets) in Pali. The first cycle of Dhamma is the Theravadin where cause and effect, impermanence, purification and liberation are taught. This path can give nirvana in seven lives. The second cycle of Dhamma is Mahayana where *sunyata* is emphasized that implies infinite emptiness and radiant openness. This is the Bodhisattva way to enlightenment. Compassion, wisdom of emptiness, altruism and fearless courage can lead to nirvana in a few lives. The third cycle of the Dhamma wheel is Vajrayana that emphasizes Buddha-nature- non-dual tantra, inseparability of nirvana and *samsara,* the sacred and the mundane, the heaven and earth. This path can give nirvana in a single life itself.

A fourth cycle was developed in Tibet, the Dzogchen- a direct non-dual method of awakening of the Buddha within. They say that nirvana can be reached in seven years. The Dhamma of Self-realization is one that can be obtained in many ways- each according to his choice. Knowing Truth is Buddha, expressing Truth is Dhamma and living Truth is the Sangha. These three correspond with the three methods of Hindu practice- *sravana, manana* and *nidhidhyasana. Sravana* means knowing the Truth from a teacher or by study, *manana* is contemplation on the Truth and *nidhidhyasana* is the practice of what has been learnt. Only by doing nothing will you be able to do all that requires to be done.

## The Eight-fold Path:

The four noble truths are:

1. Life is difficult or full of suffering (*duhkha*- sorrow).
2. Life is difficult because of attachment and craving.
3. Possibility of liberation from difficulties exists for everyone.
4. The way to realize the above is to lead a life of virtue, wisdom and meditation. These three trainings comprise the Eight-fold path to Enlightenment.

Everyday suffering, suffering due to changing circumstances and, suffering due to the imperfect nature of existence are the three sufferings. The individual is composed of five *skandhas*- form, feelings, perceptions, will, and consciousness. Craving or attachment can be overcome with wisdom. Enlightenment is not external. Our inherent nature is bliss. So, everyone can attain enlightenment in this life itself. Craving and the senses are related to the body. Consciousness is that which animates the body and we may call it *atta* in Pali, the same as the *Atman* of the Hindu. The fourth noble truth tells us the path to enlightenment. This is the eight-fold path. Moderation or the middle-path is what was taught by Buddha. The Eight-fold Path consists of the following:

Wisdom – Right view and Right intentions.

Ethics training – Right speech, Right action, and Right livelihood.

Meditation training – Right effort, Right mindfulness, and Right concentration.

These eight are the wheels of Enlightenment. *Prajna* or awareness leads to wisdom through right view and intention.

# Vedic Tradition and World Religions

Soren Kierkgaard said: 'In order to swim, one takes off all his clothes. In order to aspire for truth, one must undress in a far more inward sense, divest oneself of all one's inward clothes of thoughts, conceptions, selfishness etc., before one is sufficiently naked'. Buddha referred in the Prajna Paramita Sutra to the eight similes of illusion:

"Regard this fleeting world like this:
*Like stars fading and vanishing at dawn,*
*Like bubbles on a fast moving stream,*
*Like morning dew drops evaporating on blades of grass,*
*Like a candle flickering in a strong wind,*
*Echos, mirages, and phantoms, hallucination and like a dream*".

Remembering death everyday helps intensify life. Then death will not take us by surprise. Life is insipid without an ever present sense of death. The ancient *Book of Craft of Dying* says: "Learn to die and you shall live, for there shall be none who learns to truly live who have not learned to die". All Buddhists believe in the karma law of cause and effect and in rebirth. Buddha himself did not want to speculate on this and said, 'I am aware'. Buddha viewed *atta* as ego and *anatta* as ego-less-ness. The Self or Atman is not as we know it, and it does not exist. *Anatta* is no-self. Scholars interpreted this as Buddha denying the Self. Nagarjuna clarified the point by elaborating on the philosophy of no-identity. The body has an identity, the self has none. This is because the self is part of the universal consciousness. This Hindu theory of Brahman was avoided by Buddha as it is speculation and cannot be proved. The Lankavatara Sutra says: 'Things are not what they seem to be; nor or they otherwise'.

*Sunyata* is emptiness. One has to empty oneself in order to realize the truth. It really means that everything is just an appearance and there is nothing behind them. Nothing is permanent, everything is fleeting. As the Zen master will say, everything is a projection, created by the mind. If there is no mind, nothing exists. The world is, because I am. Without my mind there is no world.

The four thoughts or meditations are:
- Precious human existence - should not be wasted.
- It is rare to obtain - if we squander this chance, we may not get another.
- Death, mortality or impermanence is like the cloud in the sky.
- The ineluctable law of karma. This cause and effect pursues us at death to be born again to experience the effects of such karma. But this next birth may not be as a human, it may be another species. Buddha said that whenever we go or remain at one place, the effects of our action follows us.

- The defects and shortcomings of *samsara*. We need to cross this misery of sufferings in *samsara* and attain enlightenment.

Right intentions are important as Dhammapada says: 'As the shadow follows body, as we think so we become'. Shantideva said 'all the happiness there is in this world comes from thinking about others, and all the suffering comes from preoccupation with oneself'. The chant '*Om manipadme hung*' means that the Jewel is in the lotus. This really tells us that what we seek is within us. Love, compassion and kindness are at the heart of dharma. Bodhichitta is the purified and developed heart-mind. Wisdom without love is not wisdom; love without wisdom is not love. Consider all phenomena like dreams and examine the nature of awareness. Ethical training starts with being truthful. Lies and gossip are to be avoided under all circumstances and only kind language is to be used. Chanting a mantra within oneself and being silent resound like thunder. Solitude, simplicity and silence lead to enlightenment.

Right action is doing good and giving to others. Do not steal or kill. Be generous; be celibate and refrain from alcohol. Craving is a challenge to right action. The Tao Te Ching states: 'The secret waits for eyes, unclouded by longing'. Overcome that desire; laugh and be childlike. At death, we take nothing with us but our karma.

Right livelihood is good occupation that is good for others and for the doer. The Metta Sutra says: 'Let none deceive another, or despise any being in any state; let none through anger or ill will wish harm upon another. Even as a mother protects her child with her life, her only child, so with a boundless heart should one cherish all living beings, radiating kindness over the entire world'.

The eight worldly winds blow us off- pleasure and pain, gain and loss, praise and blame, and fame and shame. Do not hope for rewards or applause. Do your good without expecting anything in return. Our conscience is the constant witness and we should listen to it. Equality of all and a simple life of sharing and loving are the best. The happiness quotient (HQ) is the balance between what we have and what we want. Benjamin Disraeli had said- 'Most people die with their music locked up inside them'. One has to find his vocation in order to optimize his contribution to society and be creative. Right livelihood is doing what needs to be done.

## Meditation Training:
Awareness, attention and focus are what make meditation purposeful. It is an unconditioned way of being and seeing and living from moment to moment. The two types of meditation are concentration and insight. Insight is the Vipassana meditation. The Zen master Dogen said: 'To study the Self is to ascend the Self; to transcend the

Self is to be enlightened by all things; to be enlightened by all things is to remove the barrier between the Self and others'. Socrates had said, 'The unexamined life is not worth living'. The spiritual path is driven by effort and inspiration. The four great efforts are:
1. The effort to avoid negative thoughts and action.
2. The effort to overcome unwholesome thoughts or action.
3. The effort to develop only wholesome thoughts and action and lead an enlightened life.
4. The effort to maintain the goodness that already is with you.

The six perfections are: generosity, virtue, patience, effort, meditation and wisdom. The balance between effort and effortlessness is the essence of Self-mastery. The Jazz Saxophone legend Charlie Parker said, 'Just perfect your instrument, then just play'.

Some forms of clinging are:
- Clinging to the ego.
- Clinging to the pleasure/pain principle.
- Clinging to narrow-minded opinion.
- Clinging to empty rites and rituals.
- Clinging to a shortsighted view that sees only this life and nothing beyond.

Instead of such clinging, one may prefer enthusiasm for life itself. 'Nothing great was achieved without enthusiasm' was Ralph Waldo Emerson's take in the matter.

Love is the pursuit of the whole- Plato. Intimate relationship is a path to transcendence. The four divine abodes are:
1. Loving kindness and friendliness (metta).
2. Compassion and empathy.
3. Joy and rejoicing.
4. Equanimity and peace of mind.

Mindfulness is the very basis and cure for all afflictions of samsara. This means paying attention to what we do. Meditation is the training in mindfulness and awareness. It is paying full attention to what is being done every moment. Coming home to 'now', is the secret of meditation. As J.Krishnamurthy used to say, 'Meditation is not a means to an end; it is both the means and the end'. Kalu Rimpoche says: 'We live in illusion, and the appearance of things. There is a reality and we are that reality. When you understand this, you see that you are nothing; and being nothing, you are everything'. Taming, training, testing, transforming, and transcendence are the five 'T's of concentration.

# Buddhism

The Nicene Council banned the Indian doctrine of transmigration of souls and Constantine transformed Buddhism into a tool of the Roman state. Prof. Thomas Mcevilley mentions 'early third and fourth century Christian writers such as Hippolytus and Epiphanius' who wrote about Sythianius bringing to Alexandria 'the doctrine of the Two Principles' from India around 50 CE. Terebinthus, a disciple of Sythianius, presented himself as a 'Buddha' and went to Palestine and Judaea, where he met the apostles, who condemned him. He then settled in Babylon, where he transmitted his teachings to Mani, who himself founded the Persian syncretic Buddho-Christianity, known as Manichaeism, which was the youthful religion of Augustine of Hippo, who later condemned it. So, despite Christian claims of their teachings as *suo generis* that came down from god without any connection with other movements, Mahayana Buddhism and Christianity have very strong 'family resemblances'.

Most important of Kerouac's understanding of enlightenment is the experience of oneness of all things, yet he allowed the persistent engagement with transformed relativity. He emphasized that 'emptiness is form' and 'form is emptiness'. He referred to the womb of Tathagatha and is comfortable with Nagarjuna's *shunyata karunagarbham* or emptiness, the womb of compassion. Kerouac wanted people to convert to the grand wisdom vision of the divinity within, and of the natural love and kindness in relationships.

Buddha was dated 563-482 BCE though Tibetans date in the ninth century BCE. Buddha's Nirvana was neither the extinction of the light of the candle (*nirvana*) nor the light of the candle (*samsara*) as it is beyond both. This is profound non-duality. Kerouac says, 'death comes from birth, birth comes from deeds, deeds come from attachment, attachment comes from desire, desire comes from perception, perception comes from sensation, sensation comes from the six sense organs, the sense organs come from individuality, and individuality comes from consciousness'. 'Death pervades all time, get rid of death, and time will disappear'. Destroy birth, thus will death cease; destroy deeds, then will birth cease. Destroy attachment, then will deeds cease; destroy desire then will attachment end; destroy perceptions to end desire; destroy the contact of the sense organs to end sensation; destroy the six entrances of the senses, individuality will cease.

Buddha tells Sariputra and the assembly: 'At certain times, at certain places, somehow do the leaders appear…whose view is boundless, at one time or another, preach a similar law. Neither abstinence from fish or flesh, nor going naked, nor shaving the head, nor wearing matted hair, nor dressing in a rough garment, nor covering oneself with dirt, nor sacrificing to fire, will cleanse a man who is not free from delusions… It is not evil to satisfy the needs of life, to keep the body in good health is a duty, for otherwise we shall not be able to trim the lamp of wisdom, and keep our mind strong and clean'. Kashyapa, Kaundinya and other Rishis joined Buddha. 'Wake up! The river in your dream is evil desire, the lake is the sensual life, its waves are anger, its rapids are lust, and the crocodiles are the womenfolk'.

The difference between Vedanta and Buddha's philosophy of life is in respect of the 'I' or the Atman. This difference is quite narrow because Buddha's Self is the ego due to which sorrows arise. But the Self of Vedanta is the Brahman or Universal Consciousness itself. This Self is an observer and that is all. But Buddha says there is no 'I'. This is the essential difference. Buddha did understand the Vedantic view but did not want to enter into a speculative argument on it; if the source of the 'I' is known and realized, then that is enlightenment that stops the birth cycle.

Buddha said that there are four young creatures that are not to be despised because they are youthful. These are- a noble prince, a snake, a fire and a monk. 'Essential mind is everywhere. It is like open space, permanent and motionless; the dream of existence is like particles of dust shifting and appearing and disappearing in open space'. This unchanging mind is the Brahman of Vedanta. This is also the Self or Atman. For Buddha the defilements are: of discriminating ignorance, of form, of desire, of grasping, of decrepitude. The essential mind of non-death is non-rebirth and this essence is the holy reality, all else is a dream. For, when it is realized that there is nothing born and nothing passes away, then there is no way to admit being and non-being, and the mind becomes quiescent. This indeed is the philosophy of no-identity of Nagarjuna and this is also the essence of Vedanta. After Buddha's death, Maha Kashyapa became the first Patriarch who organized the Buddhist church and the compilation of the Tripitaka.

Broadly, the Buddhist views can be summarized as follows: We have the capacity to love and care about each other but have a strong inclination to sleep. We can move to go forward with clarity or towards confusion. Are we living with further aggression and self-centredness or are we adding some much needed sanity? We are deeply concerned about the state of the world as everything is in a mess. The only way is to work on ourselves and be more conscious about our minds and emotions for a solution. We need to make a commitment to ourselves to let go of old grudges, not to avoid people and situations that make us uneasy. Trust in our basic goodness and that of others. While talking to someone or a family member we do not agree with, we tend to be angry and spend energy. But such anger or resentments are not our basic nature. To love and be kind is healing and this is transformative. We can see our family members and others are driving us crazy just as we do to others. When we get

# Buddhism

worked up, we can make a choice to be cool or be aggressive. To be cool, we need three qualities of being human- natural intelligence, natural warmth and natural openness.

1. Our intelligence can guide us to be happy and peaceful if we will. For this our emotions need to be controlled.
2. Natural warmth is our capacity to love and to empathise and to have a smile on our lips; our capacity to feel gratitude, appreciation and tenderness. These can heal relationships with our selves and others.
3. Basic goodness is natural openness and spaciousness of our minds that is a mind which is expansive, flexible and curious. When there is a preference it shows that our mind is pre-conditioned or prejudiced.

Just breathing deeply and cooling down can contain our emotion. Emotions do not allow balance to think in a cool way. Pause and reflect before acting. Our negativity should be erased. 'Sanity is permanent and neurosis is temporary' according to the view of Chogyam Trungpa. This choice and the attitudes that follow are like a medicine that can cure all suffering. Meditation can also help us to pause before we talk or act. This is just being present, fully aware of our own Self. But our thoughts continue and we need to observe the thoughts without interrupting them. The thoughts then disappear. In the case of poison ivy, we tend to scratch. Instead of helping us, the whole body needs scratching due to the spreading of the itch. The solution is not to scratch at all. It will go away. The restlessness in the urge to scratch should be overcome. The root cause of our discontent is self-absorption and our fears of being present. The ego is like a cocoon, and we are always afraid of our feelings and reactions and what might happen to us. By trying to escape from pain we get into continuous pain. Everything is impermanent, while we look for a permanent reference point. If we tolerate uncertainty, the feeling of insecurity will go. Then we get profound freedom. Reality is just being present that requires being alert and attentive. Our tendency to escape will go. When we are distracted, problems arise.

*Shenpa* is attachment. The itch is one such. If we ignore it, it will go. If we are detached *shenpa* will disappear. When you dislike someone, shenpa appears. Why should we dislike someone? We are all part of the same family and we should just learn to live with everyone. No one is perfect. How can we expect perfection from others? Accepting people as they are, without judgment is what will help. *Shenluk* or renunciation is a beautiful idea. Once we renounce something it never bothers us. Full attention to problems will help to solve them. Bias is due to ego. We are entitled to our opinions but we get attached to a self-image of failure. The only way to ease pain is to experience it.

The individual is a bundle of contradiction in which kindness and aggression and other pairs of opposites are present. Behind these we have the dynamic energy that is always there, not affected by our reactions. It is to this energy (atman) that we should remain connected. We should learn to be comfortable with whatever experience we undergo being present during such experience is the awakening of constant awareness of our dynamic energy. All *shenpu* must be considered as an opportunity for transformation and awakening. It takes courage to stay calm amidst all negative influences. To be free of suffering is simply to live through it.

We are not permanent in this world. Our thoughts, actions, events, are all constantly changing. Labelling someone is useless since they will be changing constantly. Dalai Lama used to say that compassion for oneself leads to compassion for others. The three steps to this are: *maître* (friendliness) or loving kindness, communication with others from the heart and helping others without expecting anything in return. Peace is our essential nature and it does not depend upon good or bad events in our lives. Bad events should not affect our peace and good events should not make us overly happy. That is equanimity. Dalai Lama recommends fasting once a week to put ourselves in the shoes of those who starve in the world. Making friends with our experience and loving oneself will help in loving others.

The human spirit has a reservoir of courage. Caring for others selflessly and sharing our good with others is also the message of Mother Theresa. Putting the welfare of others before ourselves is the secret. Since everyone feels the pain and insecurity in life, why should we put the emphasis only on ourselves? Awareness is the awakening within us the dynamic energy present all the time. Love and joy are in our essential nature. Being joyful all the time helps us to tune into our own inner Self.

Dhamma is truth and the path to discover truth. The Buddhist morning chant is:

*Ehipasiko, opanaiko, paccatang veditabbho vinu hilfii'*. The dhamma of liberation is 'immediate, open handed, timeless, visible to the wise, to be experienced here and now by each person in their own heart'. We live in illusion and are carried off by the appearance of things. There is a reality, but we do not know this. When we understand this, we see that we are nothing; and being nothing, we are everything. This is what Kali Rinpoche had said. Shunryu Suzuki said- 'If your mind is empty, it is always ready for anything; it is open to everything. In the beginner's mind, there are many possibilities; in the expert's mind there are few'. Meditation helps us to realize our true nature which is always there. We only discover what is already within us. That is our unchanging essence. It is like the iceberg of which we see only the tip as the major portion is submerged in water. Pleasure is not happiness but contentment and

# Buddhism

true freedom is in not clinging to the 'I' or 'mine'. There is never anything but the present, and if we cannot live there, we cannot live anywhere, so said Alan Watts. Jiddu Krishnamurthy had said- 'To be free of all authority, of our own and that of others, is to die to everything of yesterday, innocent, full of vigour and passion. It is only in that state that one learns and observes. And for this, a great deal of awareness is required'. We see from what has been said above that Buddha reflected and repeated what the Vedanta of Hindus emphasized in the Upanishads.

Wheel is the symbol of Buddhism, 'set in motion the wheel of the Doctrine', symbolizing the sun, eternity and the cycle of life. Theravada Buddhism is the teaching adopted in Sri Lanka and elsewhere. In North India, Mahayana took roots (the Great Vehicle) and it was regarded as superior. Buddha did not believe in ritual and this was the major difference between the Hindu tradition and Buddha. As a Hindu prince, he observed human suffering and decided to leave the palace and his wife and started his teachings. Being a Hindu, he believed in the Hindu scriptures and quoted verbatim from Mahabharata and other texts in his Dhammapada. Neither Buddha nor Christ would have imagined that there would be religions in their name as they were essentially reformers of society.

Buddhist salvation is Nirvana or the Hindu Self-Realisation. Universal Truth for all is the Buddhist Dhamma (Hindu Dharma). Buddha never talked about god except perhaps obliquely nor did he say anything on creation or origin of the world and how ultimate reality is to be described. The very idea of a god as creating or in any way ruling the world, is utterly absent in the Buddhist system god is not so much as denied; he is simply not known. The power that controls the world is *karma*, literally action, including both merit and demerit. Buddha is said to have stated once that 'The future condition of the Buddhist is not assigned him by the Ruler of the Universe; the *karma* of his actions determines it by a sort of virtue inherent in the nature of things- by the blind and unconscious concatenation of cause and effect...Nothing is stable or real on earth. Life is like the spark produced by the friction of wood. It is lighted and is extinguished- we know not whence it came or whither it goes...There must be some supreme intelligence where we could find rest. If I attained it, I could bring light to man'. The Theravadins considered gods as humans (as did the Hindus), subject to change. Buddhism inculcates morality. Morality is totally devoid of supernatural sanction or support. The most essential virtues are truthfulness, benevolence, kindness, purity, patience, courage and contemplation. There is no promise of divine grace and everyone has to strive for himself. 'Be ye lamps unto yourselves. Rely on yourselves and do not rely on external help. Hold fast to the truth as a lamp. Seek salvation alone in the truth'. There is no question of sin or guilt as in Christianity or Judaism. Man's state is the result of past *karma* or actions and he has to erase the *karma* by selfless action.

Theravadins did not believe Buddha as supernatural and only accept his pure doctrine. Both sexes were equal and there were nuns and monks. Buddha prescribed precepts for them:

1. Do not destroy life.
2. Do not steal.
3. There should not be sexual misconduct.
4. Do not lie.
5. Do not drink alcohol.
6. Do not eat after midday.
7. Do not dance, sing or amuse yourself.
8. Do not wear ornaments.
9. Do not sleep on comfortable beds and,
10. Do not accept money. These also explained the eight-fold path. These precepts were increased to 227 rules later on.

The Sangha had no political activism as the objective for monks was Nirvana. For lay people, the first five precepts are mandatory.

Mahayana Buddhism of 2000 years ago strongly influenced China and thus began widespread following of Buddha's teachings there. Taoism and Confucianism also had their impact. In Mahayana, Buddha was deified. It taught the monks to delay Nirvana for helping those still struggling on earth. Buddha taught that everything was *anicca* (*anitya* in Sanskrit) impermanent and the human quest is for realization or liberation from worldly materialism. Monks should help in serving the sick and be kind to all. All ethical issues are subject to the eight-fold path and so abortion and other issues like homosexuality are to be viewed on that basis.

*Nyingma* is the oldest Tibetan text, derived from Tibet's pre-Buddhist, Shamanic religion 'Bon'. This is the *Tibetan Book of the Dead* from which we are about to glean briefly herein. According to this book, bodily death does not spell total death for humans. Reincarnation is accepted in Buddhism and its source is Hinduism but it only hints in the Kabbalah of Judaism that refers to it. Christianity tolerated it. The knife edge between past and future is the transient present and this is the basis of this teaching. That is how we take control of our lives. Karma or the law of cause and effect is central to Hindu and Buddhist thought. 'Everything we are, is the result of what we have thought', and possibly 'what we have wanted done…Don't look at your past lives or the future, just look at your present body'. The present it is that becomes the past.

# Buddhism

Jealousy, complacency and sloth become titans, demigods and animals respectively. It is possible to be enlightened in this birth itself. The book shows the way. We must know the unlimited that we really are.

The book tells us how to prepare ourselves for the inevitable death. Tibetans see the six in-betweens: The intervals between,

Birth and death- life between,
Sleep and waking- dream between,
Waking and trance- trance between,
Death and rebirth- death point,
Death and rebirth - reality point.
Death and rebirth - existence point.

Tibet is the land of Bo or snow. In the beginning they had shamanism or an animistic religion, with a priesthood that centred on royal fairy. Later on Buddhism entered and they started studying mathematics, astronomy and other sciences under Indian influence. The 13th and 14th centuries saw the Mongolians ruling most of Eurasia and Tibet but Tibet was left to itself. The Sakhya hierarchy was put in place by Kublai Khan but this was more a spiritual one. By the end of the 14th century, the Mongol empire fell apart as also the native dynasty of Pagom.

One of Tsong Khapa's younger disciples, Gendun Drubpa led the new order and it was known as the Lama Gendun Gyatso. His subsequent reincarnations and miracles led Sonam Gyatso in the 16th century after a historic visit to Mongolia in 1573, when he was named Dalai Lama (oceanic master) by the Emperor Altau Khan. Including his two predecessors, he was known as the third Dalai Lama. In 1642, the fifth Dalai Lama was crowned the king of Tibet founding the Ganden Palace victory government that is still considered as their legitimate government, though in exile in India. Manchus, the pan-Asian emperors of the era, guaranteed Tibetan independence and integrity. They were the Tungusic people of Korea who conquered China in 1644. The Dalai Lama was considered an ally due to his nearness to the Mongols and encouraged them to practice Buddhism. The demilitarization and pacification of the Mongols was a remarkable achievement of Dalai Lama.

Buddha founded the tradition of inner or mind science (*adhyatma vidya* of the Hindus). This science found the continuity between former, present and future lives leading them to prepare for death. Buddhists also believe in Yama (the god of death of the Hindus) and Chamunda, the goddess personification of the fearsome energy of Yama. Manjushree Bodhisattva tames this death as Padma Sambhava, the historical saviour of Tibet. Vivid awareness of death brings true freedom to man.

Karma is not fate as westerners wrongly believe. It is the cause and effect law, like that of Newton in science. Because only in the human life form can one attain immortality or enlightenment, this form is considered a treasure, hard-won, an achievement not to be wasted carelessly. This is precisely the advice of Adi Sankara in the beginning of the text, *Viveka Chudamani*. Consciousness is beyond dualities of finite and infinite, time and eternity, subject and object, ignorance and enlightenment. Realization of pure consciousness is the cessation of suffering. This indeed is truly the Hindu way followed by the Buddhists. For Descartes, the subject cannot be the object. 'I think therefore I am' is what he says. But the subject merges into the object and the two are one and the same in realization of the Self.

The four types of meditation are calming, insight, therapeutic and imaginative. There are other types of meditation as well like the daily active meditation. There are also four stages of spiritual development:

1. Extreme enlightenment teaching.
2. Relationship with a qualified teacher for esoteric practices.
3. Cultivation of creative imagination.
4. Mastery of the perfection stage.

'The purpose of meditation is to find the meditator; you will find silent emptiness. The mind stops', says Adyashanti. Buddhist texts tell us that compassion, love, kindness, sympathetic joy and equanimity are called the 'divine abodes'. It is foolish to run away from the world as to run after the world; both extremes have their roots in the illusion that the 'world' is something separate from ourselves, says Lama Anagarika Govinda. They can help convert eons of lives into one life.

The four types of wisdom:

Form (anger)- Akshobhya- diamond- mirror wisdom.
Sensation (pride) - Ratnasambhava- gold- Equalising wisdom.
Conception (lust) - Amitabha- ruby- Discriminating wisdom.
Cognition (delusion) - Vairochana- sapphire- Reality perfecting wisdom.
The ten merits are: seed mantra (*Om ha hum*), evocation, invitation, salutation, offerings, confession, congratulation, requesting teachings, request not to depart into Nirvana and dedication.

In effect Buddha's teaching essentially boils down to suffering and the 'ending of suffering'. Suffering arises from clinging as already mentioned. If the mind says 'I am' or 'I am not', there will be suffering. When the mind is silent, it becomes peaceful and free. Nirvana is the absence of suffering. It is empty and void of concept. It is here and now. This is how Maha Ghosananda summarises the philosophy.

We will conclude this dissertation on Buddhism with the following statement- The discerning reader would have understood by now that there is no difference between the Hindu Tradition and Buddhism except for the rituals. But rituals were not part of the Tradition till Brahmins introduced them later on based on the separation of Rig Veda into four or five Vedas. The two Vedas, Yajur and Sama both contained verses from the Rig Veda only with some hymns added later on to them. The Yajur Veda dealt with rituals and the Sama Veda was the musical Veda set to musical chanting and Indian music itself is said to have originated from it. (Please see chapter on music in the book *Ancient India* by this author).

## References:
1. Awakening the Buddha Within- Lama Surya Das, Broadway Books, NY.
2. Wake Up- A Life of Buddha- Jack Kerouac, Viking (Penguin).
3. Taking the Leap- Pema Chodron, Shambala, 2004.
4. The Buddha is still Teaching- Ed: Jack Kernfield, Shambala.
5. Ethics of World Religions- Arnold D. Hunt, Mary T. Crotty and Robert B. Crotty, Greenhaven Press, San Diego.
6. History of Ancient India-A Reappraisal- 2nd Edition, SriSriPublications, Bengaluru, 2015.
7. Tibetan Book of the Dead- Translated by Robert A.F. Thurman, Quality Paperback Book Club, NY.

# CHAPTER 4
# THE EGYPTIANS

A classic spirituality embraced by Taoists, Druids, Kabbalists, Buddhists and others who search to understand why we are here- this is the Papyrus of Hunefer, found at Thebes in Egypt and brought by the British to the British Museum in 1852, and it measured 18' X 1'3 3/8". In the 18th Dynasty, Kha-M-Wat carved a message to future generations at the entrance of the inner chamber of his tomb. In the Papyrus of Ani, the chief scribe of Pharaoh Seti I, it says: 'Men do not live once in order to vanish forever. They live several lives in different places but not always in this world and between lives, there is a veil of shadows. Our religion teaches us that we live for eternity. Thus, since eternity has no end, it cannot have a beginning. It is a circle. God has many faces… all these faces are merely the face of the One God. Our *ka*, which is our double, reveals them to us in different ways. By drawing from the bottomless well of wisdom, which is hidden in the essence of everyone, we perceive grains of truth which gives those of us with knowledge, the power to perform marvellous things'.

*The Book of the Dead* describes how the soul after death goes to *Dwat*, the nether world and then to the spiritual world *Nut* or heaven, either to be born again or to become one with the perfected souls who are not subject to the incarnation laws. Egyptians believe that the Book of the Dead was written by Tehuty, 50,000 years ago. Ancient Egyptians did not believe in many gods and goddesses but in one god only. Mythology is the earth of eternity and rituals, the earth of time. The divine qualities in nature are reflections of the natural laws of Netru, and are part of the Self (*Neter*- principle of law, masculine, the *yang*). *The Book of the Dead* says: 'I know in my heart that I have gained power over my emotions. I have gained power over my arms. I have gained power over my legs and I have gained power to do what pleases my spirit. My soul, therefore, shall not be imprisoned in my body…Death is the result of ignorance alone…The wickedness of the soul is ignorance and the virtue of the soul is knowledge'. Egyptians had many gods and goddesses who are not to be confused with the One God. These are divine angels with extraordinary powers as is found in the Hindu Pantheon but they are also the manifestations of the One God.

The Egyptian Empire collapsed in 525 BCE after which they embraced Christianity on the preaching of St. Mark the Apostle in Alexandria in 69 CE. Budge wrote: 'The priests and theologians saw nothing incompatible in believing that God was one and that he existed under innumerable forms'. Mariette Bey, describing the monuments at the Museum at Bulak in Cairo says: 'At the head of the Egyptian Pantheon soars a god who is one, immortal, uncreated, invisible, and hidden in the inaccessible depths of his essence'.

Dr Brusch in his *Religion and Mythologie* says: 'The Egyptians themselves held that the gods were only names of the various attributes of the One God'. Tehuty said: 'None of our thoughts are capable of conceiving God nor any language of defining Him, that which is incorporeal, formless, invisible, and cannot be grasped by our senses… God is ineffable'. 'Atum-Ra (God, the source of all light) existed before there was any notion of space-time. This power wanted to make itself known and so it uttered the sacred word to create (sound). This in turn led to the creation of primordial water of *Nu*…which contained everything in the embryonic form. *Nu* was shrouded in darkness and contained the male and female of absolutely everything that was to exist in the future'. The sound brought the world to life, in the form of an egg, out of the water of *Nu*. *Ra*, the light of god in nature was manifest on earth through the disc of the sun, Aten, and appeared for the first time in the form of *Dsher* or the sunrise at the beginning of life on earth. This light vanquished all darkness and the first humans were created (four male and four female). They were depicted as Baboons who sang to the creator upon the rising of the sun. They were also depicted as humans with the heads of frogs (males) and the heads of cobras (females), symbolizing that they were immortal. The four pairs, the first couples, procreated the four races as follows;

Born at dusk- Kek and Keket- the black race.
Born at dawn- Hek and Heket- the Asians.
Born at noon- Nun and Nunit- Europeans.
Born at sunrise- Emen and Emenet- Egyptian forefathers.

Among their offspring was Tehuty, who carried the divine intelligence within him and brought language and divine speech into existence. Ptah was the first craftsman on earth and Knemuh, the master builder who brought Tehuty's commands to fruition. There was no evil in Etelenty (Atlantis?) and people followed the laws of nature. They saw the creation of the moon out of the soil of the Atlantic Ocean, and the creation of plants, animals, birds, and creeping things. The earth was unstable and Tehuty, knowing that Etelenty would be submerged by the ocean, ordered the emigration of the four families that formed the population of the land. This emigration took place around 50,000 years ago. The families of the four couples went respectively to Africa,

# The Egyptians

Asia, Europe and Egypt. The priesthood of Emen and Emenet with Tehuty, Ptah, and Khnemu went to Egypt and built the Pyramids of Giza as the Temple of initiation and induction of priests.

The Nine Principles of Eunu (Heliopolis) in the life, death and resurrection of the soul are:

1. *Shu-* air (masculine, separating the three worlds).
2. *Tefnut-* moisture, the sister of *Shu*.
3. *She-* earth, the offspring of *Shu* and *Tefnut*.
4. *Nut-* heaven, daughter of    -do-   .
5. *Oser-* son of heaven and earth; the first king of Egypt, who suffered at the hands of his brother Set, and so preferred to be the king of after-life, in the constellation of Orion.
6. *Heru-* Ur (Horus the Great), subdued Set and brought him in chains to Heliopolis.
7. *Set-* killed his brother Oser, cutting the body to 14 pieces and scattering them all over Egypt. He is the emblem of indolence and rebellion. He was defeated by Heru-Sheriu (Horus the younger), the son of Est and Oser and was arrested by Heru-Ur and brought to the Hall of Justice.
8. *Est-* Isis, wife of Oser residing in Sirius (Dog Star), by the side of Orion, her husband's home. She is the symbol of knowledge and authority and ruled for 25 years in the absence of Oser.
9. *Nebt-Het-* Nephthys, emblem of peace and sister of *Est*.

In the judgment scene, the dead regains life in the tomb and stands before the 42 natural laws and Oser, the king of after-life (*Yama*?). Tehuty is also present to record the deeds and future of the deceased soul while Enpu (Anubi) holds the scales of justice upon which all the deeds are weighed against the truth. The bodily organs of the dead are witness to his deeds. If during the past life the deceased succeeded in identifying with the laws of nature, there is no further birth. Else, they have to take another body as per their past deeds. The soul travels to the garden of reeds-*Sekhet-Earu*, in the Orion constellation. The field of peace, *Sekhet- Hetep* includes Orion, Taurus and Leo. The soul then travels east to Sirius, accompanied by the children of Heru (the spirits in the stomach, lungs and intestine). The soul further travels north to the Great Bear, where it is purified by the Great Ennead (the Nine Principles) and the lesser Ennead. The soul that has accumulated a higher level of consciousness on earth ends its travels.

## Vedic Tradition and World Religions

There are at least four different recensions to the *Book of the Dead*:

1. The Heliopolitan version- this is lost but five copies are inscribed on the walls of the chambers in Pyramids of the Kings of the 5th and 6th Dynasties at Saqqara (Unes, Tete, Pepi I, Pepi II, and Mentu-M-Sa-F). They were excavated in 1880 and 1884 by Mariette and Maspero and the hieroglyphic texts known as the Pyramid Texts were published in Paris between 1882-1893.
2. The Theban Version- used between the 18th and 20th Dynasties.
3. The Generic version number one- closely allied to the Theban- used in the 20th Dynasty (written in Medu-Netru and Hieralic).
4. The Saite version- written as above and used from the 26th Dynasty till the Ptolemic period. Their chapters were arranged in a definite order.

## The symbolism of *Hedu-Netru:*

It is in hieroglyphics or symbolic writing. The original language of man was founded in Atlantis by *Tehuty* (Hermes). It had ten symbols but later *Beli Mawr* (the Great), the celtic god of the sun, added another six symbols. It was the Britain Gwydiar that introduced the sixteen letter symbols to Greece. The crocodile is written by drawing a crocodile. The female has bird like qualities, lays eggs, its heart and kidneys are similar to the birds but its lungs are those of a mammal. The crocodile therefore reflects duality in nature. It spends the night in water and day on land and so it is a solar animal emerging on land when the sun rises and getting into water when the moon rises (moon is a watery sign). The female carries the eggs for 60 days, broods on them for 60 days; it has 60 vertebrae and 60 teeth and lives for 60 years. The number sixty is the basic unit in astronomy, the measurement of time in 60 seconds, minutes etc. Sebek means crocodile and *seb* represents the principle of time. Time goes forward, never backward. The symbolism of some other things-

- Snake- *epep,* a water reptile.
- Water cow- represents earth.
- The twins *Shu* and *Tefnet* (dryness and moistness)- lion and lioness
- Virgin woman- female vulture as it became pregnant by mere exposure to the wind.
- The provider- goose.
- Leader or king- honey bee (*Bt* also means honey), symbolizes the substance of The soul (*ba*), from which the English word bee is derived.
- The artist- represented by a scarab as it continuously regenerates.
- The physician- represented by an ibis bird since it administers enema to itself.
- The Judge- by a mouse since it eats the best part of a bread, by a jackal since it hides its food in earth, once putrid, brings it out to eat and also a baboon as it

cries in the absence of the moon and rejoices when it appears. The wig used by the British represents the wig of the Baboon.
- Mystic initiate- by a grasshopper since it makes a sound using the spinal cord and not from the mouth.
- The seer- by a frog *(heqat)*, since it predicted the inundation of the Nile. Ptah was represented as a frog-headed man for creative power.
- Light of the sun- by a circle.
- Orion- *saah*.
- Innocence and simplicity- *chick*.
- Life- a looped cress (*ankh*).
- Mystery- leopard (*abu*)

During evolution, the causal energy becomes minerals, minerals become vegetables, vegetables become animals, animals become humans and man becomes superman (the sage or the immortal). The underlying quality in the above is suffering due to separation like the mineral suffering separation from the original cause, plants suffering separation from the mineral's life and so on. This suffering is consciousness undergoing the process of transformation of itself.

## The Book of Hunefer
It was written during king Maat-Men-Ra (Seti I) in c. 1400 BCE. It contains some chapters of the Book of the Dead and includes:

1. A hymn to the rising sun.
2. Declaration of Tehuty and an account of what good he has done for Oser (Osiris).
3. The Judgment of the deceased.
4. Chapters 1, 22 and 17 of the Book of the Dead.
5. Chapter on the opening of the mouth of Oser.

The Egyptian spiritual system is based on faith on the One Almighty Creator, founded by Tehuty. 'None of our thoughts are capable of conceiving God, nor any language of defining Him. That which is incorporeal, formless, invisible, cannot be grasped by the senses. God is ineffable'- Book of the Dead.

'I achieved purification of the body and soul in the time of my youth, when other people were busy with the dazzling illusion of life' (Plate 4 of the book of Hunefer).

## The Papyrus Of Gerusher, Column I
The circulation of earth energy is one of five types of circulation, which affect our lives physically and spiritually. The subtle energy of the earth enters the human body

through the feet, hips and kidneys, and has five currents. These currents mix with the energy generated by the soul (ba), which resides in the marrow of the bones, feeding the twelve inner organs in a cycle during the day and night. Each organ is fed for 2 hours each:

Colon (*er-maat*-N-F)- 5-7 AM.
The Stomach (*Dua-Mut*-F)- 7-9 AM.
The Spleen/Pancreas (*Heqa*)- 9-11 AM.
The Heart (*Er-Maaty*0- 11 am-1 pm.
The Intestine (*Qeb-sen-ef*)- 1-3 PM.
The Urinary bladder (*Er-Ren-F-Des*-F)- 3-5 PM.
The Kidneys (*Hud-Hnd*)- 5-7 PM.
The Pericardium (*Kedt-Nu*)- 7-9 PM.
The Glands (*Ery-N-F*)- 9-11 PM.
The Gall bladder (Aha-Shp-Aha)- 11 PM-1 AM.
The Liver (*Mesty*)- 1 AM-3 AM.
The Lungs (*Hapi*)- 3-5 AM.

## Papyrus of the Royal Mother Nezemt

It contains forty two negative confessions starting with 'I have not committed sins', robbed, stolen, and so on ending with 'I have not scorned my city principles'. These can be considered as forerunners to the Ten Commandments of Moses which became human law for the Christians while the forty-two were the responsibility of individuals.

The Papyrus of Ani, found in Thebes in 1888 and bought by the British Museum, is the longest, measuring 78 ' X 1' 3". They contain hymns to *Ra* and *Oser* and the judgment scene. The hymns are similar to those contained in the Vedas.

Unlike the Christian belief that the sins of men are redeemed by Jesus Christ, the Egyptian religion believes that no one can redeem the sins of others. It is built upon natural laws, not upon individual lives. The laws of nature are the true language of god. A mango seed does not spring upon wheat. The sun rises in the east and sets in the west. These cannot be changed by men.

This old document has reference to the lost continent of Atlantis which has inspired Plato to write on it. Atlantis submerged in the Atlantic Ocean millennia ago. The Egyptian Temples, paintings in the Temples and columns as in Luxor, Cairo etcetera and the hieroglyphic texts have survived for millennia because it was neither ravaged nor plundered by outside forces. India, however, was plundered by the Moghuls and other invaders for more than thousand two hundred years, during which most of the ancient texts have been destroyed and many have gone under the sea in a number of geological convulsions that submerged the Kumari continent south of Cape Comorin.

A brief summary of Egyptian Religion and its basic principles have been given above and it would be easy for a person with knowledge about the Vedic Tradition to find parallels between the two. The latter is practically timeless as it has existed since the advent of civilization in India that goes back to at least 15,000 years. The many gods in both traditions are but enlightened beings and only the One God that is beginningless, formless, all-powerful is the single reality and all else are but manifestations of the One like all gold jewellery are names and forms which ultimately are reduced to gold only. Similar is the case of clay and the pottery and other objects made from it known by different names and forms but are only clay.

## References:
1. The Egyptian Book of the Dead- (Translated by Dr Ramses Seleem, Sterling Publishing, New York.
2. Science Philosophy and Religion- Ramakrishnan Srinivasan, Citadel, Calcutta.
3. History of Ancient India- A Reappraisal, Ramakrishnan Srinivasan, 2nd Edition, SriSriPublications, Bengaluru.

# CHAPTER 5

# THE GREEKS

Since about the seventh century BCE, there have been many scholars and thinkers in the Grecian archipelago many of whom have visited and/or studied in Indian universities of Taxila, Vikramashila or Nalanda. These were the first universities in the world and people from different parts of the world studied in them to acquire knowledge of the sciences and other disciplines. First, we give an overview of the scientific and philosophical development in Greece and then go on to study some thoughts of the important philosophers and finally study the ethics of Aristotle in some detail. Most of what is given here is based on the scholarly book of essays edited by Brunschwig and Geoffrey Lloyd titled *Greek Thought*.

The key to the unparalleled originality of the Greeks may be that their culture, by definition, did not have the Greeks behind it. Its basic elements were borrowed from the Phoenicians. The latter were the 'Panis' of the ancient Tamil country who were essentially bards and roving philosophers. In fact the word Phoenician itself is derived from these bards (Panis). Their culture pre-dated the Socratic idea of 'KnowThyself'. The Greeks' debt to preceding civilizations represented by the Egyptians or the despotic Mesopotamians was however compensated by their quick absorption.

The Socratic fallacy is this- One could not say whether an individual was courageous or not, so long as one was unable to say universally what courage is. Wisdom is a kind of knowledge that is at least necessary, if not sufficient, for having a good life. The pre-Socratics from Thales to Democritus tried to provide an account of reality or theory of nature. Socrates relied on three things:
1.  The notion of the soul as what guides our behaviour.
2.  The presence of such things as justice and piety.
3.  The presence of a thing as a good that reflects on how people behave.

Though the Stoic, Aristo and many Cynics accepted this nomad vision, Plato rejected this and affirmed that ethics has to be embedded in, and supported by a theoretical account of reality. The soul is conceived as pre-existing and temporarily attached to a body. In the process, it forgets itself and its own needs and lives for the needs of the body making it its own needs. The Stoic, Phyria is governed by an immanent divine rational principle that arranges the world down to the smallest detail for a perfect world. Given that the soul can see the truth unimpeded only if it disentangles itself from the body, asceticism seems to be the way to see the truth.

The question of being- being denotes some single permanent, unchanging, fundamental reality, to which is opposed the inconstant flux and variety of visible things. Thales raised the question- what is the one constituent of all that we see about us? The salient features of this are: 1.It was assumed that things were not what they seemed to be. 2. That there was only one thing that objects really were or came from. Aristotle decried this concern with the material cause of the earlier physicists and wanted to consider the efficient cause also.

Parmenides, the father of western philosophy says: Being is one, motionless, uniform, and eternal. Non-being is unthinkable. The Hellenistic concept of Being was thoroughly materialistic and this-worldly and Aristotle's successor in the Peripatetics subscribed to it. It was the Neo-Platonist Plotinus that declared- the One, to be above the intellect and Being, these being identified as the intellect and the soul constituting a third.

The Greeks identified knowledge with sense perception especially, visual. 'I know because I have seen'. Aristotle designates 'nous' as the cognitive state that apprehends principles, that is more exact and true than demonstrative knowledge itself. To know what man ought to be is to know the purpose of life. Aristotle said that the highest state a human being can attain is one of contemplation of the divine. Virtue is related to knowledge. Man's wickedness originates solely in his ignorance according to Socrates, though happiness is defined as pleasure, the ultimate goal. This requires a life of virtue.

Writing appeared, borrowed from the Phoenicians, the source of the Greek alphabet. The first theory of political regimes was developed by Herodotus from the conversation of three Persians- Otanes, Megabyzes and Darius. It was opposed to tyranny and it was preferred to place the city-state in the hands of the best people (*aristoi* is the aristocracy), few in number (*oligoi*), known as an oligarchy. Otanes wanted people's democracy, Magabyzes, an oligarchy and, Darius advocated a monarchy. The last being a tyranny in Greece, the choice was between democracy and oligarchy. Solon appears to be the founder of democracy. He abolished servitude of the peasantry and drafted laws that applied to all. According to Plato, a city state had about 30,000 citizens during the 6th century BCE.

# The Greeks

The earliest use of astronomy in Greece was in the poems of Hesiod and Homer in the 8th century BCE. However, Greek musical activity is known from textual, visual and archaeological documents. Stringed, wind, and percussion instruments are shown in ceramics, unearthed in numbers, and about fifty musical scores in papyrus or inscriptions give us a picture of musical activity. Music and politics were closely linked and laws governed musical practice and education in Sparta, Thebes and Mantinea. Young men were taught musical theory and to play the 'kithara' with or without plectrum. Singing with kithara as accompaniment was popular. Musicians were honoured by the state. Bacchus in his Introduction gives six kinds of consonant intervals in harmony. They are the fourth, the fifth, the octave, the octave plus the fourth, the octave plus the fifth and the double octave. Music was sister to mathematics and astronomy, as a science of numerical relations governing the musical intervals. Ptolomy in his Harmonika reconciled acoustics, physics and harmonics in a cogent theory for the first time. Harmonics is the first component where it precedes rhythm and metrics. The seven sections of harmonics are: sounds, intervals, systems, genera, tones, *metabolai* and musical composition. *Metabolai* is modulation. But their harmonics lacked musical notation. With notation, Greek music is reborn.

From Hellenistic logic came determinism or sufficient cause. The epistemological principles led to the modern sciences, especially, physics. Greeks were fascinated by the near east and Egypt and the inquiry into being and nature resulted from Thales and Anaximander. Physics designates first of all, the primordial substance from which everything is derived. Physics is also a process of growth and differentiation of things out of their original substance. The process of growth or coming into being is physics. Anaximander shows that from a primordial substance, infinite pairs of opposites are ejected. Everything derives from water through condensation and rarefaction; for another, everything derives from air and a third, from fire. Certain pre-Socratics conceived the universe as having infinite extension in time and space.

The first challenge to ancient physics came in the 5th century BCE, from Parmenides of Elea (the Eleatic school). In Nature, he saw all things derived from a single principle. Thus the 'infinite' is indeterminate and so is not a being, though it engenders all things. He says being cannot come from non-being. Intelligibility belongs to what is eternal and immutable, while what is perishable belonged at best to opinion. Aristotle, however, saw that the atomist hypothesis of Leucippus and Democritus, reintroduced the possibility of plurality and movement while retaining the central core of Eleatic philosophy. The atomists imagined infinity of particles that are whole, indivisible, eternal, and in constant movement in an infinite void that is non-existent. Aggregations of these atoms produced various entities. Of all mortal things none has birth or any end in accursed death, but only mingling. Empedocles said that everything is made from new combinations that are eternally unmade and that arise from four fixed elements- air, water, fire and earth. Anaxagoras stated that 'nothing comes into being nor perishes, but is rather compounded or dissolved from things that are'. From this was derived the principle by later scientists that matter can neither be created nor destroyed but can only be redistributed. This was what was stated by Krishna in the Bhagwad Gita more than 5000 years ago.

Socrates stated that the science of nature is greater than the powers of the human spirit or that it is by design that the gods have left us in the dark on this subject. Plato was the first to give a creationist view rather than an evolutionist one, though, Diogenes gave the idea that the order of the world was optimally devised by a divine intelligence. Aristotle's theory is that everything is set in motion by an 'unmoved mover' and this is divinity. The first sky is moved by desire, because the perfection of the Prime Mover makes it also desirable.

Xenophanes (570-470 BCE) said, 'Homer and Hesiod have attributed to the gods everything that is a reproach among men, stealing and committing adultery and deceiving one another'. The Sophist, Protagoras averred, 'About gods, I cannot know either that they are or that they are not. For, many things prevent one from knowing- the obscurity of the question and the life of man, which is short'. Democritus, one of the first agnostics, said in his *Sisyphus* that 'religion was invented as a tool of law enforcement'. Plato reports in Cratylus that Socrates insisted that we know nothing about the gods.

The Stoics' explication of providence was as fierce as the Epicurean hostility. The three ideas of Stoics:
1. Doctrine of the cosmic city; humans and gods share the capacity to love according to reason, and so making a community under moral law.
2. Because gods care for men, they give us signs as premonitions of the future and the means of understanding them.
3. Providence led to a theodicy, i.e., explanation as to why a deity who cares for men should allow evil in the world. There cannot be good without evil.

Different kinds of agnosticism can be seen in the following among Greek scholars:

Protagoras- No means of knowing.

Skeptics- Reason cannot establish theological truths but that should not threaten conventional beliefs.

Xenophanes- 'We do not know but can make reasonable conjectures…if cattle and horses…had hands or able to draw with their hands…horses would draw the form of gods like horses, and cattle, like cattle'.

Theology as a discipline came about because of the philosophical doubt about the gods. Aristotle and the Stoics insisted that the common belief in gods, universal among humankind, was already a testimony to their existence. The former opined that 'There is a general idea of just and unjust in accordance with nature, as all men in a manner are divine, even if there is neither communication nor agreement between them'. Critias wrote that 'a wise and clever man invented fear (of the gods) for mortals, that there might be some means of frightening the wicked, even if they do anything or say or think it in secret'. Thus the divine was invented, saying 'god had immortal life, able to see all that is done'.

The pre-Socratic legacy provided subsequent attitudes of philosophers to religion. Their three options were:

1. Co-existence of philosophy and religion.
2. Annexation of religion by philosophy.
3. The rejection of religion.

Socrates was the pivotal figure in this evolution. Plato reveals that Greek religion was devoid of spirituality. Socrates inaugurated the trends that included respect for religion and the control or domination of philosophy over religious thought. Aristotle believed that religious festivals are moments of relaxation for citizens. Critias and the Cynics however, rejected religion. Euhemerus (340-260 BCE) held that gods were but divine men.

The Hellenistic period saw the decline of religion and the growth of individualism. Anaxagoras the Eleatic, like Parmenides, dismisses the use by men of 'birth' and 'destruction'. To come into being is just as impossible as to be annihilated, for nothing arises from non-being nor does being return to non-being. Things that are, are not born nor do they die but they reunite and dissociate themselves. 'All things were together, infinite in regard both to number and to smallness; for the small too was infinite'. Everything just IS.

We shall now very briefly look at the ideas of the major Greek thinkers and get a bird's eye view in what follows:

## Antisthenes (445-365 BCE):
He was important next only to Plato. For him, the sovereign good is life lived according to virtue; virtue can be taught and once learnt, cannot be lost; virtue suffices for

happiness. The inner freedom is based on tireless enquiry into the nature of things, governed by reason, and on the Socratic 'force' that prevents the body from asserting its hegemony over the rational soul and over truth.

## Archimedes:

His ideas mainly follow the exhaustion method of Eudoxus. He studied the circle, a sphere inscribed in a cylinder and many other mathematical problems. The sphere inscribed in a cylinder that he explored had the surface area of the two were in the ratio of 2:3. He also studied the principle of leverage for moving large bodies. He devoted himself to the beauty and precision of pure inquiry.

## Aristotle:

Aristotle was a scientist, astronomer, and political theorist rather than a philosopher. St. Thomas Aquinas reconciled his work with Christian doctrine in the 13th century CE and only after this, his influence spread in Western Europe. A student of Plato's Academy, he later started Lyceum after Plato's death. He is considered as the father of empirical science and the scientific method. He always considered the views of others before detailing his own arguments. He denied that there could be exact laws of human nature but maintained that certain metaphysical categories- quantity, quality, substance, relation etc., were applicable in the description of phenomena. The common thread in his work is teleology or purpose or goal. Every activity has a purpose. Modern evolutionary biology uses this to describe the behaviour of genes. He said that everything has a natural function and strives to fulfil that function. He ties his ethics to his physics claiming reason to be the natural function of man and to reason in accordance with virtue.

While strolling about in a thunder he found the noise in the clouds and described it as 'an extension of fire in a cloud', revealing its cause and its essence. He associated knowledge (*eidenoi*) with conviction (*pisteuein*), coordinating them by a strong tie which marks a bond between the two realities of the same nature. But, for Plato, conviction is inferior knowledge. In Aristotle's closed, finite and eternal world, the very idea of emergence of the total being, or of cosmic order from chaos disappears. Parmenides shows that this cannot be even envisaged. Secondly, Nature is no longer either all of being or the most important part of being. The whole of nature, a closed system of self-propelling realities, draws its movement from outside itself (the immovable prime mover). The heavens move because they are animated by a movement of desire towards the prime mover. The supernatural is thus necessary for the existence and the coherence of nature. In his phallo-centric view of animal reproduction, the male provides the form and the female the matter.

Aristotle's substance is an individual person or thing, a combination of form and matter and only the formal element is knowable and constant. So the substance is the essence of a thing. Matter is 'progressively informed' first as a simple element, say, earth, then as a species of earth. Like clay and its forms of pottery and forms or gold and its jewelry. Ultimately all forms of matter are reduced to its original element- earth. The four causes of form are: 1. Materials like bricks, earth etc., 2. design or shape, 3. their efficient function- that which originates the process, and finally, 4. the final cause—the end or purpose of the operation. The last three are closely related and are barely distinguishable from the formal cause.

Change is either a substance of quality (1), of quantity (2), and of place or locomotion (3). These are described as movement. Ultimately the essential form is lost and the original element only is there like gold or clay. All forms disintegrate over a period of time. The antithesis of potentiality and actuality is that of matter and form viewed dynamically. Bricks are not actually but potentially a house and gold its jewelry. The seed is potentially a tree and the fertilized ovum is an animal or human. A habit like aptitude for music can remain dormant and only when in full use does it become actuality or activity. Change involves a lapse of time (1), and when complete, they cease over time (2). One can see the ancient Hindu idea of gold and clay as the essential material and all objects made from them are but names and forms. The Upanishads often cite one or the other of these examples including fire and the sparks.

## Aristotle's Nature and Theology:
Nature meant growth with the emphasis on origin and development. Nature includes everything and exhibits process. The grades of soul—nutritive, sentient and intellectual- and the accompanying forms of life range upwards from plants, mollusks, insects, fishes, etc., to higher animals and man. Movement is due to external attraction. From the astronomer Eudoxus, Aristotle derived the mechanical nature of cosmic bodies, themselves moved by the 'Unmoved First Mover', the ultimate reality and pure form, mind or god, whose ceaseless activity is self-thinking thought since no other activity is worthy of him. He is the final good, the object of love and desire that he ultimately causes and sustains all movement and life in the cosmos. Aristotle identified *eudoimonia* with contemplation.

## Aristotle's Pleasure and Process:
Speucippus had argued that pleasure consisted in supplying the deficiency of a malady resulting therefrom. That is the remedial process. This was objected to by Aristotle-
1. Good or bad may not be such for a particular subject in particular circumstances.

So a process that is pleasant to one may be unpleasant to another. 2. Deficiency only impairs a part of one's state, the rest remaining healthy.

Pain (evil reality) -> via pleasure (a process)-> absence of pain (good reality). So pleasure is a process from pain to its absence.

## Democritus (460-370 BCE):

When matter is divided continuously, it reaches a point when it cannot be further divided. This is the atom. He had extensively travelled in India, Egypt and other places and was known as the laughing philosopher as he was always cheerful. His universe was infinite and hence had no centre. In the 5$^{th}$ century BCE, he invented the atomic theory along with Leucippus. The theory is that the universe is made of atoms and void. 'The fundamental nature of the universe consists of indivisible atoms in constant motion'. Unlike Zeno, he held that atoms, though divisible, are only matter containing spaces- parts of the void between the atoms. With Heraclitus, he agrees that both change and motion are possible and necessary states of nature. Even thoughts are a concatenation of atoms. He agreed with Parmenides and Zeno that motion would be impossible if the universe consisted of nothing but matter. The only true non-being is the infinite void, the absolute space in which atoms are eternally in motion. This is somewhat contradictory as void is the absence of being or existence. But he held that the infinite void was merely absence of matter and independent of the existence of atoms. Later Newton would uphold this idea of absolute space as a kind of receptacle for matter. Leibniz thought of space as merely a relation between physical objects. Democritus also held that all events are due to the impact of atoms upon each other. A version of this theory is 'determinism' that is mostly defended or denied by recent philosophers.

He was the first to talk of multiple universes. There was no design of creation of the infinite universe. For Anaxagoras, the huge universe had a mind as the 'moving agent'. Empedocles reduced it to the four elements- air, water, fire and sky. Democritus reduced the basic ingredients to Being and non-being, a dualism. Aristotle reduced the void as the locus of movement of atoms or 'beings'. Man is separated from reality- we know nothing about anything; belief is for us reshaping sight, hearing and so on that are illegitimate knowledge. Legitimate knowledge is separate from them. For Democritus, the soul is made up of spherical atoms as fire is. The gods do not make the physical world. 'Nature and teaching are akin; for, teaching reforms a person and by re-forming, creates his nature'. His physical theory was transmitted through the medium of Epicureanism.

## Epicurus (341-270 BCE):

His ethics is the pursuit of happiness and elimination of pain. He follows the atomism of Democritus but with one modification. He suggested that atoms in the void moved in parallel lines but some atoms swerved from their course due to free will. The resulting collisions give rise to myriad forms of things and the phenomenal world. This helped to reject determinism as an explanation of human behaviour. Mental pain is more harmful than physical pain that abates. He was not a hedonist as he urged prudence and temperance in his philosophy. Wisdom was the greatest virtue as it helped to discriminate between desirable pleasures and undesirable ones. Without virtue there cannot be complete happiness. He rejected the idea of anthropomorphic gods. He asked- 'Is god willing to prevent evil, but not able? Then he is not omnipotent. Is he able and willing? Then how can there be evil'? He was a theist who rejected divine intervention and the survival of the soul. Lucretius was his staunch follower, and he had 600 years of following before the Stoics eclipsed him.

The ten propositions of Epicurus are:
1. Nothing is born out of what does not exist.
2. Nothing dissolves into what does not exist.
3. The universe has always been and will always be the same.
4. The universe is composed of bodies and space.
5. Bodies consist of atoms and aggregates.
6. The universe is infinite.
7. Atoms are infinite and space boundless in extension.
8. Atoms of identical form are infinite but their differences in form are indefinite in number, not infinite.
9. The atoms are in constant motion.
10. Atoms have but three properties common with bodies- form, volume and weight.

Atoms pass through the void at the 'speed of thought'. All our actions tend towards an ultimate end i.e., happiness. Pleasure of the soul is superior to the pleasure of the body. Variability of the norms of justice is not an argument against the objectivity of justice.

## Euclid (3rd century BCE):

He gave to the world the theory of whole numbers. Modern mathematics evolved from the 'elements' through a dialogue and integration with the old. Euclidean Geometry was prevailing till the 17th century and it was superceded by modern geometry.

## Galen (b.129 BCE):

His study contributed and covered medicine, logic, philosophy and philology. Anatomy was his special area of study. For him, a good doctor must also be a good philosopher.

## Heraclitus (560-500 BCE):

He was thought to be from Ephesus, was an Ionian and so a Milesian. After extensive travels, he returned and remained a hermit, probably due to the Hindu influence after his visit to India. His basic dictum was 'all things pass', in the eternal flux or flow or movement, like the water changing continuously in a river or man changing constantly in life. The only permanence is impermanence. Being or reality consists in always 'becoming', not in stability but in change. This eternal movement is the eternal strife of opposites. Thus oneness emerges from multiplicity and multiplicity from oneness. Harmony of the universe is of contraries like the lyre and the bow. Fire is the underlying principle of nature due to its subtlety, mobility, and ability to penetrate and devour all things, its power of giving warmth to living bodies, and the life-giving power of the sun. He then calls it the Thunderbolt or Eternal Reason or law or fate. The Eternal Creation in which fire descends to its cruder elements of water and earth, only gets resolved again into fire. In breathing, man draws the vital element of all being in which we all have our consciousness.

He recognized a baser element of moistness in man of unreason and so his communication with the divine on the dryness or elevation of spirit that is within. For those that are base, the living fire is invisible and so, see only death. Their spirits are dead. The highest good for man is his perception of his Self and the eternal unity and harmony and constancy amidst change.

Hegel and Heidigger were indebted to him and his theory of 'unity of the opposites'. Three examples are: 'people step into the same rivers and different waters flow onto them'. This implies that one bathes in a river but every time it is a different river as the water keeps flowing and it is not the same waters. 'A road uphill and downhill are one and the same'. And, 'the sea is water most pure and most polluted; for fish, drinkable and life-giving and for humans, undrinkable and deadly'. These are paradoxical but true. Day and night are the same only in the sense that they are different temporary states of the same thing. The cyclic process implied in the soul and the cosmos is seen here. 'The same thing is present inside as living and dead, as sleeping and awake, as young and old; for, these change to become the other and they change to become yet another'. 'The best choose one thing in place of all; glory ever flowing of mortals; but the many are glutted like cattle'. The cosmos too, goes cyclically through decay and renewal. The river example is the image of the permanence through change of the cosmos or the individual soul.

He said that 'war and strife between opposites is the central condition of the universe'. He criticized Homer, Pythagoras and Xenophanes among others. Fire, earth and water are the principal elements with fire being primary, modifying the other two. The counterpart of cosmic fire is the human soul, which in weak men, is tainted by watery elements of sleep, stupidity and vice. The virtuous soul can survive death of its physical body and rejoin the cosmic fire. The dynamism between the opposites was the driving force and eternal condition of the universe. This corresponds with the Yin and Yang of the Chinese and the *dvandvas* of the Hindus. Even with such variance, there is an underlying unity/harmony as with the bow and the lyre. Change is continual but the universe itself is eternal.

## Herodotus (480-420 BCE):
The Persian Empire rose, Athens and Sparta came to prominence. Politically, 'eunomy' (equal law with a well constituted government) was replaced by 'isonomy' (equality of rights for all) and democracy. His *Histories* covered Persians, Libyans, Babylonians, Arabs, Indians, Scythians, etc. It is a meditation on the drive for conquest and the destiny of the conquerors. He travelled more to confirm his representation. The Greeks rediscovered writing, borrowing the Phoenician alphabet but it was in Herodotus that the historian emerged.

## Hippocrates (5th Century BCE):
He comes from a long line of physicians. In his Regimen, he recommended diet and exercise with lifestyle changes for a good health, never more relevant than in the 21st century. What Aristotle is to philosophical thought, Hippocrates is to medicine. The Hippocratic Oath is well known in the medical world even today.

## Parmenides of Elea (510-440 BCE):
He was a student of Xenophanes and Ameinias, a Pythagorian. He inaugurated the history of ontology or the science of being. 'To think and to be are the same thing'… 'The possibility of thinking and the possibility of existing are in fact the same thing'. It is impossible for non-existence to be. His goddess speaks of the path of truth that has many signs (*semata*), equivalent number of characteristics of Being; unborn, imperishable, whole of limb, unshaking, unendable, one, and continuous. It cannot have an origin for, if it had, it should have gotten it from non-being or from being; but non-being is not and being is already, and thus cannot originate it. Being is bound up in the chains of justice, firmly. Being neither was nor will be, it just IS now. It is eternal

subsisting in a timeless present. It is continuous since it is not divisible because it is the same everywhere. This is the clearest expression of the Hindu concept of Brahman, probably borrowed from them. He expressed his idea in a poem through the goddess. He had said, 'one cannot know that which is not, that is impossible'. He countered Heraclitus by saying that change is impossible and that reality is singular, undivided and homogeneous. Change is impossible because if something will exist in the future, it must be present in your mind when you are thinking about it. So, coming into being and passing away are illusory- Everything is one and eternal. That is the only reality. He distinguished between what exists in reality and that which exists in the mind. He was the first to give deductive reasoning.

His disciples Zeno and Melissus took over from where he left. Zeno refuted multiplicity and becoming. He was the first to argue by the logical technique of *'reductio ad absurdum'*. He gave two arguments against the plurality of things and the idea of motion. All objects can be divided repeatedly to get the basic substance. Anything can be divided *ad infinitum*. Therefore matter must be continuous, not discrete. Similarly in motion, he came up with the famous Achilles paradox. This paradox was tried for a solution by Kant, Hume and, Hegel without much success. Only the modern set theory (abandoning Euclidian geometry of a line as a series of points) can give a reasonable answer to Zeno's paradox of Achilles and the Tortoise.

Melissus interpreted 'being' as a unique mass of matter and conceived it infinite in space as well. Other philosophers like Empedocles, Anaxagoras, Leicippus and Democritus, were also influenced by his ideas. He was later opposed by the Sophist, Georgias, who affirmed that being is not thinkable and not communicable. Being is nothing more than non-being, which is also identical to itself. The principle of identity is known through his writings. Hegel observed that Being by being identical to itself, is nothing more than non-being and is thus reduced to the latter, that are the blueprints of the ephemeral phenomena of experience thereby giving rise to 'becoming'. Heidigger exalted Parmenides for his exposition of Being.

## Plato (429-347 BCE):
Plato is said to have travelled extensively to India, Egypt and other countries during his lifetime. He was the forerunner of modern western philosophy. The world of experience is illusory since only the unchanging and eternal is real, an idea borrowed from Parmenides. There must be a realm of eternal unchanging forms that are the blueprints of the ephemeral phenomena of experiences. Men, animals, birds are all made in the one universal form of man, animals etc. the Christian idea of anthropomorphic concept of man is borrowed from this. In *The Republic*, he gave

the idea of a utopian society where the ideal citizen understands how best he can use his talents for the benefit of the whole society. There is no thought of personal freedom or individual rights for everything is controlled by the guardians for the good of the state. Bertrand Russell considered this as the precursor to communist thought. Much of Plato's discussions centre round knowledge and the conditions for it and the metaphysical nature of what is known besides morality and ethics. Socrates admired expert knowledge as a unified understanding. In men, knowledge appears as a recollection that has forms as objects. He conceived the entire world as we perceive it as belief rather than knowledge. Mathematics is knowledge not dependent on sense experience. Socrates' search for knowledge is also a search for virtue. 'Virtue does not come from possessions. It is from virtue that possessions and all the rest become good for people, both in private and in public'. Plato suggested three classes of people- guardians, auxiliaries and the producing class. This somewhat compares with the Hindu classification of Brahmins, Kshatriya and Vaisya. The individual soul will exhibit this three part relationship- reason, spirit and desire. These may correspond with the three *gunas* (nature) of Hindus- *sattva*, *rajas* and *tamas* that are attributed to the three classes. The guardians will have no property, no private life, and no lasting personal relationships. They know what is right and hence the capacity to rule, though they may not want to rule, but must be compelled to do so.

Plato's Theory of Forms: Parmenides insisted that what is, is One, changeless and eternal; the world of the senses is manifold, mutable, and transient; either not real at all or more probably corresponding only remotely to reality. Only what is, can be known. Heraclitus and Empedocles felt the need for a formal cause for the differentiation in world stuff. From all these sources, Plato inherited the belief that nothing in the sensible world is knowable per se, but only in so far as it corresponds to some intelligible reality. So, what is the relation between the sensible and the intelligible? It is in the context of form. The soul in its disembodied state between one life and the next apprehends the form directly, although this knowledge is lost at birth. This was the Pythagorean view. From this Plato developed his theory. He made it clear that the forms are much more like formulae, expressing the laws that govern the physical world. They are the forerunners of Aristotle's essence or substance, genus and species. Plato conceived of goodness in a comprehensive way; that excellence or perfection to which anything can approximate in its own kind, which is the final cause in a teleological system.

## Plotinus (b. 205 BCE in Egypt):
He founded Neo-Platonism but considered himself a Platonist. He was more interested in the search for the way to achieve the best life for the individual. He divided the

intelligible world into the One, intellect and soul. The One is ineffable and transcends Being and can only be defined by the negation of all the aspects of Being. Clearly this refers to the Upanishadic way of *'neti, neti'* (not this, not this) to describe Brahman the One, without a second. It is also called the good and responsible for the being. The One is responsible for the existence of others without any other relation to them. The others emanate from the One.

The first product of coming into being is the intellect, which is essentially form and being but is initially unformed and indeterminate and so pre-existent. It turns back to the One and contemplates over it. Thus it bestows form and being without itself having them. Plotinus insists on the duality between what knows and what is known and hence different from the One. This compares with the kshetra and kshetrajna or field and knower of the field of the Bhagwad Gita. Since intellect is pre-existent, it is eternal like the One. This is strict monism, 'The simultaneous and identical omnipresence of what is'. The soul remains unaffected by its involvement with the body. All souls are one- soul as a hypothesis, the World-Soul, and the souls of individuals. Soul is separate and superior to the body, which is only an instrument or medium. Soul is to the body, as heat is to the air. Heat may affect the air by warming it, without itself being affected. Once it is understood, then contemplation can free the soul by merging with the One forever. Plotinus follows Plato in most of his arguments. His thoughts became a crucial part of the Islamic and the Jewish philosophy that was written in Arabic and through Latin translations, finding its way to the western tradition in the middle Ages. Here is a clear parallel with Vedanta which is more than five thousand years old and hence has influenced Greek thought and philosophy.

## Polibius (b.208 BCE):
He wrote Universal History and had an unflagging interest in Geography. He said that the lessons of history can be applied to the present. His *Histories* is exceptional in storytelling.

## Protagoras (b. 492 BCE):
His agnosticism follows from his relativism. His arguments deal with the 'impossibility of knowing the gods'. He first dealt with the fate of the soul after death- the invisible field. The second was the visible- Cosmology, Ontology, Politics and Art. But starting from a position of doubt, Protagoras may have ended with belief in the gods. Even if he could prove that the gods exist, we could not know how they look. Georgios uses similar arguments in his Treatise on Non-being. By different paths, he arrives at the same conclusion as Socrates who said, 'And that I am speaking the truth, you too will

know, if you do not wait until you see the shapes of the gods, but if it is enough for you when you see their works, to revere and honour the gods'.

## Ptolomy (c.90 CE):
Ptolemy, and Hipparchus before him, had followed the Babylonian theories based on arithmetics of high sophistication. Besides he also wrote on astrology (*Tetrabiblos*). He wrote *Planetary Hypothesis* and other works. His works strongly influenced posterity in mathematical methods and astronomical sciences.

## Socrates (470- 399 BCE):
Laeritus wrote that Socrates 'was nearest to the gods in that he had the fewest wants'. One of his paradoxes is- 'It suffices to know the good in order to do good and no one does evil knowingly'. Another, 'the only thing that I know is that I know nothing'. The duty of the individual toward the state stops at the point when the accomplishment of that duty threatens to alter the quality of his soul. Socrates was concerned more with the practical aspects of life- how to live a good life, an ethical life of virtue. He is considered the inventor of the branch of philosophy called ethics. He asked people to define the meaning of terms like 'beauty', 'piety' etc., and showed that the definitions led to paradox or absurdity. He developed critical thought and wanted us to question our concepts. Again Laeritus said- 'After Socrates' death, the Athenians felt such remorse that they charged the other accusers but put Meletos to death'. Cicero calls the Athenian judges, 'scoundrels' and Marcus Aurelius calls them 'vermin'. We know that Socrates was given hemlock to drink and to die as a punishment for being truthful and refusing to admit something for which he was wrongfully accused.

## Thucydides (b. c. 454 BCE):
He was convinced that human actions are primarily motivated by fear, prestige, and self-interest. He favoured the politics of human intelligence, a product of rationality, operating without appeal to transcendent powers, but was open to an understanding of what the limits of rationality are, and also aware of the obstacles that stood in the way of attaining it. He was very much concerned with morality. He wrote an elaborate history of the period but could not complete it.

## Xenophon (c. 430 BCE):
He was a brilliant military strategist. He was interested in justice and how might a good life be secured for the individual, the household, and the city-state or the empire. He wanted people to help one's friends and harm enemies. He wondered whether virtue is teachable. He cited Socrates for his nobility of character. The art of

ruling others starts with the art of ruling oneself. With Plato put against Aristotle, he agrees that the art of ruling oneself, the household or the city is fundamentally the same.

## Xenophanes of Colophon (570-475 BCE):

He along with Zeno of Elea and Parmeides formed the Eleatic school. Xenophanes of Colophon moved to the Ionian colonies of Sicily and to Elea where he formed a school that was to become the Eleatic School of philosophy. He said god is one, eternal, incorporeal, without beginning or end. This was the single deity that 'caused all things by the thought of his mind'. He wrote against Hesiod and Homer and said that oxen, lion and others, if they had hands would have shaped gods to their likeness like the anthropomorphism of Homer. His criticism of Homer had a lasting impression on later thinkers. The pairs of opposites are not applicable to god as he is above them. This eternal being was like a sphere, equal everywhere. His logical proof: the Self-existent cannot have attributes that influenced him or influenced by him. The prevailing dualism was the ultimate theory of the universe, unthinkable and hence false. Outside of the Self-existent, nothing else exists, otherwise each would be conditioned by the other and the Self-existent would be gone. He did recognize a world of phenomena or guesswork or opinion (*doxa*), earth and water being the sources from which we spring. For him, the first principle of the nature was mud. He anticipated Heisenberg's 'Uncertainty Principle' by saying that philosophical certainties cannot be had, for even if we chance to hit upon the truth, there is no way of knowing for certain that things are as we think they are.

Parmenides argued for monism and Zeno against pluralism. He famously said - How can something become without ceasing to be, or without not yet being? On difference- How can something be the other without yet ceasing to be the same? And division- How can something be divided if nothingness and emptiness do not exist? Thus being exists absolutely, immutably and permanently, one and identical to itself, indivisible, all of a piece, a fullness of being that is motionless and unique. Indivisibles can have no size. For Zeno, the thesis of the plurality of beings is intrinsically incompatible. He invented dialectics as agreed by Laeritus, Aristotle and others. His ideas have influenced later thinkers like Spinoza who says-Time measure and number exist in the mind, as modes of thought. Kant evokes Zeno in the 'cosmological conflict of reason with itself'.

We now go on to study some systems of thought.

## Currents of thought in the Academy of Plato:

The Academy had a number of famous students like Speucippus, Lacydus, Carneades, Clitomachus and Philon of Larissa. With Arcesilaus, the Academy moved from dogmatism to skepticism. His key to philosophy is 'suspension of judgment'. Carneades was the founder of probabilism. He judged that one cannot state with certainty about any representation that it is true. Heisenberg's 'uncertainty principle' echoes this idea. The word 'probable' however, comes from Cicero. Neo-Platonism arose from these two.

Aristotle himself was a student of Plato who ran the Academy after the latter's death. Aristotle's 'unmoved mover' was not accepted by Theophrastus but held that the heavens are ensouled. Aristotle maintained the infinite divisibility of matter, and absence of any void. The nature of divine involvement with the universe forms the climax of his work. He had no place for providence in our lives and argues that fate is the individual nature or character that determines what happens to them. But the stoic concept of fate as inexorably determining everything is ruled out. Aristotle defined the soul as the form of the living creature. That which makes everything is imperishable and that which becomes everything is perishable. Strato located the 'pneuma' not in the chest (as Epicurus and the Stoics did), but in the head between the eyebrows. This is the Hindu Yoga view known as the *ajna chakra*. This is the sixth energy point with the seventh energy point in the head known as *sahasrara chakra*.

## Cynicism:

Diogenes of Sinope 400-325 BCE, (called the dog) and his disciples started this movement in 4th century BCE. He was described as 'a Socrates gone mad'. He professed a single life and preferred to give devotion to the masters of the Self. He reviled metaphysics and claimed that happiness could result only by living 'according to nature'. This meant living a minimalist life with basic requirements. He was called the 'dog' for his vagrant lifestyle. According to him, masters of the Self required constant practice to be happy by abandoning possessions and family ties to minimize the illusory emotional and psychological attachments. He was partly influenced by Hindu thought like his predecessors, as it prescribed detachment and renunciation. His philosophy may apply to a few but cannot be universal as society will collapse. It is rather elitist.

For Diogenes, only the individual matters. To ensure his happiness, he must be shown the way to the individual revolution. He rejects all prohibitions of society and urges a return to nature. Man's weakness is due to his passions, pride, fear, and attraction to pleasure and to the aggressions of the world around him. 'It was the privilege of the gods to need nothing and of god-like men to want but little'. To achieve the happiness of the beetle and the ease of the ant are enough. The universe was not made for man and gods are insignificant in life. Agnosticism allowed man to preserve his apathy and to achieve his happiness by will power alone. The path to virtue is asceticism, based on training for the health of the soul. A frugal life with life's bare necessities ensured happiness.

## Hellenism:

Hellenism has as much connection with Judaism as with Christianity since the language of all texts was in Greek. Clearchus of Solis says that Aristotle had told him of Jews from the Asia Minor with their capital at Jerusalem, who were like the 'Brahman sages of India'. This also clearly suggests the influence of Hindu Brahmins and their philosophy of Vedanta on the Greeks as it implies that Aristotle and others were quite familiar with that philosophy.

## The Milesians:

Thales, Anaximander and Anaximenes were the three citizens of Miletus (6$^{th}$ century BCE) in the Ionian coast that formed the Milesians who studied the science of nature. Theirs was the School of Miletus. Herodotus and Thucydides were influenced by them. Aristotle recognized them as his predecessors in Natural Science. They used only the 'material cause'. Thales said that everything was made of water, the originating principle of everything while to Anaximenes, it was air. They searched for an account of everything. They postulated the spatial and temporal infinity of the universe. They assumed that the universe was an object of study and that it is knowable and intelligible as a whole.

The foundation of Milesian theory was the 'fundamental entity' seen as the material cause by Aristotle, which was essentially uniform in the large scale and long term. They saw symmetry, both reflection and radial symmetry and uniformity in space and time. Earth was at the centre of this universe as it was an infinite universe. It was not only infinite but also filled with infinite number of worlds. The present scientific theory of multi-verses was apparently anticipated by Anaximander. Because it is infinite, we may not consider ourselves privileged since there may be many more universes scattered uniformly throughout the infinite extent. Thales' water and Anaximander's air were not ordinary but enriched by the properties of life and intelligence. This infinite was also living and intelligent. In this scientific theology, the divine formed part of the natural world.

## The Greeks

The three important phenomena of the Milesians were:
1. The existence in our cosmos as a living, intelligent and purposive beings. Something living and intelligent from which the other beings are derived.
2. Change and movement. The divine as a living thing, a source of movement.
3. Order and purposefulness exist in the cosmos due to the purposeful planning of the divine.
4. Aristotle reported Thales as having recorded that 'all things have a soul in them, in virtue of which they move other things and are themselves moved, even as the magnet by virtue of its life or soul, moves the iron'. Anaximander invented the sun-dial and with Hecateus, constructed the earliest geographical maps. He said everything is part of the infinite and from its formlessness, everything came to be; and into that same infinite, they return. This infinite has always been there and is the only reality that is without beginning or end, underlying all, governing all. Matter and form remain very much the same infinities like the originating infinity. He seems to have formulated motion as eternal also. The idea of difference in relation to unity or change inheres in the infinite itself. He also formulated two principles of existence- mind and matter. He postulated an inherent tendency of the infinite which compelled it to develop contrary characters like hot and cold and other pairs of opposites. Consequently, fire came into being that enveloped air which in turn enveloped the earth, each being like the 'husk' of the other or like the bark that encloses a tree. Thus he envisages the sun and the stars as hanging in balance in relation to each other. Man emerged from lower forms of life that came from moisture.

Thales was the first western thinker who used the scientific method and postulated that water was the fundamental nature of the world, the single causal principle behind the natural world. He further said that the earth floats on water, anticipating the plate tectonics that proved that islands and continents have been moving. He also predicted a solar eclipse in 587 BCE during a battle between Medes and Lydians. He claimed that god is in all things.

The Milesian philosophy formed the framework on which later philosophers built their theories. Pythagoras and his school suggested that the cosmos began with a fire in the centre of a sphere that led to the astronomical system of Philolaus. In this, the earth is made a planet orbiting around the central fire along with the sun, moon, the five planets, fixed stars and a counter-earth totalling ten orbiting bodies. Copernicus refers to Philolaus as his precursor.

## The Sophists:
Protagoras, Georgias, Prodicus and Hippias formed the group of Sophists who had a collection of doctrines and philosophy that was neither sound nor serious. They were masters of eloquence. Nothing is, and if it is, it is unknowable or as Sextus put it, it cannot be grasped by men. If it is knowable, it cannot be communicated to others. It may be like the *atmajnana* of the Hindus that means knowing the source of the 'I' in us which cannot be communicated in words but can only be experienced. If not-being is not being, not-being is no less than being; for, not-being and being is also being so that things exist no more than not exist. Socrates was not a Sophist though he was accused of being one. Sophists were professional teachers who derived earning from it. Some of them challenged accepted views about religion and morality. But Plato and others considered them superficial, concerned more with expedience than with truth.

Socrates believed (against the Sophists), that knowledge is possible, and was against atheism and agnosticism, and had firm faith in divine providence; he was against materialism insisting that the soul is superior to the body and that goodness is something positive and absolute. So, he stood for everything that was against the Sophists. Seeking knowledge was a necessary and sufficient condition for all the virtues and of moral goodness. He invented the concept of inductive arguments and general definitions and had an important bearing on Plato's thought.

## The Stoics:
Zeno of Citium (334-262 BCE), Cleanthus of ASSOS (331-230 BCE), and Chrysippus of Soli (280-208 BCE) were the main philosophers of this school, whose ideas have survived to this day. To them, 'physical speculation is to be undertaken for no other purpose than for the discrimination of good and evil' as stated by Chrysippus. They saw the world as a sort of energy, penetrating bodies and passing through the whole universe. Virtue is enough for happiness, because being happy is less a subjective state of satisfaction than an objective state of success.

## Pythagoras of Samos (570-480 BCE):
He travelled to India, Egypt and Babylonia and his theorem was already known in India. He was a pure vegetarian. For him the ultimate nature of reality is numbers, based on his theory of music in which he proved that the intervals between musical tones could be expressed as ratios between the first four integers. Music has a special power over the soul infused as it is into the very fabric of the universe. Ten heavenly

bodies revolved round a central fire. The ratio of the diagonal through a square to its sides is not a whole number and this 'incommensurability of the diagonal' led to the discovery or invention of irrational numbers.

His religious order was founded in 530 BCE at Croton in Italy. He had drawn his mathematical knowledge from Babylonia. He taught that the human soul is immortal and akin to the soul of the cosmos and souls are subject to transmigration with sin in one life being punished by downgraded incarnation in the next. This is the original theory of the Hindus taken to Babylonia and on to Egypt, Greece, China, etc. Philosophy by contemplation emancipates the soul. Justice is equated with reciprocity. This view transmitted by Plato influenced Aristotle as we would see afterwards.

To him, the universe has no character but can take up a character; and things or forces can impose such character. From these two, all knowable existence came into being. All known things have a number- odd or even- the known is odd or even or the union of the two. He mentions ten pairs of opposites: definite/indefinite, one/many, right/left, male/female, steadfast/moving, straight/ crooked, light/dark, good/evil, and square/irregular- the first of these is ordered or defined principle in nature. The second is unordered, neutral, passive principle. The first is form and the second is matter. The first is the source of all knowledge and of all good. The one above these pairs of opposites is god, the One, eternal, immovable, the supreme reality the odd- even or many in one or one in many, in who are gathered all opposites of lower existence. He is the soul of the world and the world is god in process- a living creature with circumference of pure fire and between these circle the sun and planets, whose ordered movements produce the 'music of the spheres'. So also the living being is a soul. The change or flux is also visible in the relation of soul and body. This bodily life is in bonds or in a prison from where we cannot go forth till god calls us. This soul was divided into pure thought, perception and desire or reason, passion and desire. But the first duty was truth through which alone one can approach the divine; falsehood was of the earth, and the real life of the soul must be in harmony with the heavens.

## References:
1. Greek Thought- Ed. Brunschwig and Geoffrey E.R. Lloyd, Harvard University Press.
2. A Short History of Greek Philosophy- John Marshall, e-book.
3. Science, Philosophy and Religion- Ramakrishnan Srinivasan, Citadel, 2008.

## Vedic Tradition and World Religions

4. Vedic Tradition- Ramakrishnan Srinivasan, Bhavan's Book University Series, 2000.
5. Philosophy-100 Essential Thinkers- Philip Stokes, Arcturus Publishing Ltd.
6. A Classical Dictionary of India- John Garret, D.K.Printworld P Ltd, Delhi, 1999.

# CHAPTER 6

# THE HEBREWS

*Talmud* is the set of divine instructions through Moses revealed at Mt. Sinai, 3300 years ago. For Jews, the Old Testament is the scripture consisting of twenty four books – 5 books of *Torah*, 8 books of *Navi* (prophets), and 11 *Books of Ketuvim* (writings). *Talmud* is considered as the oral instructions of God transmitted by Moses known as the Torah. There were 613 Commandments (including the Ten) brought down by Moses. Of these 248 are positive and 365 are negative injunctions. In the Exodus 24.12, God's oral instructions to Moses are referred to. This is an unwritten Tradition till recently (during the Roman Era, 5th century CE). Today the various pages of the Talmud contain interpretations by various sages from time to time. *Pilpul* refers to the hairsplitting arguments documented in the Talmud. The chain of transmissions of the sages starting from Moses covers 120 generations until the 5th century CE. The Talmud presents conflicting viewpoints that may raise more questions than answers. Many centuries ago, a Jew would go to Yeshiva or Rabbanical Academy to study the Talmud and families considered this an honour to house these scholars. The sages studying the Talmud are not in paradise but paradise is in the sages. In 70 CE Jerusalem was destroyed and the Jews were exiled.

Jacob was Abraham's grandson. He had twelve sons who were the twelve tribes of Israel including Levi. When Moses was tending the sheep of his father-in-law, a Midianite priest, he encountered the god of Moses' forefathers. This god had made a covenant with Abraham, Isaac and Jacob and asked Moses to lead the Hebrews out of Egypt to the Promised Land as he was empowered to do so. Moses and his brother Aaron pleaded with the Pharaoh to release the Hebrews but he refused. God unleashed ten plagues, each worse than the earlier one. But at the tenth, the slaughter of the first born, Pharaoh allowed the Jews to leave. Though he changes his mind and sends his army after them, they escape through the Red Sea and god helps to almost destroy Pharaoh's army. After two months of travel through desert, they reach Mt. Sinai. Moses goes up to the mountain where god appears before him and tells him that if the Jews listen to his words, he will consider them as his own and give special favour. On his agreement, god embarks on a 40 day conversation with Moses when he gives the 613 Commandments comprising the Oral Law. This was written on stone tablets during 39 years that they wandered the desert, god dictating to Moses. Moses taught the Jews these laws during the period. These were the five books- *Genesis, Exodus, Leviticus, Numbers* and *Deuteronomy*. These, along with the Hebrew Bible, are also part of the Christian scriptures but the Oral Law was always the property of the Jews. They then reached Canaan, the Promised Land. But Moses was not allowed to enter it for many reasons and he delivers a number of farewell addresses and Joshua was made his successor. Then he climbs the nearby mountain looking at the Promised Land and dies. The Talmud teaches that Moses wrote 13 Torah scrolls, 12 for the 12 tribes and the thirteenth to be placed in the Ark of the Covenant- a chest that was the symbol of god's presence in the Tabernacle, the portable sanctuary built by Israelites in c. 1450 BCE under Moses' supervision. This scroll was the standard for all the subsequently written scrolls. The Law is the Pentateuch, the 5 books of Talmud. There were a million prophets until the time of the fall of the Temple in 70 CE. The prophets were to prevent the people from straying from the Talmud. After they settled in Canaan, the Philistines settled in South Canaan and took over making the Israelites captive, but David the second king of Israel defeated the Philistines, besides others in the Middle East including the Romans who harassed them (Romans had occupied Canaan in 63 BCE). Due to this Roman persecution, the Oral Law had to be recorded. Rabbi Yehudah Hanasi put the law into writing. He, a descendent of David, befriended Marcus Aurelius and for some time there was peace. The Seven branched candlestick or Menorah that once stood in the Temple of Jerusalem was removed by Romans in 70 CE when they destroyed the Temple. It is the symbol of Judaism, the Tree of Life.

Ancient Israelis did not appear to have discussed issues of philosophy and have only produced prophets. Their ethical system was based on religious experience. Their God Yahveh demanded good and the desirable and forbade evil. About 2000-1800 BCE, the Patriarch Abraham was invited to undertake a journey, leaving behind his family heritage to seek a new life in Canaan. He had a son Isaac who succeeded and in turn was succeeded by Jacob (Israel). The latter had twelve sons by four wives. When famine came, they all moved to Egypt. Though welcomed first, they were seen as a threat and so began genocide by Egypt. Moses assumed leadership and left for Mt. Sinai with guidance from Yahveh, with whom he then made a covenant in which the latter made a promise of protection if the Jews obeyed him. Joshua succeeded Moses and defeated the locals and took possession of the land. Historians however say that in 3000 BCE, there were waves of Semitic migration into the arc of land bounded by Mesopotamia, Egypt, and Canaan. This is known as the Fertile Crescent.

# The Hebrews

Archaeology has established one such wave that arrived between 2100-1700 BCE. This was the time that the River Saraswati in northwest India that drained into the Gulf of Cambay, dried up (c. 1900 BCE) and people migrated to the west, east and south in India from the northwest. The above reference may be to this wave. Among this group was Abraham of Urs, who was said to have been hounded out by the Brahmins for not following the Vedic fire ritual. There could have also been groups led by Isaac and Jacob. Research by Matlock, Anastasias and others suggest that Abraham was a Brahmin who married his sister Sara (Saraswati). Upon arrival they adapted their religious practices there. Before this migration, they practised a clan religion that was simple and protected by a God without any priesthood. Since there was no religion other than the Hindu Tradition, it may be to this that reference is made. However after settling, they became Canaanites. They had a whole Pantheon of gods (again, only Hindus had such a Pantheon). The main god was El whose son Ba'al, was the god of storm and fertility. The Semitic people came into contact with this god El and identified their clan gods with him. Historians also say that the third transformation of the Semitic clans was connected with Egypt. Evidence of Semitic people living in Egypt is aplenty. They were taken as prisoners and sometimes famine in Canaan drove them there. They were used as compulsory labour by the rulers. Though they could have seized the throne, the Egyptians must have recaptured it and found the Semites as a threat and forced their exodus. Moses, their leader saved them by taking them to Sinai. His wife, a Midianite and her clan might have worshipped Yahveh who was like El. Through his father-in-law Jethro, Moses came to know the power of Yahveh and went to Egypt to his clan and told them that Yahveh would help them leave Egypt. They did leave Egypt and this is attributed to Yahveh and Israel came into being with the religion of Abraham being adopted by them. They looked to the patriarch Abraham and some to Isaac, Jacob, and Moses. Yahveh sided with Israel and showed '*hesed*' (covenant love), the undeserved care and concern of Yahveh for these people. This was followed by unswerving love for '*emeth*' or truth. The Israelites showed '*emunah*' or faithfulness to Yahveh. The moral demands of the covenant were the '*derek*' or the way. The way of Israel was also known as The Torah or the law-. The Torah consists of the first five books of the Bible. By the 7th century BCE, the semi-nomadic life of the tribes was gone. Mercantilism spread with dishonesty, exploitation of the poor and growing disparity between the haves and have-nots. Bribes and deprivation of the righteous were abominable practices in Israel. The Law or the way was given by Yahveh to Moses that was developed over the period of the twelve tribe confederation. By the time of monarchy in the 10th century BCE, it would have reached a permanent form. Doubtless, some of the materials were borrowed from neighbouring cultures, particularly laws that maintained order and stability in society. This is a clear indication mostly of borrowing of Manu's laws from India.

The Covenant however, shows that there were to be no class distinctions though slavery was accepted. The Code of Deuteronomy was set down centuries later when the monarchy and institutions were in place. There were Ten Commandments:

1. There shall be no god besides Yahveh.
2. No idolatry or worship before other gods forbidden.
3. Yahveh's name should not be misused.
4. Remember to make the Sabbath day holy.
5. Respect your parents.
6. You shall not kill.
7. You shall not commit adultery.
8. You shall not steal.
9. You shall not bear false witness.
10. You shall not covet your neighbour's wife or property.

The Talmud was composed in the 4th century CE and is a collection of Jewish traditions. The many codes of Israel- the Covenant, Deuteronomy, the Ten Commandments, the Book of Leviticus- all showed how the *emunah* could be practised. During the Common Era, the Pharisees group had a marked influence on Jewish ethics. This is the group that broke away from the Maccabees who succeeded in the struggle against the Greeks but who later became corrupt. So the pious Pharisees broke away. Caring for Jews and non-Jews alike was recommended in the Talmud.

In modern times Judaism has seen divisions, mainly the orthodox and reform (liberal) Jews. The reform group was mainly due to the persecution of Jews in Europe when they suffered at the hands of Christians. After the Napoleonic wars, religious freedom and toleration spread and Jews at last received their full rights. They got involved in civic rights and changes overtook them. Dietary practices changed and Hebrew, their language of worship was replaced by the language of the people. Women however, are seen as subordinate to men, though emancipation has been taking place. After 70 CE, Pharisees saw sexual sin as the cause of sullying holiness.

The Mishna of the Rabbis was arranged topically into six sections (*seder*). These are:- *Zeraim* (seeds), *Mo'ed* (time or season), *Nashim* (women), *Kodshim* (sacred things), and *Taharot* (purity). These were divided into subdivisions (tractates) and each of these into several chapters. Besides these, other teachings began to appear in writing. The Oral Laws were cryptic in a kind of secret code (Talmud code) that only seasoned scholars could understand. These are probably like the sutras in Sanskrit that are like pithy aphorisms. After the Rabbi's death in 200 CE, the Mishna was expanded upon by generations of scholars (*amoraim* meaning explainers), and around 400 CE, the Rabbis of Palestine gathered the Mishna into many books or recensions (Talmud Yerushalim, Babylonian Talmud etc) and by 499 CE, the Talmud was fully preserved. Each tractate starts on page 2, as there is no beginning or end in the Talmud. From 220 CE to the tenth century, the major centre of Jewish learning was Babylonia (Iraq). Printed editions of the Talmud first appeared in Spain in 1508 CE.

*Pesach* is Passover, signifying the freeing of Jews and birth of their nation more than 3000 years ago. *Matzah* is the specially unleavened bread (flat) eaten during Passover. *Yom Kippur* is the Day of Atonement.

Seder Nashim has seven tractates that deal with women and their rights, marriage, divorce, or adultery. *Ketubak* is the pre-marital agreement that gives certain rights and protection to women. *Get* is divorce. Jewish marriages had *kiddushin* or betrothal and *Nisu'm*, the marriage itself. A widow may marry her husband's brother if she wants and this is levirate marriage. Naziriters are those who live apart from others like the Hindu *vanaprastha*.

The three gates are- *Baba kama* (direct/indirect damages), *Baba metzia* (losses, loans etc), and *Baba batra* (real estate, property etc). Sanhedrin is the Jewish Supreme Court. *Kodushim* are the holy laws on construction of temples etc. Animal sacrifices, common in older times have now been discarded. *Tithing* is the payment of 10% of income for supporting a religious house. *Kosher* instructs as to what kind of food to eat and what is prohibited. Slaughtering animals or fawn should be ritually followed. Fish is considered as a vegetable. *Mikwah* contained rainwater, considered as primordial water and hence pure.

In forty days, the fetus gets human form after conception and receives human soul. Forty means cataclysmic change and new creation. *Harayun* is pregnancy for 271 days starting one day after intercourse. *Kabbalah* refers to mysticism or a body of mystical writings. Its study required ego-lessness and a minimum age of forty.

## Creation:
Originally there was only the infinite. When god withdrew, it left a place for the cosmos to come into being. God projected a beam of light from which a mass without form appeared. From this mass, all kinds of reality came into existence. God left an 'imperfect unity' of his own creation. Through prayer and right action, this creation became perfected (*Tikkun Olam*). This is a brief description of Jewish creation story. The *Zohar* (Talmud tractate) says that there are seven earths. They are separated by a

firmament and all of them have inhabitants. At least some form of intelligence is in them. This is comparable to the seven worlds of the Hindu scripture (*saptaloka*). The tractate *Mo'ed Katan iba* has a sage *Ulla* who says, based on the Song of Deborah in the Book of Judges (5:23): 'Cursed is Meroz…cursed are its inhabitants'. He further says that *Meroz* is a star or a planet and it has intelligent beings.

*Midrash* is the exploration of the scriptures. From this came the Islamic Madrasa, where the Quran is studied by students. *Midrush haladin* deals with legal court rulings. *Midrashim* helps gain moral values. Talmud has a science section where the value of *pi* is given and the calendar calculated. It also has a section on animal husbandry. It talks of twelve constellations, each with 365,000 of myriads of stars. The total number of stars has been given as $1.6434 \times 10$ to the power 18 in the Talmud. This is very near the estimate made by Edwin Hubble which is 10 to the power 18-20.

In *Rosh Hoshana*, Rabban Gamliel said that the lunar month is 29 1/2 days. NASA's estimate is 29.530388 days. There are more lunar months in a year than solar (12.4 to 12). A 12 month lunar calendar loses 11 days in a year, while a 13 month lunar calendar gains 19 days in the 4th century. Hillel II developed the calendar and added an extra month during certain years in the standard length of the month.

Talmud also has a medical section that deals with hygiene, healing with good scents (aromatherapy), surgery etc. The sages agreed with the Greek that diseases are caused due to the four humors of the body- phlegm, blood, yellow bile, and black bile. This is the Hindu system of Ayurveda borrowed by the Greeks. William Harvey's findings on blood circulation in the 17th century were already foreseen 2000 years ago by the Hindus.

The Talmud does not believe in Original Sin. *Kadosh* is holiness that is separateness. Darius the King of Persia had held a competition on the strongest thing. After many foolish answers, David rose and said 'truth' and he got the Prize. Rabbi Shimons in his *Ethics of the Fathers* says that silence is most beneficial to man. These can be seen to be a reflection from the Sanatana Dharma of The Hindus where truth and silence are valued very high. God gave the code of conduct to Adam and Eve, handed down to Abraham, then to Noah and then to Moses. The Hindu scripture describes how the Vedas and the various living species were saved by Vishnu from the Flood by the use of a large boat that the first incarnation of God as fish (*matsyavatara*) had guided to safety. Many of the Hindu legends find a place in the Greek, Christian and other religions. (Please read this author's book on *Vedic Tradition*)

# The Hebrews

The seven Noachide Laws include six 'thou shalt not' and one 'thou shalt. These are:

1. Idolatry.
2. Blasphemy.
3. Murder.
4. Robbery and theft.
5. Immorality and forbidden relationships.
6. Removing and eating a limb from a live animal.
7. Establish a judicial system, including courts for enforcing the above six. The first six are of course, proscribed.

These are similar to the Ten Commandments. Out of the 613 commandments in the Talmud, only 271 can be fulfilled today since the Holy Temple of Jerusalem is not there and also the Jewish Supreme Court with 71 elders are also not there and so the other *Mitzvat* do not now apply. Judaism teaches tolerance of other faiths and creeds. Some Talmudic sages suggest that Adam was to eat vegetables and fruits only till the Flood after which he was allowed to eat meat. Blasphemy was to be punished with death. In the Hindu scriptures there is no blasphemy at all as all beings are considered divine. God tells Noah-'whoever sheds blood of man, by man shall his blood be shed, for he made man in the image of god'. While idolatry is prohibited, murder is punished by death. Destiny and pre-destination are accepted since we are born without our willing it. Free will or accountability is ruled out. But even the depraved can change to a better man through teaching and precepts. So, man does have some free will. While the life term is fixed, it may be extended by good deeds.

Talmud had many words on ecology, in reuse of waste, preserving natural reserves, dying to live, preserving body's resources, order and balance (*feng shui*), sleep, energy flow and so on. It teaches of an afterlife- death is a transition from one life to another. It says our experiences in this life will shape what our afterlife will be. It further talks of one unified soul with three characteristics-

*Nefesh*- Near the physical, vital life force.

*Ruach*- Wind, breath, the passions of a person. It also helps a person to change.

*Neshama*- supra-rational powers of the soul.

Two additional levels of the soul are:

*Chaya*- Origin of wisdom that is higher than consciousness.

*Yedvida*- Spark of god, the highest level.

The above five levels correspond with the five sheaths in the Hindu philosophy, mentioned in the chapter on the Hindus, starting with *annamaya kosa* and ending with *anandamaya kosa*. The soul is severed from the body immediately at death. For righteous persons, this is painless. For others, the soul bounces around for some time before travelling onward. *Gehinnom i*s an intermediate stage where the soul is purified before its next level of existence. Reincarnation is accepted in the Talmud.

Essentially, the Talmud suggests a way of life in which one has good behaviour, serves others, values teachers and friends, and learns from life. This involves character building and lifelong learning. Only good association helps a man in this. One could easily find similarities between the older Hindu texts and the Talmud including many of the legends. For instance, the story of Rabbi Yehoshua Ben Levi asking Elijah the Prophet to accompany him to learn virtue and the prophet blessing a couple who were hospitable even with the death of their cow and other such legends. Comparison can be made with Krishna and Arjuna staying with a poor couple and their hospitality, while on a tour of some villages.

The similarities between the Talmud and Hindu texts leads one to believe in the origin of Abraham as a Hindu Brahmin in Urs, being driven out for not performing the Fire rituals of Brahmins and ultimately his leaving Urs with some of his followers, going first to Egypt and then to Canaan. Of course more research needs to be done on this.

## References:
1. The Talmud (Oral Torah) - Rabbi Aaron Parry, Alpha Press (The Idiot series).
2. Ethics of World Religions- Arnold D. Hunt, Marie T. Crotty, and Robert B. Crotty, Greenhaven Press, San Siego.
3. Vedic Tradition- Ramakrishnan Srinivasan, Bhavan's Book University Series, 2000.
4. Science, Philosophy and Religion- Ramakrishnan Srinivasan, Citadel, Calcutta.

# CHAPTER 7
# ZOROASTRIANISM

Three thousand five hundred years ago, Prophet Zarathustra, a priest of the then Iranian religion, started rejecting many of the religious beliefs and preached about one Supreme God Ahura Mazda. It was a religion of personal ethics, where people's actions were more important than rituals and sacrifice. Zend Avesta is their scripture.

About 200,000 people worldwide practise this religion. Their Fahavahar symbol represents the link between the spiritual and physical worlds. The human form is encircled by a ring that represents the eternal soul. The head reminds people of their free will, a mind and intellect to choose the good. The right hand points upward to lead people toward *Asha* or the path of Truth. The left hand is a ring symbolizing the just power of *khshathru vairya*. The wings help the soul to fly towards progress. It has a tail that serves as a rudder to balance between good and evil, shown as the curved hooks on either side of the tail.

The good religion reveals its vision in a series of psalms or *gathas*. The one god created the world and humans. The twin spirits, Truth and falsehood, represent consciousness and knowledge of good, the spirit of Truth (*spenta mainyu*). With the physical world (*Getig*), evil came in the form of ignorance and lies. This is *angru mainya* or Ahriman. The struggle between these opposing forces governs human thought and activity. Ahura Mazda gave the gift of free will during creation. Their main prayer:

*Ashem vohu vahishtem asti ushta asti ushta ahmai, hyat ashai, vahishtai ashem.* (Asha is good, it is best. It is happiness. Happiness comes to the person who is righteous for the sake of utmost righteousness YS. 28.1).

The Persian Sage Zarathustra's (Zoroaster's) Zend-Avesta gives us the doctrine of dualism and the worship of fire. He attributes the evil in life to the Devas and the good things to the 'Holy Immortal Ones' who are found standing around the Presence of Ormuzd. His code considers burning the dead as pollution of fire and it is equally wrong to commit the corpse to the waves or to bury it in earth; it is tantamount to committing an act of violence. The dead are exposed in high places to be devoured by the birds of the air and swept away by the streams into which the rain should wash their remains.

His hymns furnish abundant imagery of the wonders of nature like the running stream. He relies for his cosmogony on the traditions of the past gathered from other nations and reduces them into conformity with his dualistic creed. He was the predecessor to Mohammad and his beliefs were trampled out in Persia by the force of Islam in the seventh century CE. The Persian Zoroastrians fled to India in the West Coast and are known as Parsees, who were integrated into the Indian life stream. Their dualism involves two powerful creative beings, the one good and the other evil that have control of the universe. They are the Ahura Mazda and Ahriman representing the Holy Mouru and the evil of plunder and sin respectively. This constant struggle of the two divinities with their armies of good and evil spirits formed the background of Zoroastrian Supernaturalism. Their worship is of the powers of Nature and especially of fire, although water, air and earth are also addressed in the litanies of the Zend. The sun is also invoked.

All activities of the world are to result in the triumph of the good over evil. Zoroaster taught that the life of man has two parts, that on earth and that beyond the grave. After his earthly life each one is to be punished or rewarded according to his deeds. The Zend cannot be dated earlier than the first century CE and it consists of four books of which the chief one is the Vendidad; the other three are liturgical and devotional works. The Vendidad contains an account of creation and counter-creation of Ormuzd and Ahriman. After this, follows a detailed history of the beginnings of civilization under Yima, the Persian Noah. The revelation is shown as directly made to Zoroaster, who, like Moses, talked to God. Ahura Mazda told Yima, son of Vivanghat,: "Well, fair Yima, be thou the Preacher and the bearer of thy Religion'. Yima replied: 'I was not born, I was not taught to be the preacher and bearer of thy Religion'. After this follows praises of agriculture, injunctions as to the care due to the dog, the guardian of the home and flock, the hunter and the scavenger. It includes an elaborate code of ceremonial purification resembling the Leviticus of the Bible, and it prescribes also the gradations of penance for sins of various degrees of heinousness.

As the Parsis are the ruins of a people, so are their sacred books the ruins of a religion. It was the old enemy of Persia, the Greeks, who first studied the Avesta. Aristotle, Hermippus and many others wrote of it in books of which only a few fragments have come down to us. The clearest and most faithful account of the Dualist doctrine is found in the treatise *De Iside et Osiride*, ascribed to Plutarch. But Zoroastrianism was never more eagerly studied than in the first centuries of the Current Era. As Xanthos the Lydian, who is said to have lived before Herodotus, had mentioned

Zoroastrianism, there came to light, in later times, scores of oracles, styled '*Oracula Chaldaica sive Magica*', the work of neo-Platonists who were but very remote disciples of the Median sage. Zoroaster and Plato were treated as if they had been philosophers of the same school, and Hierocles expounded their doctrines in the same book. Proclus collected seventy Tetrads of Zoroaster and wrote commentaries on them. Prodicus, the Gnostic, possessed secret books on Zoroaster; on the whole, it may be said that in the first centuries of this era, the religion of Persia was more studied and less understood than it had ever been before. The real object aimed at in studying the old religion was to form a new one.

Throughout the Middle Ages nothing was known of Mazdaism except the name of its founder. During the Renaissance, real inquiry was resumed. Barnabe Brisson completed the task of collecting information that could be gathered from Greek and Roman authors. French, Italian and English travellers in Asia followed it up in the next century. Pietro de Valle, Henry Lord, Chardin and others found Zoroaster's last followers in Persia and India and made known their features in Europe. Gabriel du Chinon saw their books and recognized that they were in different languages, their original holy writ being understood only in its translations and commentaries in another tongue. It was Thomas Hyde, the Orientalist Oxford professor who made an attempt to restore the history of the Old Persian religion by combining the accounts of Mohammedan writers with the true monuments of ancient Persia. Despite its defects, his book was the first complete and true picture of modern Parsiism. From that time scholars started studying it in its own home.

In 1754, Anquetil Duperron, a scholar of the *Ecole des Langues Orientales* in Paris, saw a copy of the Oxford Vendidad and gave both the books of Zoroaster and the first European translation of them. He later went to Surat after an eventful and dangerous travel through war-torn areas, and stayed with Parsis for three years and after getting their books, returned to Paris with the whole Zend-Avesta and deposited it at the *Bibliotheque Royale* along with copies of several traditional books. After studying them for ten years he published the first European translation of Zend-Avesta in 1771. Though it was not received well and criticized by Voltaire and others; Kleuker, a professor at Riga, published a German translation of Anquetil's Avesta. He then authenticated the Zend books. He showed that it had no Arabic elements in it, and that Pahlavi itself does not contain any Arabic but only Semitic words of the Aramaic dialect.

Sir William Jones, the then President of the Royal Asiatic Society, and the creator of the comparative grammar of Sanskrit and Zend wrote: 'I was inexpressibly surprised to find that six or seven words in ten are pure Sanskrit and even some of their inflexions formed by the rules of *Vyakaran*, as *yusmacam*, the genitive plural of *yushmad*.' Since Anquetil did not know Sanskrit, he could not have invented the words and thus it was that Jones confirmed that the Zend was genuine. He further said that the language of the Zend was 'at least a dialect of Sanskrit, approaching perhaps as nearly to it as Prakrit…which we know to have been spoken in India two thousand years ago'. In 1798, Father Paulo de St. Barthelemy further developed on Jones's remark on the antiquity of the Zend language by showing its affinity to Sanskrit with a list of such Zend and Sanskrit words as were least likely to have been borrowed. Another list of eighteen words from the liturgic (read Vedic) language used in India and Persia was also given by him. *His conclusions were that Sanskrit was spoken in Persia and Medea in the far antiquity and that Zend was derived from it* (Italics by this author). Significantly the Gathas of Zend and the Vedas were considered as similar when chanted and the hymns in both were considered similar. Be that as it may, the roots of ancient and later religions definitely could be traced to the Hindu tradition.

Peter von Bohlen, in 1831, agreed with Jones, Leyden and Erskine that Zend was a Prakrit dialect. Eugene Burnouf who studied Aryan languages gave a comparative mythology of the Avesta and Veda by showing the identity of the Vedic Yama with the Avestan Yima. He also deciphered the Persian inscriptions at Perseapolis and Behistun as they were done by Lassen in Bonn and by Sir Henry Rawlinson in Persia.

The Zend contained creation stories and the words of Ahura Mazda spoken to Spitama Zarathustra. It described the lands he created, the myth of Yima and so on. Some of these are given in what follows. On the earth, Ahura Mazda said: 'It is the place whereon one of the faithful steps forward, O Spitama Zarathustra! With the log in his hand, the Baresma in his hand, the milk in his hand, the mortar in his hand, lifting up his voice in good accord with religion, and beseeching Mithra, the lord of the rolling countryside, and Rama Hvastra'. He goes on to describe how, on earth, the faithful erects a house, brings up a family, sows corn, fruit, and grass, grows cattle to thrive, fodder to thrive and so on. He then describes the contracts and outrages, punishments for breaking contracts and other ethical and moral issues. Also, he talks of funerals, cleansing and purification, and other such matters. Mostly they are questions by Zarathustra and answers by Ahura Mazda and they also include the nature of Devas, worshipper of the Devas, how to cleanse the unclean, spells and how to recite them for cleansing, recitation of the Gathas and such matters. Prayers for sanctity, rain, helpers, fire, the Bull, to the waters and light of the sun and moon, and the stars and to the immortals.

To help people choose truth, each one is born with *fravashi*, the guardian spirit of discrimination. This is more than conscience. It is more like the soul as it is with men all their lives and then leaves to return to keep the company of other *fravashis*. It is a link between the living and the dead. It is the divine essence. The battle between Ahura Mazda and *Angra Mainya* or Ahriman, the evil spirit, will go on for thousands of years. At the end of time, a saviour or *Sashoyant*, will come to lead people against forces of evil and ignorance. In later mythology, the battle will result in the world being destroyed by fire. Molten metal will cover the earth like water. The righteous will wade through it as if it is warm milk, but the unrighteous will be consumed. Evil, sin, and death will be defeated and the world will be purified as perfected. In the renewal of the world, all the dead will rise. The gates of hell will be open and these souls too will rise, purified and redeemed. People will live together in harmony for all eternity. This time is called *Frashogard* or renewal.

Zoroastrianism is not a congregational religion. It has rich rituals in sacred places of worship and lay people are not expected to attend. They mainly gather for the New Year (*No Roz*), and six major festivals or *gahambars*. Otherwise prayers are done individually. The day is divided into five periods or *gahs*. At each of these times, they repeat a prayer from the Avesta. Fire is the sacred symbol of Ahura Mazda. The most sacred fires are consecrated fires, containing fire from sixteen different sources including lightning from Ahura Mazda. It is however, not worship of fire.

Three types of Fire Temples are there- Atash Behram (eight in India and two in Iran), Atash Adaran and Atash Dadga. The first is the highest named temple called the Fire Cathedral. At the entrance hall, there is a washplace for bathing exposed hands and feet. At the centre is the fire room containing a large urn *afargan*, to hold a blazing fire. Fire burns day and night. No statues are there and the faithful can observe the ritual through iron bars/grill work. They also have meeting rooms, lecture halls and library. The Atash Adaran has fewer rituals performed and the Atash Dadga is similar to a household fire. No high rituals are held here and may not have a full time priest. It is a monotheistic religion.

## References:
1. World Religions- Paula R Hartz
2. Sacred Books of the East- Zend-Avesta, Translated by James Darmestetter.

# CHAPTER 8
# CHRISTIANITY

Christianity started as a sect of Judaism. The apocalyptic way of thinking in Judaism was in anticipation of Yahveh coming to them to change things. This is the difference between 'this age' and the 'age to come', (*ha'olam hazzah* and *ha'olam habbah*). This age is the period of lawlessness and evil where the anti-Yahveh forces had control. But in time, Yahveh would come and usher a golden age. This is comparable to the statement of Krishna in the Bhagwad Gita in which he says 'whenever dharma is destroyed and evil prevails, He will incarnate again and again to establish virtue'. In fact so deep was their faith that a sect of Jews went to the arid areas around the Dead Sea, Qumran, to await the coming of the Messiah who will be sent by Yahveh. This never happened and the Monastery of Essenes at Qumran was destroyed by the Romans in 68 CE. A similar group, in 35 CE or so, announced to the Jews that the Messiah had already come, and was executed in the Cross and had been resurrected during the battle against the children of darkness that was taking place. These were the Christians and their Messiah was Jesus (Messiah- Christos). So the apocalyptic group eventually accepted for establishing practices of worship and a Christian ritual system to which all Christians should subscribe. Yahveh was the father and Jesus the Messiah. The way of Israel was to be replaced with the new way of Christ. They talked of a new law, a new commandment, a new covenant or a new teaching. The Torah was said to have been reformed. The early Christian church had no systematic ethical theory. They just lived a good life. Since the professed end did not come, they later on established moral codes from the society along with domestic virtues for the survival of society.

Paul converted to Christianity because the Torah just did not give enough assistance to him. There was a new covenant in which love would destroy sin. He said: 'Love is patient; it is kind; love is not jealous; it does not put on airs. Love is not proud; love is never unbecoming; it does not seek its own ends; it does not stir up anger; it does not seek revenge. It does not rejoice in what is not right, but rejoices in the truth. Love can put up with everything; it can trust to the end; it has infinite hope and it endures all things' (1 Corinthians 13:4-7). Paul insisted that this love should be directed toward all humanity. He also said that one should not esteem self above what is proper but be modest. Each one had a specific capacity like ministering; prophesying, teaching and so on (see Romans 12:3-7). Paul accepted society as he found them. He accepted homosexuality and slavery. Divorce was prohibited in Mark's Gospel because the union of man and woman made them one, not two. Matthew's ethical guide came with the Sermon on the Mount. He describes the Christian group as the poor of Yahveh-

'Blessed are the poor in spirit because the rule of God belongs to them.

Blessed are those who mourn…

Blessed are the lowly…'

The sermon contrasts the old and the new righteousness- The response of Israel and the response of the Christians. The Christian group is assured that their righteousness fulfills the requirement of Judaism. To the old rule of not to kill was added that one should not be angry or to call a companion a fool or 'unfaithful fool'. To adultery was added anyone who looks lustfully at a woman. Lying is forbidden and so no need for oaths. To the call for retaliation in the Torah, it was replaced by non-resistance to evil; to love the enemy as also the neighbour and pray for the persecutors. Right action like giving alms should be done without publicity and in secret. 'Do not let your left hand know what your right hand does, but let it be done in secret'. (Matthew 6:1-4). Be practical and do not judge others. The new Christian law did not abrogate the Torah but fulfilled it. In fact, in Luke 10:25-37, there is a conversation between a lawyer and Jesus in which the latter says that to inherit the life of the age to come, he must follow what is written in the Torah. As for loving one's neighbour, Jesus says that a neighbour is not one who is insensitive to others, nor a priest who is also insensitive but the man, the Samaritan who helps someone in suffering by giving him his care, and feeding him. People should consider possessions as belonging to all and not as personal belongings.

John's Gospel was the last, probably completed decades later than the others. He said- 'Do not love the world or anything in the world; if anyone loves the world, the love of the Father is not in that person' (1 John 2:15). John called the manifestation of the power of Yahveh as the Holy Spirit. This spirit is the spirit of Truth that describes the work of god to humanity. This Gospel of John probably originated in the Asia Minor according to some authors. This appears credible since The Hindu Bhagavata says in the beginning and at the end, *satyam param dhimih* or 'Medidate on the highest Truth'. Jesus identified himself with this Truth, the truth of Yahveh, the Father.

# Christianity

These early value systems were slowly replaced by reform in later periods. Divorce, marrying a non-Christian and such other rules were adapted to suit social development. The Greek Orthodox Church formally split from the western Catholic Church in 1054 CE. The former used Greek as the sacred language and then later, Latin. The former looked to the Patriarch of Constantinople for leadership and the latter, to the Bishop of Rome or the Pope. The Slavs, Bulgarians, Serbs, and Russians had embraced the former church. John Wycliffe, Jan Hus, Martin Luther King had all challenged the authority of the Pope and Protestantism came into being. John Calvin and others removed the Catholic Church from the control of the Pope in England, paving the way for an Anglican Church. The Roman Church itself underwent a reformation at the Council of Trent in 1545 and 1563 in three sessions. This became the Roman Catholic Church. In the 17th century, other churches came up like the Methodist, Baptist, Quaker, Salvation Army and these were all non-conformists. Most of them, however, rely on the Bible and the Ten Commandments.

The Catholic ethical system originated in the Middle Ages. Aristotle and other Greek philosophers influenced Thomas Aquinas who expressed Christian ethics on the lines of Aristotle. He merely substituted Christian terms for those of Aristotle. He said that moral works were governed from both within and outside of the human person. Within were ingrained habits like prudence, justice and charity. These are virtues. From the outside, the humans are governed by the law of god with god's directing assistance. This is the eternal law directing all creatures and all creation itself. Non-rational creatures follow it blindly but rational ones sometimes resist it to their own detriment.

From the seventeenth century, the Roman Catholic Church started training the clergy using texts. This moral law could help in determining what was right and what was wrong. The Vatican Council II was convened by Pope John XXIII in 1962 for revitalizing Catholicism. Both Catholics and Protestants agree on the reference to the Bible and the concept of love as the ethical foundation of morality. Of late, the Protestant Churches have laid more stress on social justice in the world. Christians have now radically changed their attitude to the environment and consider humans as caretakers with accountability and want to protect the environment by discovering the harmony and wisdom given to it by god. This is the land-ethic that requires Christians not to think of land use. The earth does not belong to them. They belong to the earth. They should see themselves as lovers and co-creators of the world. The World Council of Churches recently encouraged Christians 'to call on the whole human family to strive for the preservation and restoration of the natural environment- especially the world's animals and plants- interrelated with each other and with us…This can only be done by awakening countries and nations to seek justice and peace for all'.

As for the status of women, there are conflicting ideas. The Torah clearly says that men are superior to women and the latter should serve them. But in Genesis 1:27, male and female are created in god's image and form one person. 'There are no longer any distinctions between the Jew and the non-Jew, the slave and the free person, the male and the female. All of you are united in Jesus the Messiah' (Galatians 3:18). The New Testament's call for a wife's subordination is dismissed as the old patriarchal religion rearing its head. The equality or non-equality is just cultural perception, some accepting and some rejecting. The west however, has seen the emergence of women as equal to men though atrocities against women continue in the world. There has been variety in Christian ethics and there is no single ethical system.

Let us now study some facts about Jesus. Jesus is from a wealthy family. Joseph and Mary, his parents, hail from the royal house of David. In 1890, a Russian journalist, Nicholas Notovitch said that Jesus travelled to India and possibly studied there. The Tibetan Text in Sanskrit, *The Life of Issa* states that Jesus was a guest in a Buddhist Monastery. Jesus left with a train of merchants when only fourteen, arriving and settling among the Aryan Indians. He went to Djaggernaut (Jagannath in Puri) in Orissa, where Brahman priests taught him to understand the Vedas, to cure by prayer, to teach scriptures and to drive out evil desires from man and make him in the likeness of god. For six years, he lived in other holy cities in India. The Gospels of Aquinas and the Dead Sea Scrolls talk of similar stories. Elizabeth Clare Prophet in *Lost Years of Jesus*, Janet Brock in *The Jesus Mystery* and Holger Kersten in *Jesus Lived in India*, all say that Jesus lived and taught in India, and returned to Palestine more enlightened. His teachings have a gentle eastern flavour.

Jesus then migrated to Buddhism, mastering the Pali language and the sacred texts. After his birth, Joseph and Mary did travel to the Middle East and India with Jesus. Buddhist schools existed in Alexandria. From the third century onwards, fanatics of Christianity systematically destroyed books and libraries that contained Hindu and Buddhist texts. A Persian work by Mir Mohd. Bin Khawand (1417) states: 'Jesus was named the Messiah because he was a great traveller'. Ikmaluddin's *The Book of Balauhar and Budasaf*, tells of Christ preaching to the people of Kashmir and surrounding areas. It clearly mentions Christ's travels in Kashmir and his death in the country of natural causes at the age of 120. Mullah Nadri in his book *Tarikhi Kashmir* wrote: 'During this time Hazrat Yuz Asaf (Jesus) having come from the Holy Land to this holy valley, proclaimed his prophethood…He declared himself to be a Messenger of God for the people of Kashmir'. He also states that Christ's beliefs were like those of the Hindus.

Dr Fida Hasnain's *A Search for the Historical Jesus* cites a Tibetan manuscript translated from an ancient Chinese document, *The History of Religion and Doctrines: The Glass Mirror*- 'Yesu the Teacher...commanded his disciples to observe ten vows among which includes prohibition of manslaughter and attainment of eternal joy through good deeds...This is one of the virtuous results emerging out of the teachings of Buddha'. The official decree of the Grand Mufti of Kashmir in 1774, mentions Jesus' time in Kashmir. He is referred to on a signpost outside his purported burial site at Roza Bal. There is also a mention of Jesus at the Takhat Suleiman (Throne of Suleiman) monument in Srinagar. Of the inscriptions in this monument we have:

At this time, Juz Asaf proclaimed his Prophethood. Year fifty and four.

((4) He is Jesus, Prophet of the Children of Israel.

There are at least thirty ancient texts covering the religions of Islam, Hindu, and Buddhists that very specifically mention Jesus- not only before his public life and crucifixion but also afterward when he continued his performance of ministry in the Middle East and India.

Mark, Matthew, and John were written in 70 CE to the 2$^{nd}$ century, while the synoptic gospels of Mark, Matthew and Luke are similar. John's is different as it names people and two episodes (The wedding of Cana and the raising of Lazarus) not mentioned in other gospels. Why were the other books not included in the Bible? The answer clearly is because, they were too controversial and many Books conflicted with the 'four true Gospels' and the idea of the Church of what Christianity should be. Modern Christianity is based on what Paul understood of Jesus (Paul never met Jesus). But being a Roman, Constantine chose his version. Christ did help with the Dead Sea Scrolls.

Christ was an Essene and a Gnostic and did what he told us to do. The Gnostic gospels' glaring comparisons between Judaism, Christianity (as per Jesus), Hinduism and Buddhism should be an eye opener. As a true Gnostic, he incorporated it all into what we still say today- loving god and doing good. Jesus had once said: 'Only in his hometown and in his own house is a Prophet without honour' (Matthew 13:57). The time Jesus spent in India was the best in his life.

Mary Magdalene, a high born woman (not a harlot as made out by many) did not know that Jesus was married and that his wife wanted her stoned for adultery. Christ not only protected Mary but also married her. At the age of 29, Jesus returned to Israel with Mary.

Jesus believed in reincarnation but this was left out of the Bible. He was influenced by the Hindu belief. Matthew 11:14 says: 'And if you are willing to accept it, he (John the Baptist) is Elijah who was to come'. In Matthew 17:10-13, Jesus again relates that Elijah came but was not known, for he was John the Baptist. It is clear that Elijah was the earlier life of John. He talks of his father's house with many mansions, meaning man can occupy many bodies.

The Acta Thomae (banned by the Church) says that Jesus attended a wedding with Thomas in AD (CE) 49, 16 years after his crucifixion. Crucifixion is only a punishment and people do not die as many have lived to tell their tale. Pope John XXII said that Christian belief should not be based on the fact that Christ died on the Cross.

Pontius Pilate, a friend of Jesus, was not happy with the crucifixion though he went with it and after three hours, Christ was removed from the Cross and Pilate 'washed the hands of this innocent man'. When Mary Magdalene came to the tomb, the angels asked, 'why do you look for the living among the dead?'. Later, Jesus appeared to his apostles and asked 'why are you troubled and why do thoughts arise in your hearts? See my hands and feet, that it is myself; touch and see…Do you have anything there to eat?' (Luke 24:36-43). This along with the empty tomb on Easter morning found by Mary, are proof enough of his survival. Also there is complete lack of documentation of the Resurrection except for Paul's account.

In Turkey, there is 'The Home of Mary', a tourist attraction where Jesus had stayed with Mary. From there, they went to Kashmir and India again. Because he was scorned in his home, he went to France where he lived with his wife till his late eighties. The Knights Templar, the Rosy Cross and the Priory of Sion were set up to protect Jesus and his family. He had seven children.

December 25th is the birthday of Mithra, who was called 'the son of god and the light of the world'. Mithra was an important Vedic god. It was also the birthday of Osiris, Adonis and Dionysius, all Pagan gods. Easter was the advent of spring and not connected with the resurrection.

New research suggests that the Vatican was originally a temple of Lord Shiva. The Vatican compound is shaped in the form of a Shiva Linga and the aerial photograph of the Vatican indicates the three lines and the third eye of Shiva. In fact the historian P.N.Oak suggests that Christ is actually derived from Krishna and Christianity is Krishna Neeti or the ethics of Krishna. Significantly about eight Shiva Lingas that were found during excavation in the area have been kept in the Gregorian Etruscan Museum, Vatican City. The word *'vatica'* in Sanskrit means a religious centre and the Vatican was probably a Shiva Temple in the pre-Christian era. The Museum has valuable collection from the Iron Age onwards and the Encyclopedia Britannica mentions that during excavations many such Lingas, stones mounted on carved pedestals were discovered in Italy. The Vatican was originally called Vatika and the Papacy, a Hindu Vedic priesthood, until Constantine killed the Vedic pontiff and installed a representative of the tiny Christian sect. Constantine himself was a sun worshipper (*sol invictus*), detailed in another chapter of this book. In fact, when they say Amen, it is really the *Pranava* sound AUM (a cosmic sound) of the Hindus which is the word that was God the Brahman. The credibility of the above is enhanced by Aristophanes (446-386 BCE) in his play *The Acharnians*. In this, Dicaeopolis tells Xanthias to 'walk behind the basket bearer and hold the Phallus well erect; I will follow, singing the Phallic hymn'. Here the basket refers to the pedestal on which the Phallus (Linga) is mounted, which was carried by a bearer for which the Spartans had high reverence. This clearly proves that Phallus worship and singing in praise of the Linga was very much in practice in Greece 2500 years ago. So the Vatican having been a Shiva temple (Linga) in the pre-Christian period appears to be quite credible. This also indicates the Hindu influence in Greece and Rome at that period and confirms the view of scholars like Max Muller that Phallus worship was the oldest known religious practice in the world. This practise continues in India to this day in thousands of Shiva temples where oblations are offered to the Linga with the chanting of Vedic Hymns.

The ancient trade between South India and Rome, Egypt, Greece and other places has been well documented by historians. Tamil was the language that existed in the whole of India even during 10,000 BCE when the Pandyans ruled. Tamil Brahmi was the source language for all other languages of India. Tamil Brahmi inscriptions have been found in potsherds at Quseir-al-Qadim, a Roman settlement in Egypt. These are dated to the 1st century CE or earlier. Professor Peacock and Professor Blue from Southampton University team of archaeologists discovered these potsherds in Egypt and the inscription reads '*paanai ori* meaning pot that is kept suspended with a rope in which butter is usually kept. Earlier excavations 30 years ago also yielded pottery with inscriptions in Tamil Brahmi. Similar potteries were found at Berenike, a Roman settlement on the Red Sea coast of Egypt in 1995. Again potsherds with Tamil inscriptions were found at the Khor Rori area of Oman in the ancient city of Sumhuram that is dated at the 1st century CE or earlier. The Italian Mission to Oman had found this during its second excavation in 2006. Dr Cherian said: 'It is unfortunate that the geographical and cultural significance of the south Arabian region and its links with ancient south India has not been properly studied for various reasons'. The Euro-centric perspectives that became dominant after the Roman Empire seem to have erased more history than they probably produced anew. In most of these potsherds, frankincense traces were found indicating the connection with South Arabia famed as the 'land of incense'. Dr Cherian wanted more such archaeological finds in peninsular India for providing textual evidence in addition to the existing body of research that have confirmed export from Pattinam port (Musiri?) and other southern ports where already Roman settlements, coins and other artefacts have been unearthed.

We will conclude by quoting Victor Hugo who said in *Les Miserables,* 'Cloisters, useful in the early education of modern civilization, have embarrassed its growth and are injurious to its development. So far as institutions with relation to man are concerned, monasteries, which were good in the tenth century, questionable in the eighteenth, are detestable in the nineteenth. The leprosy of monasticism has gnawed nearly to a skeleton two wonderful nations, Italy and Spain…the Catholic cloister, properly speaking, is wholly filled with the black radiance of death'. This is a powerful indictment but appears to be confirmed by the sexual abuse of children by priests in America and elsewhere and as compensation, the Vatican paid a staggering $168 billion to the United States in 2011 in response to a court ruling. Let us hope this leads to reform in the Church that leads to the suspension and stoppage of conversions and to a purer way of life of the priests. This rethinking is particularly necessitated if we recall the way in which books and libraries around the world were destroyed by religious fanatics over the centuries. Only from the twentieth century such aberrations have mostly stopped but the loss of valuable books and scriptures has proved to be very costly as it has prevented the present generation from knowing various historical teachings. This has resulted in the imagination of some scholars running wild thereby falsifying such universal truths as are considered invaluable for the spiritual progress of all humanity.

## References:
1. Ethics of World Religions- Arnold D. Hunt, Marie T. Crotty and Robert B. Crotty, Greenhaven Press, San Diego, USA.
2. History of Ancient India- Ramakrishnan Srinivasan, 2nd Edition, SriSri Publications, Bengaluru, 2015
3. Sacred Books of the East- Zend-Avesta, Translated by James Darmestetter.

# CHAPTER 9

# ISLAM

The word Islam in Arabic essentially means surrendering to god and to acquire peace in your soul. The Koran does not believe in forcing someone to convert. In fact it forbids it. Factually however, there have been forced conversions in India after the Moghul invasion in the 7th century. In 622 CE, Mohammad gained control of Medina and since then Islam had been expanding till the 16th century. Though they lost Spain in 1492, the Mongol invasions of the 13th century saw the Christian world losing all of North Africa, the Middle East, and much of Eastern Europe to Islam. The Crusades however, showed that the Christians could wrest land from the Moslems by the invasion of Palestine in the 11th/12th centuries. Though the Crusades failed, the Europeans came back with a vengeance in the 18th century and by the close of World War I, came to dominate 95% of the Moslem world.

Islam has seven fundamental beliefs- belief in god, in angels, in the revealed Book of God, in god's many prophets, accepting there will be a Last Day, in the divine measurement of human affairs, and belief in life after death. In the Koran, there is a statement that tells the Christians and Jews: 'We believe in the Revelation which has come down to us and in that which came down to you; our god and your god is one, and it is to Him we surrender' (Sura 29:46). The Islamic concept of our place in the universe hinges on the notion that God is the only reality. Nothing else is permanent. He is eternal and uncreated. Everything else is created and they will pass away and return to Allah for review. Not even the stars will last forever.

The proof of God's existence is found in the following:

1. The natural world with its complexity and beauty is the sign of intelligence in the universe because only a designing mind could have created it.
2. Human abilities for thought, belief, invention, creativity and moral choice. Other species do not have these faculties.
3. The God's revelation shows that there is a right way and a wrong way to live life. Prophets, holy book, flashes of insight, all serve as proof that guidance is real and purposefully directed.

4. Our inner feelings propel us to seek the meaning in things and show us that we have a soul that seeks harmony with nature, the universe and a higher power. The humans will seek the answer to questions that concern more than mere physical existence.

Jinns or spirits are the real cause of supernatural and paranormal events, not ghosts. Their dimensions cannot be seen. Islam teaches that all angels are good and cannot be corrupted. Just stating the testimony of faith in the presence of two witnesses is enough to convert. Islam holds that all are born good but our weakness of desire for pleasure and aversion to pain leads us to weakness in committing sin or wrong. God will judge after our physical death and resurrection on the Day of Judgment, and reward or punishment follows.

Three levels of self-development are passed by men. These are- the Animal Self with basic instincts and desires, the Accusing Self of a higher order of questioning of our purpose and the Restful Self that transcends worldliness as a focus. The Koran accepts the original Torah, Psalms and Gospel as original revelations from God and so the Jewish prophets and Jesus are accepted. The final stage is when the soul becomes the Restful Self, awaiting the meeting with the Creator. There is no place for monasteries or asceticism. While still maintaining normal life, he does not live for satisfying himself but realizes the higher purpose of life. Charity, self-sacrifice, truth and the simple beauty of life blend to create peace and wisdom around people.

No previous revelations from God have survived without alteration by humans and the Koran is the final revelation that cannot be changed. There is an awareness of more than hundred vices and virtues that can be found in Islam. The major sins are- idolatry, stealing an orphan, adultery and fornication, disobeying parents, collecting interest on investments, accusing falsely a chaste woman, false testimony, murder, suicide, infanticide, enslaving a free person and slander or gossip. The virtuous deeds are- truth, kindness to family, honouring parents, charity, poor feeding, fighting injustice, freeing slaves, returning borrowed property, studying and learning and kindness to animals. All sins can be restituted by remorse, asking for forgiveness, making restitution, and resolving never to do it again. For some sins that harm others, penalties must be paid- Cutting off hand for repeated theft, flogging for fornication etc., and capital punishment for murder or treason. All other sins can be restituted by the four methods given above.

God or Allah has no form. It is just monotheism. Idol worship is taboo. God is one without a second or partners. He is the god of all creation. There is no son of god as in the Judeo-Christian faith. The pagan Arabs before Mohammad accepted a Supreme God over all demigods they worshipped, but believed that Allah was too powerful and remote to make any difference in their lives. An informal tradition of quasi-agnosticism was practised by some, and they were nicknamed Hanifs. They believed in God but shunned idolatry and even well developed religions like Christianity. Every soul draws the results of its actions on none but itself; no bearer of burden can bear the burden of others (Surah 6:164).

Islam considers Jesus as a prophet of God born of Virgin Mary as a miracle of God. Moslems accept the virgin birth but consider the lack of a father in Jesus' creation at the same level of lack of parents for Adam's creation. The 'likeness of Jesus in the sight of God is that of Adam. He created him from dust and said 'Be' and he was'. The Koran denies that Jesus was killed on a cross. Islam flatly rejects the notion of original sin. Adam and Eve sinned but god forgave them when they asked for his mercy. The word *taqwa* means consciousness or awareness of God in life. Prayer, fasting, reflection on life and its brevity and selfless action can cause our *taqwa* to grow. Islam looks for god's quality instead of His form. His actions, nature, manifestations are all in His many names.

"Call on God or call on 'the compassionate' by whatever name you call upon Him (it is well), for to Him belongs the most beautiful names" (17:109). There is a list of 99 names for Allah, like Merciful, the Living, the Faithful etc. God is neither male nor female because He has no form. Because there is no Arabic name for 'it', they use the pronoun 'He'. Life arose for a purpose. Humans have the free will or choice to accept God or not. Free will is our great burden and there will be rewards and consequences because of it.

Human life begins at conception and life after birth is a crucial testing ground where contentment or frustration will be our lot. The four stages of life are- life in the womb, in the world, in the grave and in the next life (hell or heaven). Our Soul or *ruh* is other-worldly and the angel of death takes hold of it and pulls. If the person denied god, the soul is torn. Death is not final, merely passing on to another stage of life. A good soul will be gently clothed with shrouds from paradise. Then the angels are told "take him back to earth because I promised them that 'from it I created them, unto it I will return them and from it I will resurrect them onceagain'". If a person rejected Allah he will be taken to hell and then returned to earth for the same reason. The non-believer is a *kafir*. *Jannah* is paradise. *Jahannum* is hell, described in detail in Islam.

The Creation in Islam: Allah said 'Be', and a ball appeared and he split it into pieces. This initial explosion caused the pieces to be the building blocks for all things in the universe. From this interstellar gas arose, planets and stars were formed. 'By the rotation of the stars and orbits and settings of the planets, by the night as it falls and the morning as it passes, certainly, this is the speech of an honoured Messenger' (81:25). The Koran identifies the sun as the giver of light and the moon as the reflector of light (munir). God completed creation in six days or segments and then mounted the throne to govern. He never rests. One day of god is 1000 earth years. At another place it says, the time it takes the angels to ascend to god for Judgment Day will be a day equal to 50,000 earth years. God made time.

God created the first man Adam and woman Hawwa or Eve from dust and placed them in a tropical garden, a paradise. God taught Adam everything in the environment then asked the angels to bow to Adam. He told Adam to guard against Shaytan as he could corrupt him. Adam and Eve were prohibited from going near one particular tree. But Shaytan came into the garden and tempted them to eat from the tree. He told them it will give eternal life to both. This was the first lie of Shaytan. God said 'they did wrong'. They then began to feel ashamed of their nakedness and used leaves to sew into clothes. They were expelled from the Garden of Eden, but later were forgiven. He gave instructions to them to pass on to their descendents.

"If there comes to you guidance from me, whoever follows my guidance will not lose his way, nor fall into despair. But whoever turns away from my message, certainly he will have a life narrowed down and we will raise him up blind on the Day of Judgment' (20:123-124). Adam is considered as the first Prophet of God on earth.

Islam has a concept of divine measurement, which gives hope that they can affect the future with personal effort explaining why things happen the way they do. There is no destiny as free will gives the ability to shape our own future. Mohammad said-'Work as you are able because if you did not help yourself, God won't help you either'. Islam does not believe in astrology; it advises living from day to day without bothering about the future since god knows the past, present and the future as he had created it. *Qada* is determination and *qadr* is measurement as God has power over future and controls it. We have control over how we feel and respond to events; patience (*sabr*) or panic, what is our reaction? This appears to be another variation of the Hindu concept of karma- accept what comes to us without trying to influence it.

Georg Wilhelm Frederich Hegel said-'There are patterns of history, and those who do not know the past are doomed to repeat it'. Islam says that all true religion began with God. History for Islam is no less than playing out episodes in a cosmic script culminating with the inevitable journey of all people back to their Lord.

# Islam

According to Mohammad, 'There is no superiority of a white over a black or of a black over a white. All of you are children of Adam and Adam was made from the dust' (Hadith). Mohammad had commented that this colour of the skin is due to hot and cold climates only, which is also the scientific explanation. From 1800 to 1960, most of the Moslem world was ruled by France, the Netherlands, Russia and England. Only after that date the occupation of their land ended.

The Jewish Old Testament warns Jews of God's wrath and destruction of Zion and later rebirth of the Messiah. The Christian New Testament warns of a great disaster to befall believers who will later be saved by Jesus. Islam has a tradition of downfall of the Moslems until a hero, Mahdi (guided One), comes along who will revive the community. All the above are a reflection of Krishna's statement that God will descend again and again after every Yuga when evil overtakes humanity. Many Moslems feel that the end of the world is near and expect a *Dajjal* or Anti-Christ to incarnate at the right time. Mohammad also said that Islam came to the world as a stranger and will end up as a stranger one day. Other signs for the end are:

1. Abundant riches (oil?) under the Euphrates River in Iraq and people fighting over it.
2. Children will no longer obey parents.
3. Poor nations will compete with each other to build tall buildings even as people starve.
4. It will be hard to tell men and women apart physically.
5. Women will outnumber men by a huge margin (50:1).
6. Religious knowledge will decrease dramatically and real pious scholars rare.
7. Wealth will be widespread and corruption rampant.
8. The worst people will be chosen leaders.
9. There will be family turmoil in every home.

We can easily see that most of the above are already seen as reality in the world. When the leader Mahdi appears, all Moslems will be unified under his banner, and many campaigns against enemies of Islam will end in unification of the Middle East, and prosperity will come to all. The main base of Moslems will be Palestine and after a certain period *Dajjal* will appear. Prophet Jesus, with the army of Mahdi at Damascus will vanquish *Dajjal* and strike him down with a lance and the reign of tyranny will be over. Jesus will then speak to Jews and Christians and convert them to Islam (*Dajjal* will have an army of 70,000).

The next challenge will be from the nations of the East, the Yajuj and Majuj, known as Gog and Magog in the Bible. They will invade massively and Jesus will command the faithful to Mt. Sinai in Egypt because no one could withstand the onslaught of the invaders. Jesus will then pray to God for deliverance and will be answered with a pestilence outbreak on the invading army which will crumble and Jesus will come out with his followers and many more will convert to Islam. But before this, Jesus will pass away. He will be buried in Medina next to Prophet Mohammad. Three massive sinkholes will open up in the East, west and Arabia. A mysterious haze will envelop the world making people hot with fever and the sun will rise in the west. A fantastic beast will rise from the earth and warn people about the end of the world. A ground fire will ignite the land of Yemen and people will flee to Syria. The earth will start to quake and mountains will crumble. 'Everything will be a commotion. A trumpet will be sounded and all will perish except the chosen ones. A second trumpet will be sounded when they will be standing on the Plain of Judgment (39:68). The stars will fade, skies will roll up, the seas will rise and terror will grip the remaining people. The earth will be crushed and God will create a new universe with a new earth but for humanity the game is over. Everyone will stand before God for Judgment. This Islamic end of the world has similarities with the Christian Armageddon and the Jewish Day of Judgment.

The five pillars of Islam are:
1. *Shahadah*- Testifying allegiance to God.
2. *Salat*- Daily prayer, five times.
3. *Zakat*- Annual charity.
4. *Saum*- Month-long fasting.
5. *Hajj*- Pilgrimage to Mecca.

Humility is a valued asset in Islam. The pilgrimage to Mecca is to perform rituals at the Kaba'h, the Temple of Abraham where Abraham is said to have prayed to God. Umrah is a preliminary ritual after which the next day the Hajj begins by going round the Kaba'h seven times anti-clockwise. They need to have two white garments unstitched, around them (like a Toga) without straps, and women are allowed any dress. The station of Abraham (Maqami Ibrahim) is the place after the seven rounds and then to go to the fountain that saved Hagar and Ishmael from perishing. It is the well of Zam that gives mineral water to be taken by the worshippers. Then they move to the covered walkway between the two hills where Hagar ran back and forth in desperation. After the walks, they spend the day in prayer. Men and women follow the same ritual.

Jihad means the struggle to work for something with determination. Mohammad said- 'You have left the lesser Jihad, now you are coming to the greater Jihad, the struggle against yourself'. Jihad can only arise from an established country with a leader of Islam. But groups have risen in response to oppression. The Hamas after

# Islam

Israel was created, Al Qaida, after Soviet invasion of Afghanistan, and Moro rebels after Christian colonialism in Northern Philippines. These are political grievances in the guise of religion. Jihad is a godly campaign for truth and justice. It is not meant to be misused. Many levels of Jihad include social activism to improve society as the Jewish Tikun Olam or perfecting the world. Moslems oppose alcohol, pornography, drugs, pollution and littering, gossip in media, corruption, pedophilia or spousal abuse and cruelty to animals.

The western hostility to Islam started with the Byzantine during the Prophet's time. This has continued as a cold war as Moslems started to bite off more and more territory. Moslems in the non-Moslem societies are bound by Islamic law, to live peacefully with their neighbours as no injustice is being done to anyone. Crime and vice must be opposed regardless. Terrorism, *Hiraba*, is forbidden. Though such small groups are there, the majority do not support or condone such acts.

Moslems call Christians and Jews 'people of the Book'. The Books of God are brought by Gabriel from the 'Mother of the Book' kept by God. The main ones are- *The Scrolls of Abraham (Suhuf), The Law of Moses (Taurah), The Psalms of David (Zabur), The Gospel of Jesus (Injeel),* and *The Reading of Mohammad (Koran).* During the first fifteen years of Islam, Moslems were told to pray in the direction of Jerusalem. After a year and a half in Medina, a revelation instructed them to pray in the direction of Mecca.

Judaism holds that Jesus is a false Rabbi but the Koran called him the Jewish Messiah and a messenger of God who was called to make the wayward Jews come back to the true faith. Though Mohammad engaged in talks with the Jews in Medina, the latter became increasingly hostile to Moslems. The first Jewish tribe to fight was Banu Qaynuka who had to leave and settle in Palestine. The second tribe to fight was Banu Nadir which even tried to assassinate Mohammad. This tribe was also forced to leave for Palestine and some went to Khaiber in North Arabia. The third tribe was Banu Qaraiza which wanted to live in peace as per their treaty. But Banu Nadir sent ambassadors to Mecca, the centre of idol worship. A coalition of Arab tribes were sent to Medina who even had an agreement with Banu Qaraiza and Mohammad came to know of this and after fierce fighting, Banu Qaraiza agreed to surrender subject to the judgment of the Arab tribe. Banu Qaraiza's warriors were taken into custody and clan leaders were executed by the verdict of their own religion. Mohammad ordered Moslems to be kind to Jews and to share their food with them. He had business dealings with Jews who continued to stay in Medina even for centuries after Mohammad's passing. One of Mohammad's wives Safiya was Jewish. Subsequent expulsion of three organized Jewish tribes was due to their own duplicity and treachery. Even then many

Jews lived in Medina but only a tax *Jizyah* was imposed on them for not drafting in the army in times of need. Moslems also paid the *Zakah*. The Moslem Empire had Jews as palace physicians, finance officers, and even viziers or ministers. The Islamic Millat allowed them to follow their own religions.

Christianity has not yet accepted the validity of Mohammad's message and hence knows little about Islam. This is now changing. The Koran says-'You will find that the closest to you in love are those who call themselves Christians because there are priests and monks among them who do not behave arrogantly' (5:82). The Christians of Arabia were known not as paragons of virtue. At Mohammad's time, the few Christians were not organized. A generation before him, Christianity was all but made illegal by the reigning idolaters who feared the loss of their religion.

According to Mohammad, 'every Prophet sent by God has been a shepherd. Moses was a shepherd, David tended animals and before I became a Prophet, I also was a shepherd'. It is significant that Krishna was a cowherd. Beyond disagreement with a few Christian concepts, the Koran accepts and promulgates many teachings that are accepted in Christianity. Mohammad never went to a school of divinity, never read the Bible and could not read. Both Judaism and Christianity are given equal coverage in the first nine chapters of the Koran. 'And we made Jesus, the son of Mary, and his mother a sign for mankind' (23:50). The fierce opposition to Jesus came from the Jewish leaders, records the Koran. The Koran was very enthusiastic about inter-faith dialogue. *Futuwwat* was the chivalric Moslem code by which a Moslem soldier would give quarter to an injured opponent, protect women and children, and fight with honour at all times.

The second Vatican Council of 1962-65, opened the door to fellowship with Moslems and the Lumen Gentium says: 'The plan of salvation also includes those who acknowledge the Creator, among whom are, in the first place Moslems. These profess to hold the faith of Abraham, and together with us, they adore the One, Merciful God, judge of humankind on the Last Day' (LG 16). Pope Paul IV and Pope John Paul II opened the door for full dialogue with the Moslems. The latter even apologized for the Crusades. He was the first to visit a Mosque in Syria and allowed the construction of a small mosque in the Vatican City. While other religions had ancient sources, Islam derived only from two sources both of which passed through man and completed in 25 years.

From 610 to 635 CE, Mohammad was receiving revelations from God. First he was asked to read. He said he cannot read. Again the same and the third time he had received divine grace to be able to understand the revelations. First he ran home to his wife Khadija in fear. The word Koran means reading or recital. Mohammad would ask people to write the revelations dictated by him. There are 114 chapters (Surahs) comprising 6000 verses called *ayahs*. The content revolved round monotheism, virtuous living and the eventual triumph of Islam, though it was a persecuted religion. The revelations were received through dreams, revelations in his heart, loud ringing in his ears with flowing verses and last through the archangel Gabriel appearing as a man. The first 13 years, the revelations were in Mecca, the second after migration to Medina. Initially it was an oral tradition and only later was it put down in print. The first Caliph Abu Bakr faced a rebellion and 70 of the memorisers were killed. He was then prevailed upon by Umar bin al Khattab to prepare the Koran as a single book. This was done under the supervision of the Prophet's secretary, Zayd bin Thabit, who utilized paper from China. The book was kept with one of Prophet's widows.

Later, during the third Caliph Usman ibn Affan, disputes on the pronunciation arose and Usman released the official edition from the Prophet's wife; it was duplicated and a copy each was sent to every Moslem city. A Hafiz is one who has memorized the Koran. Two copies of these Usmani Korans exist in Museums in Turkey and Tashkent. Mohammad's life example, Sunnah, represents his interpretation of the Koran. Hadith is a different book of pronouncements given by the Prophet. Imam Bukhari collected 600,000 Hadiths but included only 2602 as he could not prove the authenticity of the rest.

The crescent is a symbol associated with the moon worship taken over by Moslems after they conquered Byzantine in 1453 CE. The Byzantine's got this symbolism from the Hindu settlers who worshipped Shiva, generally worshipped in the form of a Phallus (Linga) in India. Shiva had the Crescent moon on his head along with the Ganga and the legends concerning these are well known in India. Mohammad considered Islam as a restoration of an ancient faith, probably the Hindu one, as the Crescent may suggest. Allah had revealed himself in ancient times to Abraham, the Patriarch of Judaism and to the other prophets of Israel including Jesus prior to Mohammad himself. He felt that both Judaism and Christianity had strayed from the law of God, first revealed by Abraham. The prophets and Jesus sent by Allah were unsuccessful and hence Mohammad established the Law, as the last of the Prophets.

The Arabian Peninsula had attained a high degree of culture in the southern region and a series of states were established, ruled by Priest Kings and other leaders. By the seventh century, there were many fine temples, castles, dams for irrigation and so on. They had three main gods- the sun, moon goddess, and another, probably Venus. In the north, a more ancient way of life existed. Tribes had a solidarity and honour and they did good, avoiding evil. A tree or a rock surrounded by a sacred enclosure was the place of worship. This included the worship of the Linga or the Phallus stone, which is known to be the oldest form of worship in the world going back to more than 6000 years. By the end of the fifth century, the tribe of Quraysh seized the Mecca area and honoured a shrine called the Ka'aba (cube) built around a large stone, possibly a Linga. There were other images of gods that was destroyed in the eighth century and only the large stone still remains. The tribal leaders were ruling amid great tensions but trade flourished, making people rich. Mohammad was born in Mecca and by the age forty, he had transformed due to some revelations. He then became a preacher and a *Rasul* (apostle). He became a threat to the traders facing rebuff and almost succumbed when his wife Khadija died. His followers from Yathrib invited him and he moved there (known as *hijra* or migration). He established the community of Islam there. In 630 CE, Meccans attacked Medina and Mohammad won this battle. He destroyed all the idols in the Ka'aba except for the stone as a symbol of his religion. He died in 632 CE but by then Islam was established and the Qu'ran was written with the Hadith, his teachings. Sunnah became the custom of Mohammad. The word 'became the Book' in Christianity and 'the word became the flesh' in Islam. Every Surah began 'in the name of Allah, the compassionate, the Merciful' except one.

The Surah 17 has among other things the following: 'Your Lord gives abundantly to those he selects and sparingly to others' 'To kill is a terrible sin'. The public opinion of the community expressed by jurists agreed on the right or wrong of a practice, it was upheld if it did not conflict with either the Qu'ran or Hadith. The Moslem Law or the Shariah is the pathway to Allah.

After Mohammad many disenchanted people sought a spiritual way of life. And these were the Sufis. They aimed at a personal union with god. The leader of the Sufis, the Sheik, became a model. An uneasy alliance between the Sunnis and the Sufis ensued in the twelfth century. Their focus on the hereafter, meant that Islam lacked the interest in the human body, the vehicle of life, discarded at death. Men had authority over women. When Islam came into contact with the Byzantine Greek society of Syria, the practice of women wearing a veil came into being.

Sunni Laws:

The Hanafi - (700-767) of Abu Hanifa Sunni.

The Shafi - Mohd. Al Shafi I (767-820).

The Maliki – Malik ibn Anas (716-795).

The Hanbali – Ahmed ibn Hanbal (780-855), the most conservative Sunni sect.

# Islam

## Shia:

The Jafari- Imam Jafar as Sadiq (699-765), School of Islamic Law.

Allowed activities- Halal. Prohibited activity – Haram.

Music, other than immoral, lewd or suggestive is permitted. Intoxicants, gambling are prohibited. Women had equal rights and suffrage. Countries ruled by the king are prohibited by Islam. In other countries, women vote freely. Iran has more women in government than in the United States. Harem is a prohibited place where women enjoy privacy. Honour killings have no sanction in Islamic law. Woman is half of man and inherits half the property. Wearing a burqa or *niqab* (veil on face) is not required in Islam. Neither socks nor gloves are required. Purdah or female seclusion is also not required in Islam. The Koran promoted democracy. Abu Bakr was elected the Caliph after Mohammad. Only Ali ibn Abi Talib, cousin of Mohammad, objected initially but later relented. His followers however dissented and broke away as Shi'as.

Islam promoted study and learning. Moslems were famous for calligraphy, the arts, sciences, architecture and so on. Their science hall of fame includes: Mohd. Al-Khawarizmi (d.840)- algebra and trigonometry.

Hasan ibn al Haitham (d.1040) – optics and linking algebra with geometry.

Abu Raihan al Biruni (d.1048) – circumference of earth and study of speed of sound and light.

Ibn Sina (d. 1037) – Medicine and speed of light as constant.

Ali Ibn Rabban al-Tabari (d.870) – Encyclopaedia of Medicine.

Jabir Ibn Haiyan (d.803) – Father of modern chemistry.

Abu Abdullah Al Battani (d.929) – Earth was round, length of solar year, astronomy and mathematics.

Mohd. Al-Razi (d. 930) – Madicine, Classification of organic and inorganic compounds.

Mohammad said, 'Acquire knowledge, it enables its possesser to distinguish right and wrong'. By the close of the 14th century, progress in science came to a halt. The Mongol devastation, the Crusades, and civil wars caused the end of the influence of the Ulema. 85% of the Moslems in the world are Sunnis and the rest Shi'ahs.

Shia's consider themselves as the only fit people to guide Moslems as they are the descendents of Ali. Sufis are the gentle people, introspective and highly spiritual.

They may be Sunni or Shia. The Whirling Dervishes are Sufis, following the teachings of Jalaluddin Rumi (d.1273).

Sufis:

Sufis took Indian Mysticism to Islam. The major doctrines of the Sufis are:

a. God alone exists; He is in all things and all things are in Him.
b. All things are emanated from Him and have no real existence apart from Him.
c. All religions serve a purpose, as leading to realities. The most profitable is Islam, of which Sufism is the true philosophy.
d. There is no distinction between good and evil, for God is the author of all.
e. It is God who determines the will of man; therefore man is not free in his actions.
f. The Soul existed before the body, in which it is confined as in a cage. Death is to be desired, for then the Sufi returns to the bosom of the Deity.
g. Apart from the grace of God no one can attain to this spiritual union; It may however be obtained by fervent prayer.
h. The principal duty of the Sufi is constant meditation on the unity of God, the remembrance of divine names and progressive advancement in the tariqat or journey of life, so as to attain union with God.

All the above except c and h is identical with Hindu Vedanta.

In spite of the Sufi saint's progress in mysticism, it is not a part of Islam's natural growth but has originated in India from the Upanishadic principles. Mysticism also penetrated into Judaism in the middle Ages and can be found in the Book of Zohar (brightness) and other works known generally as Kabbala.

Kabir was monistic and Ahmed Shah emphasized this. Some of Kabir's poetic passages reflect his agreement with Visishtadvaita or modified Monism. This regards the universe as a creation of Maya and allows some individuality to the soul after its absorption into the Supreme.

Sufism is of Islamic origin and the Sufi saints were Muslims. But orthodox Islam did not tolerate Sufis and we know that Hallaj was executed for his assertion that he was the truth. Prof. R.C. Zachner of Oxford in his *"Mysticism- Hindus and Muslims"*(1969) writes: "Islam was not a congenial soil in which a mystical tradition of any kind could take root. Sufism met with the hostility of orthodox theologians from the beginning and both Dhul Nun of Egypt and Sbul Hussayn al-Nuri are said to have been arraigned before the Caliph on suspicion of heresy". Zachner established after careful research that Sufi mysticism or Monism is derived from Hindu Monism. The phrase *"takuna anta dhaka"* is a literal translation of *"tat tvam asi"* from the

Chandogya Upanishad. Zachner concludes: "Abu Yazid was directly influenced by a totally alien stream and it was through him that Vedantic ideas became part and parcel of later Islamic mysticism". It is clear that the Upanishads influenced Islam as it did Christianity and Buddhism besides Greek thought.

Bahais are another Moslem sect being an offshoot of Islam. They are a more benevolent face of Islam. They follow the teachings of Baha'ullah. It teaches the oneness of humanity and the recognition that everyone is part of the same family. Men and women are equal and need the same opportunity for education. All religions are regarded as coming from the same loving God and as being given to humanity progressively to spiritualise the world in stages. It revolved round peace and justice for all humanity.

## References:
1. IDIOT's Guide to Islam- Yahiya Emerick, Third edition.
2. Ethics of World Religions- Arnold D. Hunt, Marie T. Crotty and Robert B. Crotty, Greenhaven Press, San Diego, USA.
3. Science, Philosophy, and Religion-Towards a Synthesis- Ramakrishnan Srinivasan, Citadel, Calcutta, 2008.

# CHAPTER 10
# CHINESE MYTHOLOGY

The Chinese had many dynasties like the Shang, Zhou, Quin, Han etc., and their myths are interesting. The Flood myth is one in which two siblings (brother and sister) release the thunder god caught by his brother, the human ancestor. The Thunder God went to heaven after sending one of his teeth (or gourd or pumpkin), to the siblings and telling them that there will be a flood and they should do as they are told. When the Flood came, all humans were destroyed except the siblings who hid in a big gourd from the seed sent by the thunder god. To recreate humans, the siblings married and gave birth to a gourd. They cut it into pieces which in turn became humans. This reminds us of the birth of Duryodhana and his 99 brothers. Different variations of this myth or legend are found. Similar legends exist in all societies like the Brahma marrying his sister, the Noah' story and so on. Apparently this Chinese myth originated in the Miao region of the southern Guizou province (nearest to Tibet and India). Shamans played an important part in telling such myths.

Pangu as a creator of the world was born of the Cosmic Egg. Other myths tell of mothers becoming pregnant on seeing a lightning, and similar stories. One may compare this with the Hiranyagarbha (Cosmic Egg) of the Hindus and the birth of Karna to Kunti by looking at the sun. Dragon myths are very popular in China. The hero's mother marrying a dragon and producing a hero son and the black dragon killed by the goddess Nirwa are such stories. In southwest China, an ethnic group Bai says that it was a dragon that gave birth to a couple that later became the human ancestors. Most dragons were considered divine though many were not.

During the period of the Eastern Dynasty (25-220 CE) Buddhism spread in China from India. Only after this did the dragon king figure started appearing there. A deity named Naga was linked with the divine dragon originating in Chinese Buddhism. Seeing the positive feedback, Taoists also came up with such dragon myths. The Spring Festival, Lantern Festival (January 15 of the Lunar year), and Temple fairs became popular like the dragon dance and dragon boat race. The latter is a ritual to avert evil fortune. Qu Yuan, a great poet in the warring states era, drowned in the river on May 5$^{th}$ for the honour of his state and ambitions. People rowed boats to rescue him. Though Yuan died, this custom of boat race continued. However the dragon motif on clothing etc., was monopolized by emperors, and others who used the motif were executed. This ended only with the Imperial era in 1911.

The Tree of Immortality had a *chi* spring that helps maintain youthfulness. Two officers of Fang-feng, a giant god killed by the god Yu, stabbed themselves in the hearts and died. Yu was sympathetic, took out the daggers and revived them with the herb of Immortality. This elixir is also with other gods and Shamans. Yu was the hero who stopped the world flood, assembled all the gods in Mount Guuji, but Fang-feng arrived late and was killed by Yu. Feng Bo (the Wind Master) helped Chiyou in a battle against Huang Di. The Flood myths are very popular in China; three of these myths are given here:

1. Controlling the Floods- God Gong Gong caused a flood and Goddess Nuwa, using stones in the sky and accumulating reed ashes to stop the flood. The god *Gun* stole *Xirang* (the self growing soil) to dam the flood and Yu channelled the flood waters into the sea and eventually stopped the flood. (Zhou Dynasty)
2. The brother sister marriage mentioned earlier.
3. A good lady and a dutiful son and others were told by god that their city would sink and turn into a lake when a stone lion (or a turtle) turned red in the eyes. A butcher put blood in the eyes one day and the lady and son with the others went up to a mountain. The city sank and became a lake. There are other variations of this legend linking it with the siblings.

The Chinese legends emphasized the conquest of the flood and the origin of civilization, while legends of some countries stated that the flood came to punish human sin. There were also many legends in which a human body with a snake head and similar variations (Fuxi) exist. Thus people invented many human activities like hunting and fishing nets by imitating a spider's web. Fuxi and his sister recreated the world. He was respected as one of the three divine sovereigns along with Nuwa and Shennong or the divine farmer. But Fuxi is mostly known as the human ancestor. A Jingge (classic songs) has this hymn:

Remember the beginning of the world is chaos,

Without sky, without earth, without human beings;

Then the deity of the sky created the sun, the moon, and the stars;

Then the deity of the earth created the grain and grass;

Having the sky and earth, the chaos separated;

Thus appeared Renzu, the brother and sister.

# Chinese Mythology

They climbed the high mountain Kunlun,
To throw the millstone and get married.
They gave birth to hundreds of children,
That is the origin of Beijiaxing (humans).
Therefore, the people in this world look different,
Yet in fact they belong to the same family.
How wrong it is struggling for wealth and fame,
Because, you cannot bring them with you when you go into the grave.
I persuade you to be a good person, because
A good person can be blessed by the Renzu on earth.

Houtu is the earth deity having temples for her at many places. From the Han to the Song Dynasties, many emperors offered sacrifices to the Temple of Houtu in the Shanxi province. Again Huang Di is portrayed as a human with four faces. In traditional Chinese philosophy, the world is made of five elements:

East- wood- god Taihao and deputy Goumang (controls the spring season).
South – fire – god Yan Di and deputy Zhuming (controls summer).
Centre – earth – god Huang Di and subordinate Houtu (controls the four directions).
West – metal – god Shaohao and subordinate Rushao (controls autumn season).
North – water – god Zhuanxu and subordinate Xuanming (controls winter season).

Kunlun is a remarkable mountain in Chinese mythology, the earthly residence of the Supreme Divinity, a paradise of immortals and deities, one of the pillars of the sky. This mountain is supposed to cover an area of 400 sq.km with a height of 80,000 feet. The summit has nine wells, nine gates and a magic grain. The gates are guarded by the divine beast Kaiming (enlightened) and looked like a big tiger with nine heads and human faces. Nuwa is said to have married her brother in this mountain becoming the first ancestors of the world.

The east and west paradises form the two myth systems (Kunlun and Penglai). Ling lun is the culture hero, who invented music and many musical instruments. He was the governor of music to Huang Di, one of the brothers who ruled the world. Pangu was the creator of the world, born in the cosmic egg miraculously. He was born in chaos and shaped the heaven and earth. He was coiled up in the egg (*pan-* coil up). His body transformed itself into the universe after his death. He is said to have had a dragon's head and a serpent's trunk. Another myth suggests him to be a giant with a cat's head.

# Vedic Tradition and World Religions

There are twelve pillars of the sky in the Chinese myth that protects the earth from the sky falling on it. Most gods in Chinese mythology like Shaohao, are believed to have had miraculous births. Shennong is a popular hero who started agriculture, medicine, the market, Zhaji sacrificial rite, and invented many farm tools and musical instruments. Shentu and Yulu were the gate gods that supervised ghosts. Yan Di, the god of the south is one of the five August Emperors, distinguished descendents who are also famous in Chinese mythology. Yao was the first of the three sage kings. He initiated the system of abdicating and handing over the crown to a worthy person. The other two sage kings were Shun and Yu. Zhulong is a powerful deity with a dragon head and serpent body. He had a vertical eye which when open, it was daylight and when closed it was night. He was red and was 1000 li (300 miles) in length. He was the Torch Dragon. We may here perceive the similarities with the Hindu legend where Shiva (represented by a *Linga* or Phallus) is said to have become a pillar of fire/light in which the gods Bramha and Vishnu could not find the beginning or end and a dispute between the two was settled by Shiva. Shiva has a third eye, vertically on the forehead that when closed keeps the world in darkness and when open, there is daylight. In fact so many of these Hindu legends have been reflected in the Christian, Buddhist, Jewish and other legends of the world. This includes the creation story of the cosmic egg (*Hiranyagarba*), the Flood story, miraculous births and many others.

Confucianism, Taoism, Shintoism and other such variations are faiths that are practiced in China and the Far East. The main focus of Taoism is the 'Tao' or the way or path, that refers to a nameless, formless and all pervasive power which brings all things into being and reverts them back to non-being in an eternal cycle. The way of the Tao is not acting contrary to nature and finding one's place in the natural order of things. It provides the structure for making sense of the change of seasons, the creation life cycle and the place of man in the world.

The ancient cosmic symbol of the Chinese has a circle with a letter 's' inscribed within it and two dots, one on each side and the two sides represent the yin and yang, the female and male power aspects that are complementary. It represents harmony. One of the great philosophers of olden times was Confucius, in the 6th century BCE, who had a significant influence in most of South Asia. But in China today, he is now considered as a corrupting influence. Confucius was a social reformer like Jesus, Buddha and others. His attention was to this world or society. He wanted people to walk as the way of heaven itself because heaven willed and made possible the pursuit of goodness. The Supreme Being, Heaven, ordained that people should seek virtue. His teachings lay in the ethical value system he had proposed. One can go to any god that can help him (Taoist, Buddhist etc.). His ethical element formed a syncretic religion. His ethical system was rather agnostic, not concerned with religious issues like the fate of man, after death and so on. China in his time had a number of states with internal conflicts and aspirants for power. He felt that his message could banish the strife that was destroying society. His interest was education for leadership (for guiding the laity). He considered the sage-kings of China as examples to be followed. Living had priority over the dead. He said that without goodness, a man cannot enjoy prosperity nor can he endure adversity. He wanted people in their private lives to be courteous and in public life to be diligent and loyal. *Shu* was a practice of reciprocity or mutual consideration. 'Never do to others what you would not like them to do to you', Analects 15:23. This mutual consideration was amplified in the five relationships:

Father- kind, gives protection , <> son- accepts father's guidance, cares for him in old age.

Elder Brother- set an example of good behaviour <> younger brother- respects the elders.

Husband- provides for the family, honourable and faithful <> wife- meets the needs of family and is obedient.

Elders- set good examples, encourage juniors <> junior- show respect and defer to their advice; eager to learn.

Ruler- acts justly, strives to improve welfare and is worthy of loyalty.

The teachings of Confucius had influence on the Chinese family life. A sense of order with each one knowing his/her place in the family and society for the general well being. Filial piety was most important as it helps the society. Chun tsu or the gentleman had nine qualities: to see clearly, to hear distinctly, to look kindly, be respectful in manner, be loyal in words, be diligent in work, ask for information when in doubt, care for the consequences of anger and in gain, see if the pursuit is right, shun violence and find what is right. He taught that privilege entails responsibilities. Society was divided into the common people and the nobility. Authority should be exercised by a few over the many. Men of merit will have impact on the character of a society. Example or precept is the important means of maintaining moral health of the people. Education should produce gentlemen. The two terms he used are: 1. Rectification of name or fulfilment of appointed role. 2. Li or ritual, propriety, good manners and conduct. Li was sometimes with the Tao or the way. His was not a religion but a way of life for people and the government. Men and women had complementary roles with the women as subordinate. But under communism, it has undergone a change. Confucius identified women with the yin, the passive force in the cosmos.

The search for the 'Elixir of Immortality' led to the invention of the gun powder besides advances in medicine and the magnetic compass (used in feng shui). The Taoist schools have never been united under a central authority. The Chinese religion is an amalgam of Confucianism, Taoism and Buddhism. Confucianism mainly addresses matters of government and social behaviour. Buddhism provides cosmology, structured priesthood and a theory of the after-life. Taoism offers methods of spiritual and physical healing, means of commerce with the spirit world and securing protection and blessing.

Confucianism and Taoism have served as foils for each other and are examples of Yin/Yang complementarity. Taoism also made an impact on Korean, Japanese and Vietnamese societies, all of which were influenced by Chinese culture in the early centuries of of the current era. Acupuncture and the traditional Chinese medicine were affiliated to Taoism. Taoist priesthood is strong in Taiwan and its communities have reappeared in China in recent times.

The 'philosophical' Taoism arose during the late Warring States period (403-221 BCE) and religious Taoism at the end of the Han Dynasty (206-220 BCE). Lao Tse (6th century BCE) wrote *Tao Te Ching* and his teachings were based on ideas that were established much earlier like divination (I Ching), complementary forces Yin and Yang, and the notion of Chi, the vital matter of life energy of which all things are made. Other texts are- *Chuang tsu* (4th century BCE), *Huai-nan-tsu* (2nd century BCE), and *Tieh-tsu* (3-4th century CE). These texts stress mysticism, performing no action (wu-wei) that is contrary to nature, learning the tao and the pattern of the changing cosmos.

For achieving immortality, the fang shui (gentlemen with recipes), were hired by imperial courts to know the secrets. By the current era, Lao tsu was raised to a god, T'ai –Shang-Lao-Chin, or most high lord Lao. Buddhism brought the concept of retribution and reincarnation and other organized religious traditions. One group, the 'Yellow Turbans' preached a coming golden age (184 CE). This was superseded by the way of the Celestial Masters with its founder Chang Tao Ling becoming the head of a theocracy with a hierarchy. In 215 CE, his grandson relinquished authority to the new political order and received royal patronage. The Masters moved south in the fourth century due to instability in the north. This resulted in a new sect Shang-Ch'ing (highest purity) Taoism. Based on mount Mao, it was also known as Mao Shan

School. Another southern school, Ling-Pao (numinous jewel) drew from the Master's practices, Shand Ch'ing's revelations and the Mahayana Buddhist idea of universal salvation. The period of disunity (265-589 CE) saw the popularity of Buddhism rise. The rivalry between the two resulted in the change in both in the development of Ch'an (Zen) Buddhism, an amalgam of Tao and Buddhist ideas.

The T'an Dynasty (618-917 CE) made Taoism very popular with the imperial family sharing the surname Li' (from Lao Tsu's surname). The dynasty supported monasteries and temples and Lao Tse's birthday became a holiday and decreed each family to have a copy of *Tao-Te Ching*. The Sung Dynasty (1279-1368 CE) continued the tradition. Of the many schools of this period of Sung and Yuan, the Ch'uan-Chen (complete perfection) and Cheng-I (orthodox unity) have remained active with temples in Beijing. The first of the two, the leader Wang Che supported a syncretic religion of the three teachings. It mandated celibacy for adepts. Genghis Khan called upon Wang Che's disciple Ch'iu-Ch'ang-Ch'un to reveal the secrets of longevity and was told to sleep apart from the imperial harem for one night, being better than taking elixirs for 1000 days. The Chang-I school priests marry and pass the lineage to descendents. Their patriarchs are believed to be descendents of Ch'ang-Tao-Ling. The 64th Celestial Master resides today in Taiwan. The Tao's hymn of creation:

> There is a thing chaotic yet formed,
>
> It was born from heaven and earth.
>
> Silent, empty.
>
> It is self-sufficient, does not change.
>
> It goes in all directions, but is not exhausted.
>
> It could be considered mother of all creation.
>
> I do not know its name. I call it Tao...
>
> Tao follows the pattern of nature.

Aspects of the Divine:

Triads play a big part in Taoism. 'The Three Ones' reside in the cosmos and also in the three 'cinnanar fields' or vital centres of the body- breath, essence (semen), and spirit. They create an embryo of immortality, the foundation of the immortal body. 'The Three Pure Ones'- heavenly worth of the Original Beginning, the heavenly worth of the Numinous Jewel and that of the Tao and Te (Lao Tsu) - they are the abstract power of the Tao. The Queen Mother, His Wang Mu of the west referred in the Chuang tzu as one who has obtained the Tao- she is the 'queen of the immortals' and symbol of the highest Yin.

The Sacred Texts:

The Taoist Canon in its 1445th edition has 1120 volumes. There are also non-canonical texts- These are: *Tao Te Ching, Chuang tsu, Huai-nan-tsu, Pao-p'u-tzu* by Ko-Hung (320 CE) and many others. Religious Taoism is a revealed religion and its scriptures are emanations from the beginning of creation formed by the primordial breath that existed at the first stirring of the Tao. The schools of Taoism are viewed as the manifestation of the Tao on earth. Red headed Taoists are Shamans who can access the local spirits and perform exorcisms. The black headed priests are orthodox who can control celestial hosts. Contemporary fire-dwelling priests are from the black headed or Cheng-I school and can claim lineage with the Celestial Masters of the Han Dynasty. The Ch'uan-Chen school is the main monastic school till the present day and novices between 12 and 20 years begin their monastic life with menial labour in addition to daily practice of devotion. This is similar to the practice of students in the Hindu Gurukula system.

Immortals date from antiquity and many do not experience hunger or cold, and pass through fire without burning and through water without getting wet. They could reduce the world to the size of a gourd or turn it into the size of the universe. They can appear and disappear at will (evanescent). They live in caves or magic places such as P'eng-lai Island of the Chinese mainland. They are people who have realized the Tao and are free from the concerns of gods or humans. These are like the sages in India who have achieved the eight *siddhis* (powers) many of whom live for thousands of years as they have conquered death. Such saints are well known among the Hindus. They are the Jivan Muktas described in the second chapter of the Bhagwad Gita.

*Wu Wei* or non interference demands that we submit and move with natural processes and change. This is acceptance of life as it comes without influencing it. The heaven, earth and the sage are benevolent to the good and not to the wicked. Ethical behaviour is considered very important and one must be morally and ritually pure for substances to be effective. Ethics of the 'Three Teachings'- Confucianism, Taoism and Buddhism- are to be followed for the pursuit of immortality. Precepts for becoming an immortal are as follows:

1. Do not permit wicked, jealous, and treacherous thoughts to grow in you.
2. Be humane with compassion and love. Do not kill.
3. Have purity and righteousness.

4. Limit alcohol, regulate behaviour and be free from evil.
5. Do not criticize the scriptures or writings of sages. Act as if you were always face to face with god.
6. Be harmonious and conciliatory and steadfast in your deportment.

This excerpt is from the Numinous Jewel School and the adepts take these as vows.

*Ch'I* or vital matter is created from *Yin Ch'I* and *Yang Ch'I* or heavy that sinks and light that rises up. These are the female-male binary relationships. The five phases (*wu-hsing*) or elements are:

Water and metal- greater and lesser Yin.

Fire and wood- greater and lesser Yin.

Balanced centre earth.

These Pentads are significant. Mountains, caves, rivers, oceans, are considered sacred places with spiritual powers. The true form of macrocosm is presented in the microcosm of sacred drawings such as talismans and holograms. They show powerful sources of cosmic energy and their powerful structures.

Chinese time is observed as per solar and lunar Calendars. The lunar calendar is 12 months with a thirteenth month added every two or three years. The solar calendar has nodes or breaths that are the 24 periods of approximately 15 days each. They correspond with the patterns of the agricultural year. The start of each season is determined by the solstices and equinoxes. There is a cycle of 12 years (animals of the Zodiac). This is widened into a sixty year cycle. The lunar year of 360 days has 4320 hours with each day divided into 12 hours. In 4320 years the elixir of metals is finished.

Taoist practices include offering food etc., to the deceased as is done in India. The *shrardh* continues for a year and then once every year to appease the spirit and take its blessings. Death and life are but alternating parts of a cycle; these are neither sought nor feared. Secrets of immortality are in the Tao and many texts like the *Journey to the West* give details. Conserving and purifying bodily fluids and reversal of the five phases to go beyond time and transcend death.

While patriarchal system existed, Taoist cloisters allowed women (due to bad horoscope not allowing marriage, widows, divorcees and unmarried girls) were permitted to follow this vocation. Taoist women were therefore given an alternative to family life.

**References:**
1. Taoism- Jennifer Oldstone-Moore- Oxford University Press.
2. Handbook of Chinese Mythology- Lihui Yang and Deming An, Oxford University.
3. Ethics of World Religions- Arnold D. Hunt, Mary B. Crotty, and Robert B. Crotty, Greenhaven Press, San Diego.

# CHAPTER 11
# GNOSTICISM

Gnosticism is a school that did not survive though it could have been the way Christianity may have taken. In 1945, an early Christian library was discovered in southern Egypt, published as the Nag Hammadi Library (51 documents). A number of alternative systems of Christianity arose in the first centuries of the current era. Gnosticism survived more than the other forms like Valentinian, Marrionite, Martonist and others. The Gnostics believed in the superiority of the spiritual world. Gospel of Thomas and Mary, and Apocryphas of John are not found in the Bible today but these provide instructions for an ascent out of the material to the spiritual world. The early varieties of Christianity were considered heresies. The Orthodox Church stamped these out and exiled them from the church. Jesus was born in 4 BCE and crucified in 29 CE but did not die according to most researchers. During 325 CE, Emperor Constantine saw a controversy in which Arius, a deacon of Alexandria, believed that Jesus was not of the same substance as his father but had been created by him. Bishop Alexander of Alexandria condemned the notion and removed Arius from his post but his idea spread throughout the Christian world. Constantine summoned some 300 bishops, formulated a credo (NicEne) that all Christians could recite that affirmed their beliefs. However the bishops excluded many alternative forms of Christianity.

Orthodoxy is what remains after all heretical schools are removed. Paul's letters, rather than the words of Jesus, provide the earliest evidence of Christianity. Different variations of the creed, those of Mark, Matthew and Luke exist. John wrote his gospel in 110 CE that was different from that of his predecessors. These diverse elements were woven into the New Testament. Over the years, Christianity learned to incorporate different versions under one umbrella. Diversity came directly from Jesus himself. Jesus was a Jew and he never said he was god. He simply proclaimed the kingdom of god. He told people to create the kingdom of god in their own contexts. He said that the kingdom of god was within oneself. But most communities recognized him as the son of god.

Gnosticism was subtle, sophisticated and audacious. The Gnostics considered themselves as the spiritual elite. They made the conventional church look drab and boring, almost stupid in comparison. It began early in the second century and is there till the present day. But it is known through what its opponents wrote about it. The Coptic translation of Gnostic texts in Greek, were found in papyrus in 1945 by Mohammad Ali, an Egyptian and his brother at Samman on a hill on the banks of Nile. The Gospels of Thomas and Philip contained details on truth, the origin of the world and so on.

Gnosis connotes understanding, perception, insight, and learning. Gnostics know that the world they experience is illusory and wicked like a stage-set. It is a very old religion. The Gnostic of the first five centuries CE, felt imprisoned by his body and by the physical world which prevented the exploration of true insight and knowledge. Material existence was bad. The material world was a place of entrapment and the spiritual world afforded liberation. An evil Demiurge created the spiritual world and the bodies of humans. The problem of materiality and its deleterious effect on human pursuit of reality was the foundation of Gnosticism. For the orthodox, god brought beings out of nothingness (*ex nihilo*). He created the material and spiritual worlds. The demiurge created the material world precisely to prevent humans from knowing the true creator, God. When the stupor induced by this is overcome, true knowledge begins. A human being consists of the body, soul (psyche), and spirit (*pneuma*). Only the spirit, not the soul, could intuit the divine realm. Discovering the divine spark that resided in the person would lead to true knowledge. For this, the Gnostics pursued scientific knowledge. This is available only to the select few who could hear the savior's call and who had the intellectual and spiritual insight to respond to it. Gnostics were intense intellectual speakers. Their struggle is for release from the material world. They saw the world in some ways as Plato described it in the parable of the cave- as a shadowy simulacrum of a transcendent reality. Plato was not however, a Gnostic. They believed that angels and demons ruled and controlled the body. These could correspond to the *sattvic* and *tamasic* qualities in humans described in Hindu texts. In fact, Gnosticism could have followed the Hindu tradition in much of what it believed.

## References:
Gnosticism- Richard Valentasis, Three Leaves Press, Doubleday, New York.

# CHAPTER 12

# PAGANISM

Paganism includes other branches like Shamanism, Wicca, Neo-Platonism, Asatru, Druidry and so on. Paganism is described as non-Judeo-Christian or Moslem religion. But this is not true. Hinduism, Buddhism, Taoism are all very old faiths. It is better defined as that which promotes reverence for earth and/or the deities of pre-Christian religions. Neo-Paganism however, applies to Wicca and other religions created during the last two centuries. Some Druids call themselves neo-Pagan but this is not true as they are also ancient.

Paganism is fast gaining ground because it believes in many gods. The oldest image of a goddess dates back to 35000 BCE and hundreds of this goddess figures have been found. Mostly they were pregnant women. Male figures were generally phallic. This corresponds with the Siva Linga and Shakti of the Hindus, the former being the passive and the latter the active forces in creation. Linga or Phallus has been the oldest spiritual element in the world and hundreds of Lingas have been unearthed in excavations around the world. Ancient Minoans (2800-1500 BCE) worshipped a goddess with animals and a young god, her son or consort, symbolizing cycles of nature. The Myceneaens in Greece (Dorians in 1100 BCE invaded Northern Greece) and Dorians merged around 800 BCE to form the myths of the twelve Olympian gods. Pagan worship centered round a tree or spring inside a sanctuary. Later on temples were constructed and offerings of wool, oil, honey and milk were made. Oracles for the purpose of prophesy were important. The oracle of Delphi is the most famous.

The Greek creation theory states that in the beginning there was nothing (chaos) from which earth (gaea) and Tartarus (the nether world) sprung up. Then came Eros (love), night and Erebus (darkness) emerged together. From their union came day and ether (air). Gaea then created Ouranos (heaven) and the mountains and the sea and then married her. Oceanus was born as a great river that surrounded the flat disc of the earth. They also gave birth to six Titans, the Furies, nymphs, giants and monsters. Aphrodite Emerged from the foam of the sea and love and desire joined her.

# Vedic Tradition and World Religions

The Titans mated and gave birth to Isis, the Harpies and the Gorgons. One Titan married his sister Rhea and gave birth to Hestia, Demeter, Hera, Hades, Poseidon, and Zeus. To avoid prophesy that his son would overthrow him. Kronos ate each of his sons at birth. When Zeus was born, Rhea hid the baby until he grew up. Rhea then convinced Kronos to regurgitate the children, and Zeus returned to kill his father. This is similar to the legend in which Krishna the eighth child of his mother whose brother Kamsa had killed all the earlier children out of fear, was secretly sent away to be brought up by another couple, later on came and killed Kamsa and fulfilled the prophesy. Similarly other legends from India can be found in Christian, Hebrew, Zoroastrian and other religions. Van Den Bergh has mentioned nine parallels to incidents in the Gospels that can be compared to Buddha's legends like The Widow's mite, Peter walking on the sea and so on. Seydel also has given five such parallels like choosing the disciples, the Prodigal Son, and the Transfiguration. This subject has been discussed in detail in the author's book *Vedic Tradition,* (Bhavan's Book University series, 2002) and so are not repeated here.

Zeus and his siblings took up residence on Mt Olympus and waged war against the Titans. After winning the Cyclops over to his side and receiving from them the Thunderbolt and lightning, Zeus led the Olympians to victory. The Titans were imprisoned in Tartarus. Aphrodite, Ares, Hephaestus, Hermes, Athena, Apollo and, Artemis joined the Olympians while Hades took up residence in the underworld. He then kidnapped his sister Demeter's daughter Kore and made her the queen of the underworld. Dionysius is the god of wine and was not an Olympian. Apollo is the god of music and poetry, Ares that of war, while Hephaestus, the god of fire and husband of Aphrodite, made the first woman out of clay, Pandora. Hermes, the son of Zeus is the god of the sky and father of many gods. As per legend, Rome was established in 753 BCE, by Romulus but their technological advancements followed the Etruscan emigration from northern Italy 1100 years later. Romans conquered the Etruscans and their reign lasted until 476 CE. Etruscans were masters of engineering and their cities were aligned with the four cardinal points of the compass. Their deities formed a triad and the temple was divided into three parts. Among the first Roman guards were the guardians of the land, Lares, and they had no icons. Each Lare had its own shrine. *Vesta*, the goddess of the hearth was flame itself. The doorway to the home was god Janus. As the society developed, Etruscan deities merged with those of the Romans. Eventually 33 deities came into prominence. Twelve priests were responsible for performing sacrifices and rituals for peace. Romans adopted the solar calendar of ten months and the festival followed the cycle of the year. Laws were based on logic, omen and divination.

# Paganism

The Egyptian society evolved over time. Osiris was their first king. He was murdered by his brother Set and his son Horus took the throne. Each Pharaoh was Horus incarnate who became Osiris at death. The Pharaoh ruled by divine right and was divine himself. Egyptians viewed time as cyclical, not linear. The world was unchanging and recurring events were part of natural order. The death of the Pharaoh was a transition, not a time of upheaval. They were monotheist with the sun god *Ra* or *Aten* as the only One.

The Norse and Germanic people were several groups of people who had varied beliefs. Scandinavians believed that trees and water bodies were sacred. The world tree Yggdrasil linked humans with god. It stands at the centre of a disc of land surrounded by the ocean, occupied by a giant serpent and its roots reach the underworld. Divination was important. Celts are one group that branched off from the Norse. The Greeks/Romans referred to all northern people as Kettoi (Celt). For Celts also, trees played an important role in worship. Springs, wells, rivers and other water bodies had their deities and some were places of healing. Caves were seen as entrance to the underworld. While the Germanic people had a creation story and end of world scenario, the Celts had none.

The Celts had three classes of holy people- the Druids (priests, judges, and philosophers), Vates (seers interpreting dreams and omens), and bards (poets and singers). The Coligny calendar, discovered in 1897, is the oldest calendar dating back to the 1st century BCE. It spanned thirty years with five divisions of 62 lunar months and a sixth division of 61 months. A single lunar year had two extra months and dark/light halves, with the dark half coming first and the light half coming next. The single lunar year with two extra months was to realign with the solar year. The year was also divided into two halves, the dark and light halves. This is the same as the *uttarayana* and *dakshinayana* of the Hindus being the first and second parts of the year. They had three seasons with summer as the longest, winter and spring the shortest. They had no written language and what is known about them is from Julius Caesar and others besides the archaeological finds of the last two centuries.

Monotheism came to Judaism via Abraham. Canaanites were till then all polytheists. Around 2000 BCE they moved towards monotheism, when Abraham adopted the local god El as his main deity. The Bible episode refers to El requesting the sacrifice of Abraham's son Isaac to be the last of human sacrifice. Judaism continued till Jesus was born, when the Jews sought to free themselves from the Romans. After his death, a Jewish sect believed he was the Messiah, the son of god. Paul took up Jesus' message to all including Jews. The Roman persecution lasted for 300 years. In 325 CE, Constantine called the council of Nicea where Jesus was declared divine.

In 346 CE, Paganism was banned in the Roman Empire (though briefly restored, banned again). Many of the gods were recast as saints. Celtics became Christians though Pagan customs continued as folk customs. Christianity became the official religion of Iceland. Paganism continued in Norway till 1120s, when she also became Christian.

Islam emerged in Saudi Arabia in 610 CE when Mohammad received the words of the Koran. He carried the message to Mecca but the people rejected him and sent him back to Medina. He gathered followers, raised an army and after him the four Caliphs continued the holy war. By 641 CE, Iran, Iraq, Egypt, Syria and Jerusalem were conquered and converted. In Africa, the Mandinka people were brought into the faith and they continued the spread of Islam.

Neo-Pagans proudly proclaimed that they had inherited their beliefs from a long line of witches and Pagans. It has many sects like Christianity or Islam. It evolved over the last 200 years due to archaeological discoveries and a longing to return to a simpler age to recover what was lost. A common myth is that it has descended from ancient religions, that they worshipped a single goddess and that they worshipped Satan. But Pagans are polytheistic and worshipped local gods and goddesses.

While Satanists do exist as a religious group, neither they nor neo-Pagans worshipped Satan because they do not believe in Satan. Satan is a Christian construct. Satanists honour the human characteristics Satan represents. Pagans worship gods with horns or horned animals in god's form, and these gods pre-date Christian Satan. It is the Catholic Church that recast Pagan deities as demons when Pagan lands were conquered and converted. They do not practise human sacrifice nor do they worship cemeteries or molest children.

Wicca, Asatru and Druidry are the major branches of neo-Paganism. Other sects are Hellenism, Sanistragnata, Kemeticism and Thelema (Greek, Celt, and Egyptian). Druidry is ancient. Asatru is the smallest group. Druidry and Wicca are more popular in England and Asatru in northern Europe. All three are practised in the United States and growing in popularity in South America, Australia and parts of Asia.

From the 17th century onwards, magical organisations in Europe started appearing- Freemasons, Theosophical Society, Rosicrucians, Hermetic society interested in Jewish mysticism, and European Magic. Rosicrucians were an offshoot of Freemasonry. From this was born in 1988, the Hermetic Order of the Golden Dawn.

Sir James Frazier's book, *The Golden Bough* in 1890 influenced Neo-Paganism. Wicca is based on ancient beliefs and practices, but was born of modern desires to return

# Paganism

to ancient ways. In 1948, Robert Graves wrote *The White Goddess* that studied the history of the Great Mother, the pre-historic goddess and helped fuel feminist Neo-Paganism.

Asatru was largely based on archaeological finds in Iceland. It is a Norse Pantheon. The Nazis used Asatru beliefs and symbols to stir up German nationalism but Asatrus were not Nazis. John Aubrey researched Megalithic sites in England in the 17th century and said they were built by the Druids.

Wiccan Beliefs:
They have neither a fixed dogma nor a holy book like the Bible. They may or may not practice witchcraft. It is greatly popular among the young in the United States. They require an initiation ceremony. Individual practitioners require a teacher. Pantheism is the belief that divinity is in everything. Everything is sacred and all have a purpose. Often a tree before cutting is asked permission to cut it because of its divinity. Many Wiccans follow a vegetarian diet due to reverence for the sacred animals. It is however, an individual's choice. Polytheism is common to all branches of Wicca. But some believe in the One, the source of the universe. Gods and goddesses are finite beings. Kali is the goddess of creation and destruction. Each deity has specific areas of power but they are all subordinate to the Infinite One. There are many branches of Wicca like in Christianity and other religions. The different traditions with their pantheons are:

Gardnerian - Gender equality.
Alexandrian – Ceremonial magic. (Greco-Romanic).
Dianic – Mostly women. (CEltic-300 deities)
Feri (fairy) – Use American Indian folk magic. (Egyptian)
Faery – Celtic Faery Lore. (Germanic/Norse)
Strega – Roman and Etruscan deities. (Hindu)

Wiccans believe in reincarnation. Though Hindu practices are millennia old, some of their deities like Kali, Shakti, Shiva and Ganesa are invoked by Wiccans in their rituals. Personal gods or patron deities are worshipped by Wiccans for special purposes.

They have eight major festivals called Sabbats and they are based on the solar calendar. They also honour the phases of the moon. The four lesser Sabbats are the winter and summer solstices and spring/fall equinoxes. The four greater Sabbats are the cross-quarters between the solstices and equinoxes. The year begins on October 31$^{st}$ (Samhain, pronounced Sowen). It is an ancient fire festival when the sun is at 15 deg., of Scorpio. The date of Christmas is based on the European celebration of the birth of God Mithra observed on December 25. The Mithraic faith of Iran, Syria, Persia and Egypt observe this, the date of solstice in the Roman Julian Calendar.

Imbolc on February 2 is the festival of lights, one of the four fire festivals. On February 4, the sun is at 15 deg., to Aquarius when the goddess awakens from slumber and along with her, the earth reawakens. Ostara on March 20-23 is the spring equinox. Eostre is an East European moon goddess from which it is derived. The word Easter also is derived from it. The tradition of decorating eggs is from the ancient Egyptians and Persians. Beltane is a fertility festival on May1 or 4, when the sun is 15 deg., to Taurus. Dancing round the Maypole, a Phallic symbol, is practised. It is covered by a flowered wreath to symbolize a womb. In fact the Hindu Shiva Linga is placed on a pedestal resembling a womb. Litha is the summer solstice on June 20-23, the longest day and start of the sign Cancer. It is also the first day of summer. Lammar on August 1-6 is the first harvest when the sun is at 15 deg., to Leo. Mabon is the Fall Equinox on September 20-23 when Libra begins and the day and night are equal as in Ostara. This is when the harvest is concluded and winter is heralded. Yule is on December 20-31 when the night is longest and the winter solstice takes place.

The Wiccans use tools like cauldrons, athane, chalice, broom, bell, bolline, wand, symbols, The book of shadows, censer and astrology. They are used for consecration and for rituals. Wiccan symbols are a Pentacle or the five pointed star used as a piece of jewellery and the triple Moon. The four directions of east, north, west and south are represented by air, earth, water and fire respectively. Many people have permanent home altars that are initially consecrated. They use incense and practice meditation for quietening the mind and for breath control. These are practices the Hindus have been doing to this day.

Tarot cards are used in divination. I Ching or the Book of Changes for divination is a 4000 years old Chinese system. It comprises a set of 64 Hexagrams that translate the knowledge of the subconscious to the conscious mind. The six-line hexagrams are based on the binary yin/yang symbol. A crystal ball is also used.

Asatruan Beliefs:
These are based on the ancient Viking beliefs of Iceland and other Germanic/Nordic beliefs. They are re-constructionist by nature since they are based on historical documents and archaeological evidence. Most of them are also based on the 13th century collection of Norse poems (Eddas). They have a pantheon of gods and goddesses like Aesir, Vanir, Loki (a trickster god like coyote). The Norns are like the Greek Fates. They weave the thread of fate. The three Norns are Urd, Verandi,

and Skuld, being respectively the oldest or what has become, the middle or what is becoming and the youngest or what should be. They correspond with the past, present and the future. The Skuld could rip up the web and end one's life. The future is guided by Orlog, the law of the universe. Wyrd is set and cannot be changed. Past actions shape the personality and future actions. The individual can succumb to or fight disease.

Asgard contains twelve palaces of the gods. Valhalla is one of them corresponding with the Hindu Yamaloka or the realm of the God of death. It is the abode of the dead where battle heroes and Odin reside. The Valkyries are Odin's daughters (9-13). They roam the world with spears and helmets and decide who will die or live. Vanadir or Disirs are go betweens among the gods and humans like priests. They help their wards. The Wights are spirits honoured by the Asatruan. Jotnar are giants that lived before the world. The world has three realms and for some nine, where each realm is divided into three. They are the realms of the dead, humans and gods. They correspond with the Hindu *Pitruloka, naraloka* and *devaloka*.

The nine noble virtues are: courage, truth, honour, fidelity, discipline, hospitality, industriousness, self-reliance and perseverance. Oaths are very serious and are taken carefully. Life continues after death and the soul is born again in another body. It is a legally recognized religion in Iceland. Their festivals are Yuletide (Christmas), Mayday (honours the light half of the year and the bounty of spring). They carry the Maypole (phallus) in procession. May Eve is a celebration of the dark side of the year. Midsummer or the summer solstice, winter finding or the Fall equinox for harvest, winter night in mid-October or the Fall equinox on a Saturday, Einherjar on April 25 or November 11 to honour the veterans Thorrabloy to strengthen the spirit in mid-late January, Vali the feast of vengeance and rebirth on February 14, the Loaf feast celebrates harvest and Thing Tide on August 23 being marriage time.

Asatruan tools include the bowl, hammer, ring, sax (knife), and rister, the wand. Irminsal is a pole connecting the world and Thor's hammer is the symbol of fertility, Yin and Yang. Valknut is a triple triangle. They also have the solar cross and swastika symbols.

Druids:
They are a modern reconstruction of an older faith. They have no sacred texts. It is a religion and a philosophy. There are Christian Druids, Buddhist and even Wiccan Druids. They have the same three realms called the Circle of Abred, Gwynwyd, and Ceugant, the realms of the dead, humans and one God. There are also three beings- gods, humans and ancestors. Death is seen as a transition- birth, death and rebirth.

# Vedic Tradition and World Religions

The Awen symbol represents the flow of energy and inspiration. It has concentric circles with three dots and three rays. The dots signify the position of the sun throughout the year and the rays symbolize the paths of wisdom, knowledge and inspiration. To access Awen, Druids chant its name- ahh-ooh- ennn. This is similar to the Hindu OM or AUM and also sounds alike. While most Druids work with Celtic deities, many honour no deities at all and see Druidry as a path of healing and Self-knowledge. The myth that they erected the Stonehenge columns has been proved wrong. Stonehenge was built over a period of 1400 years and completed in 1600 BCE. It is not known who built it but it appears the Hindu settlers of old did it.

They believe in the divinity of all life including the land they lived in. Tolerance and equality for all beings and all systems of belief are stressed by Druids because of interconnection of everything. They honour their ancestors, genetic and of heritage, the original Druids. They seek balance by seeking to return to the earth what is taken from it. They follow the Wiccan holiday system of eight days. They use the Ogham alphabets for divination. Their tools include bowls, wand, staff, etc., like those of Wiccans. Ogham is pronounced ohum, again similar to the Hindu Aum. Their tree lore refers certain trees- the oak for strength and stability, the rowan for protection and prophesy, the birch for renewal and cleansing, the apple tree being the tree of life and at the centre of the other world and the yew for death and decay. Similarly the horse represents Epona the goddess, swan represents fairy women, raven is sacred, boar stands for war and death, stag for spiritual power, salmon for wisdom and knowledge and the eagle for connecting humans to gods. The important symbols are the Triple Spiral, three legs, and wreath with two vertical staves. The first signifies the interconnection of all things.

Vodoun and Santeria are African pagan practices that grew from the slaves in the New World and their response to forced conversion to Christianity. They are not Neo-Pagan, but are a continuation of the old pagan ways of Africa. Their tribes spoke Akan and Fan languages and lived in the Yoruban and Dahomey regions (Nigeria, Benin, Togo, Senegal and the Guinea Coast). Many of the gods are common; however the Ashanti believed in three gods similar to the Catholics - Father, Son and the Holy Spirit. They erected temples and deified their ancestors. Magic and rituals are common to both.

Shamanism:
This is not a religion but a practice and a philosophy that can be used under any religious framework. Pagans and non-pagans alike practiced the ways of Shamans. And it is this practice that led to the building of pyramids in Egypt, China, Mexico and other places. None of these cultures had contact with each other according to

some scholars. But it may be due to the Hindu settlers who are known to have moved all over the world in pre-historic times. In India, Shamans are called shamanas that refers to Jains who practised medicine in south India.

Only when one gets a call can he become a Shaman. It can come in the form of ancestral heritage or due to grave illness or injury. They achieve their work mainly by going into a trance. Chanting and drumming constantly can take one to a trance. This practice exists to this day in India where during festivals to Karthikeya, the second son of Shiva, and also Mariamman, a form of Shakti whose devotees go into a trance in the above way and they also prophesy certain events.

Australian Aboriginal Religions:
For these aborigines, symbols represent the cyclical nature of the universe. During the last Ice Age, Australia and Asia were close to each other, never more than 50 to 100 kilometres apart. The aboriginal natives arrived there between 25000-40000 years ago as per archaeological evidence, most of them from Asia like the Fijians from India, New Guinea and so on. The first whites came to Australia around 1770 CE and Captain Cook wrote from there in that year- 'In reality, they are far happier than we Europeans... they live in tranquillity... they covet not...' Their dreaming describes the great events of creation. Before creation, there was a formless substance, maybe a watery mass or a waterless desert. Ancestors detached themselves from the formless substance and emerged in various forms. The ancestor being came sometimes as a rock antelope, a river bed or a ridge. Others ascended the skies when their travels were over. They had an oral tradition which was handed down to subsequent generations. Land was sacred to them. Ancestor beings can enter a woman's body and she could conceive and the child linked to the being. We may here note that such conceptions were common in Hindu myths and the Puranas are full of such stories. Karna of The Mahabharata was conceived by Kunti through the look of the sun. The sages were considered as these ancient beings and their progeny formed the Gotra system of lineage. The sage's name is attached to the progeny's Gotra. They had sacred rituals in which group solidarity is expressed. There were no priests or ministers. It is a group concern to protect sacred sites. Women were excluded from rituals though they did have their role in the religion. Women were equal and were not treated as subservient. They had their own ethical system for individual living; truth is upheld and falsehood, vanity and deception are forbidden. People shared food with others and respected elders. Even today, they celebrate the Hindu festivals like Dipavali, Navratri and other festivals.

Other known Pagans are:
Hellenism- Greek reconstruction Paganism, and similarly, Kemeticism, Senistragnata and Religio Romano are Egyptian, Celtic and Roman reconstructionist Pagans. Then we have the modern Thelema faith of their prophet Aleister Cowley (1904). He had written a series of holy books while in a trance saying that he had received it from the spirit Aiwass. The main book is The Book of the Law. Native American traditions are not neo-Pagan but based on old Pagan faiths.

Pagans have no concept of sin and they mostly live on the basis of ethical standards set by their faiths. They take personal responsibility for their actions and their outcome. They mostly adopt the concept of karma or the law of causation of the Hindus. This theory of karma has been adapted by most faiths in the world and all Pagans follow it. Reward for action may not be immediate. It may be left over from past lives due to which one has to be born again and again until final release. Newton's third law of motion states that action and reaction are equal and opposite. The Wiccans have the Law of Three that states that everything you do returns to you threefold. This applies to physical action, magical action and energy and the effects are felt often immediately. The Christian concepts of Nemesis and retribution are similar. The witch pyramid suggests that a goal requires knowledge of it, the will to go ahead and the courage to proceed with it. Then the spell will be successful. To be silent is not to talk about the spell or the goal. In fine, Paganism is a way of life like Hinduism to which it probably owes its origins. Most Pagans are cremated because there is not enough space for burial, ashes can be spread at a spot to join with nature like a river or ocean, and the body is just a vessel and will not be needed again after death. For feasts, if you are invited, you are expected to bring something like a dish or fruits.

## References:
1. The Everything Paganism Book- Selene Silverwind, Adams Media, Avon, Massachusets.
2. Ethics of World Religions- Arnold D. Hunt, Mary B. Crotty, and Robert B. Crotty, Greenhaven Press, San Diego.

# CHAPTER 13
# SOME RELIGIOUS SYSTEMS

Arthur Goldwag in his *-Isms and –Ologies* (Random House) gives an outline of many religious systems and these are studied here. Religions are nothing but belief systems of a group of people who want to be different from others. This varies between belief in one god or many gods, dualism, monism, monotheism, non-belief in god or atheism, agnosticism and many variations of Christian beliefs. About 28% of the world is Christian- 20% Hindu, 20% Muslim and 10% Buddhist. The rest consists of other groups like atheists and so on. The Christian and Muslim worlds are not ones of unity, but in each of them, scores of different groups exist, sometimes very antagonistic to each other like the Protestant-Catholic or Shia-Sunni, anti-Semitic, and others who fight with each other and they all see a divided world. All that it tells us is that religions are more personal than universal and hence should be restricted to one's home or places of worship rather than practising outside in the streets. Hundreds of millions of lives have been lost worldwide in the name of religions over the past two millennia.

Goldwag has given details of scores of religions that include Animism, Anabaptism, Bahaiism, Calvinism, Confucianism, Creationism, Donatism, Evangelicalism, Gnosticism, and many others. Here we shall study some of these minor ones to get an idea of the divisions due to religion.

Animism:
Edward Tylor (1832-1917) in his book *Primitive Culture* regarded Animism as a first step in the evolution of religions. This belief involves the message that the world is inhabited by invisible, incorporeal beings or spirits who reside often in animals, plants and inanimate objects. The idea that people and things have souls led to the idea of Shamanism, Fetishism and the belief that physical objects can have occult power and that the bones of ancestors might be venerated and Totemism (the identification of a social group in the spirit of a plant or animal). Spirits take the identities of gods and demons leading to polytheism that leads to monotheism. Tylor's belief in the superiority of Christianity over Shintoism etc. is not shared by most thinkers today.

To quote Nietsche, 'In reality there has only been one true Christian, and he died on the Cross'.

Atheism :
Atheism finds a place in this book because it has also become a kind of religion. Atheism posits that there is no god and philosophers like Richard Dawkins are quite dogmatic about it. All beliefs that exclude other beliefs are such that they become a religion sooner or later. Agnosticism cannot be considered one because it neither accepts nor rejects god or any belief and has an open mind. It considers that the existence or otherwise of god is of no consequence to human lives. It rather emphasizes the place of reason in human life.

Confucianism:
The Confucian School has famous members like Mencius, Hsun-tsu and others from 380 BCE to 1710 CE. It encompasses different traditions and is known as the school of Ju (weak). The Golden Rule is at the heart of the school that asks people to do to others what they would have them do to them. The Tao or the Way and *Te* or virtue is a central concept. It is not a religion but a way of life based on ethical principles. They believe that 'good government obtains when those who are near are happy, and those who are far off are attracted. Jen is the quality of benevolence and *li,* the norms of decency. Respect for ancestors and tradition and self-knowledge were essential attributes. Confucius pointed to nine things for consideration:

- Eyes must see clearly.
- Ears must hear distinctly.
- Countenance must be benign.
- Demeanour must be respectful.
- Speech must be sincere.
- Business must be done reverently and carefully.
- In doubt one must question others.
- In anger one must think of difficulties that may involve him.
- Gain must be righteous.

These naturally form part of an ethical code of conduct.

Essenism :
This was followed by a Jewish monastic sect between the second century BCE and seventy CE, when the Temple was destroyed in Jerusalem. They believed in the immortality of the soul and multiple messiahs. The Dead Sea Scrolls contains a number of books in clay tablets and the sect's beliefs have fascinating parallels with Zoroastrianism.

## Some religious Systems

The Ethical Culture Movement of Felix Adler (1876), asserts that 'if god and good, and good and god be one, there is no god save what dawns upon us in the experience of doing good…the object of social reformation shall not be a mere change in conditions under which men live, but a change in human nature itself'. Fundamentalism includes Wahabism, conservative Protestantism and the like and these are known for rigid doctrines that are otherwise known as contrary to natural law.

Gnosticism:
This was considered as a religious belief that incorporated the best ideas from all religions. They are syncretic in nature. Salvation is attained through secret knowledge, rather than ritual, grace, incantation etc. the world was created by a lesser divine spirit, the demiurge. These beings were both parts of the plethora (plenitude), the source of Aeons, the divine powers that ruled the universe. The subordination of the body and the soul (psyche) and the liberation of the spirit- the divine spark that resides deep within that is the same substance as god and this is the ultimate goal of all. We could see the similarity between the Hindu Brahman which is considered as the same as the individual soul.

Hermeticism gave a theological system that was free from the Catholic dogma. Later generations of alchemists seized the occult arcane as did the Rosicrucians, Freemasons and, Theosophists. Hinduism has the fourfold aims of life called purusharthas. These are *dharma, artha, kama* and *moksha*. In a general way, they mean respectively virtue, wealth, pleasure and enlightenment. The last named is considered as the ultimate goal of man.

Humanism:
It refers to any system with a human frame of reference rather than the supernatural. Renaissance humanism refers to the revival in classical literature and philosophy that began by the end of Middle Ages (mid- 14th century). Francesco Petrarch (1304-74) was the father of renaissance Humanism. Giovanni Boccaccio, Desidarius Erasmus and others were humanists. They argued that the intellect alone gives mankind the power to ascend the chain of being. Machiavelli, Copernicus, Leonardo and others belonged to this school. Their manifesto by Raymond Bragg says- the universe was self-created and that mankind was part of nature. It denied any 'supernatural or cosmic guarantees of human values'. It added codicils on the importance of sexual tolerance, political liberty, economic equity, rights of the disabled and, the importance of the separation of religion and the state. The religious mind identifies 'truth' with god and humanists as emerging and evolving.

## Iconoclasm:

Literally, iconoclasm means the tendency to break or smash idols (eikono- image, klan-break). Taliban's destruction of the Bamiyan Buddha is an instance. Generally it applies to those who scorn society's sacred cows. A Republican, citing Marx as an economics authority, Abraham destroying idols his father had carved, the protestant Reformation, Calvinists in particular, smashing icons throughout Europe are instances.

In 726 CE, Emperor Leo III ordered the image of Jesus removed from the gates of Constantinople, later issued an edict forbidding all religious images. His son, Constantine, convened the iconoclast council in 754 CE that upheld the ban. The seventh council of Nicea, in 787 overturned the ban after monasteries and monks were attacked by iconodules (slaves to icons), and iconophiles (lovers of icons).

## Islam :

Mohammad proclaimed the oneness of Allah who called upon the prophets Adam, Noah, Abraham, Ishmael, Moses and Jesus to proclaim his message. Other obligations include eschewing pork and alcohol, avoiding gambling or lending money for profit, and eat animal slaughtered in a ritual only. Jihad is a duty to strive for god and fighting temptation or 'commanding the right and forbidding the wrong'. Shiite eschatology revolves round only twelve imams or direct descendents of Mohammad. As per legend, Mohammad al Mahdi, the 12thImam, was born in 868 CE to a Byzantine princess who had disguised herself as a slave to travel to Arabia; his father the 11th Imam, kept his son Mohammad hidden because of the persecution of Shiites by the Sunni Caliph at that time, and until it was time for him to come out and assert his claim. Then he hid in a well but kept communication with his four assistants for 70 years, known as the Lesser Occultation. When he was in his deathbed, his assistant produced a letter from him, of his intention shortly before judgment day, when he would return as the Mahdi to establish perfect justice. This was the beginning of Greater Occultation continuing to this day. Sufis are mystics and Rumi (1207-73) wrote poetry and founded the Mevlevi in Turkey (the Whirling Dervishes, who achieve ecstatic union with god through music and dance).

## Jainism :

It was founded in the 9th century BCE by Parshvanath (877-777 BCE) that absorbed elements of Hindu thought. Presumably, it was not started as a separate religion as there are not many differences between their ideas and those of Hindus. They were mainly reformers that believed in pure vegetarianism, not eating after dusk, and such like. Twentyfour Tirtankaras are considered by them of which Parshvanath and Mahavira 599-527 BCE) are the most recent. The universe is uncreated and eternal, and that history moves in vast cycles (like Hindu Yugas), individual souls are reincarnated again and again until they are purified. The universe with its unchanging laws composed of five elements- *jiva, pingala* (atoms), *akasha* (space), *adharma* (rest) and *dharma* or motion. Some consider time as the sixth element. Soul is non-material, infinite and perfect. All animate beings contain some aspects of soul in them. *Karma* sticks to the soul and prevents it from attaining its pure essence or *moksha*. Jains aspire to conquer karma through five ethical or spiritual principles. These are:

*ahimsa*- non violence, (includes kshamapana or forgiveness).
*Satya*- truth.
*Asteya*- not stealing.
*Aparigraha*- non-attachment and,
*Brahmacharya*: celibacy.

Digambar Jains are naked and believe that women cannot get moksha (release or nirvana) unless reincarnated as men. Svetambar Jains use white garments and believe that women can get moksha. They also believe that Mahavira had married and had a daughter. They value *anekantavada* or non-singular conclusivity. They generally cover their mouth with a thin white cloth to prevent bacteria in the air from entering since bacteria also have life.

Judaism:
The Tanakh or the Old Testament tells the story of the Jewish people's inter-personal relationship and special covenant with god. The Heart Temple in Jerusalem was the centre of ritual life and was a slaughterhouse for many centuries. The hereditary priests were butchers- Sacrifice, rather than prayer was the way of honouring the gods. Maimonide's (1135-1204) thirteen principles of faith are the closest thing to a Jewish creed. By 1700s, Hasidism in Eastern Europe was the spirit of enlightenment. Baruch Spinoza (the excommunicated Jew, 1632-77) anticipated by centuries the succession of Jewish thinkers like Karl Marx, Sigmund Freud, and, Albert Einstein. Conservative Jews keep kosher, but wear modern dress, ignore majority of Biblical laws, and conduct service in English. They reject the notion of 'chosenness' and deny the reality of miracles and a personal god. Their fifth and largest movement is secularism.

Kabbalism is a mystical Jewish tradition that developed a cosmology and metaphysics reminiscent of Gnosticism and Neo-Platonism. They believed in the changeless infinite and merger with god through meditation. Hasidism is an offshoot of Kabbalism. Variations of it have influenced Freemasonry, Theosophy and others.

## Manichaeanism:

Mani (216-276 CE) was raised as a Zoroastrian who joined the Essenes. He was expelled in 240 CE, after which he spent several years in India, where he was exposed to Hindu and Buddhist philosophies. After returning to Persia, he declared himself the Paraclete (Holy Ghost) and an apostle of Christ. He combined elements of Zoroastrianism, Christianity, Buddhism, Gnosticism and other philosophies and divided the cosmos into two separate realms- the light and the dark. St. Augustine was a Manichaean follower in his youth. They believed that through asceticism, vegetarianism, celibacy and faith in Christ, believers can liberate the light trapped in their bodies (soul) and return to its divine source. Clearly this is borrowed from the Hindu concept of Brahman into which souls eventually merge.

## Mithraism:

Withdrawal from society and leading an ascetic life was their goal. This was widespread in the Hindu practices millennia ago. Both eremitic (solitary) and cenobitic (group) monasticism was practised by early Christians- the Christian Brothers, devoted to teaching, Buddhists, nuns, Hare Krishnas and even Sufis (though banned by Islam) practised monasticism.

## Mormonism:

These are the Latter Day Saints who do not believe in Original Sin, practise polygamy and teach that one atones for one's own rather than Adam's sins.

## Mysticism:

This is similar to monasticism, and Sufis, Catholics, Hindus, Buddhists, and others practise meditation for release. The Zohar of the Kabbalists is filled with erotic imagery. Not all mysticism, however, is erotic, but his intensity of devotion and desire and the disintegration of the Self in the union are suggestive of rapture.

## Neo-Platonism:

Plotinus developed this system. Julian the Apostate (half brother of Constantine) renounced Christianity for Neo-Platonism. It had an enormous influence on Christian theologians from St. Augustine to Meister Eckhart. It posited primal unity, indivisible and transcendent, the fount of all existence. The Cappadocian fathers were trained in Neo-Platonism.

## Pantheism:

Giordano Bruno and Spinoza were pantheists- a system of beliefs that identifies god with the universe itself. This was the Brahman of the Hindus which is considered Universal Energy and the entire universe/s a manifestation of it. Gottfried Leibniz

## Some religious Systems

referred to the 'pantheistic opinion of those who believe in no other eternal being but the universe' and declared that the universe is divine. 'Every material thing is in all things and all things come from all, and all is in all things'.

Pharisaism:
It was a Jewish sect of Palestine that separated from the non-Hebrews observed minutiae of Mosaic law eschewed temptations of Hellenism and believed that priesthood was common to all Jews. Although Jews scorned Pharisees' sanctimony and hypocrisy, their notion that any person could have a direct relationship with god impacted the development of Christianity. Pharisaism is a religion codified by Paul of Tarsus, a former Pharisee.

Polytheism:
Essentially it is a belief in many gods and Henotheism that believed in many gods but its credo is to venerate a single god. 'Monotheism in principle but polytheism in fact' as stated by Max Muller while referring to Hinduism.

Protestantism:
This emerged in the 16th century Europe from the Reformation. There are more than one thousand distinct Protestant denominations in the United States, most of them rooted in the movements founded by Rev. Martin Luther King (1483-1546), Heinrich Zingli and John Calvin. There are four families of Protestant church- Lutheran, Anglican, Presbyterian and Free. They believed that the Bible itself is the source of truth and in the universal priesthood of believers. They believed in predestination- that people are born with their fate and only an 'elect' will be saved. But later on they believed that salvation may be available to all. In 2001, 76.5 % of Americans regarded themselves as Christians. George Barna, a pollster, noted that 75% of Christians did not believe in Original Sin. They believed that their good works alone will be enough to earn a place in heaven. Methodists today are not interested in proselytizing but in social justice.

Quakerism:
George Fox, an ex-apprentice shoemaker (1624-91) founder and preacher of the Society of Friends was sentenced by Judge Bennett to six months in prison. In 1650, Charles I was beheaded, and it was a time of political and religious strife in England. Fox questioned if Puritanism was pure after all. 'In people's hearts…his people were his temple and he dwelt in them', referring to the Lord'. He believed that every person in the world had an 'inner light'. Quakerism believed that the Bible was the words of inspired but not inerrant men. They do not take oaths, speak only truth and consider all beings as divine. They were persecuted in England and America till 1689. They

were pioneers in women's rights and stood at the forefront of the abolition movement. Quakerism comes nearest to Hindu thought among all other faiths. We may cite the first verse of the Isa Upanishad that states 'anything that moves in this world is divine'. Similarly every human being is considered a temple where the Atman, the manifestation of Brahman, the Universal Energy, resides.

Quietism:
Miguel de Molinos (1628-97) started the movement with the notion that spiritual perfection can be attained only when the soul is purged of will, desire and effort, so the divine can fill the vacant space. Forgetfulness of every created thing, even of itself, joyful simplicity, heavenly indifference, prayer and a total nakedness, a most wise contemplation, serene peace within which this happy soul of wisdom and all other graces dwell. In the 1970s, Israel forded Ahmad Yassin who founded Quietism, which posed a challenge to militant nationalism and opposition to the armed struggle of the PLO. Sheikh Yassin's movement became the Hamas.

Sol Invictus:
Christianity started gaining importance from the fourth century onwards when Emperor Constantine brought out the New Testament. Extensive research done by a team led by Michael Baigent has produced the book *Holy Blood Holy Grail*, which has exposed the hypocritical views of Christianity that has been perpetuated on humanity. This does not belittle Jesus or his greatness but the self-serving Pilate and later, Constantine (4th century CE) who brought out the largely edited and revised New Testament in the 4th century. Sol Invictus or the invincible Sun, the Sun God worshipped by some cults- a vision that Constantine was said to have got in a temple of Gallic Apollo. Earlier he had been initiated into this cult. After the battle of Milvian Bridge, the Roman senate erected a triumphant arch in the Colosseum with the inscription that stated 'through the prompting of the Deity'. This deity was the Sol Invictus, not Jesus. The state religion under him was pagan sun worship and he was its chief priest all his life. He was not a Christian nor did he convert to Christianity. He was not baptized till 337 BCE when he was in his death bed, too weak to protest.

The Sol Invictus cult was of Syrian origin and was imposed by Roman emperors a century before Constantine. The cult posited the sun god as the sum of all attributes of all other gods. Moreover it conveniently harmonized with the cult of Mithras- which was also prevalent in Rome and involved solar worship. We all know that Mithra was a Hindu god- a sun god- and this clearly establishes the Indian influence on the Greeks, Zoroastrians, Romans and Egyptians.

## Some religious Systems

Constantine's objective was unity in a strife torn empire and this cult helped him to achieve the objective as it included all other cults within it. It was under this cult that Christianity consolidated its position. Since the cult was monotheistic, Christianity also became monotheistic. In 321 BCE, Constantine ordained that the law courts be closed on 'the venerable day of the sun' and made this the rest day. This was transferred to Sunday (being the day of the sun), bringing into harmony with the existing regime while dissociating itself from the Judaic origins. This suited Christianity as well. Until the 4th century, Jesus's birthday was celebrated on the 6th January, but for the cult, the crucial day was December 25th- the festival of Natalis invictus (the birth or rebirth of the sun), when the day began to grow longer (corresponding to the Hindu Dakshinayan). In this respect also, Christianity brought itself into alignment with the regime and the established state religion. This cult meshed happily with that of the Mithras and both follow the same Sunday as holiday and December 25th as a major festival. Christianity also found points of convergence with Mithraism as the latter stressed the immortality of the soul, a future Judgment and resurrection of the dead (This is essentially a Hindu concept- immortality of the soul, transmigration and rebirth).

In 325 BCE, Constantine convened the Council of Nicea that established the date for Easter, confirmed Jesus as a god, since a mortal could not be easily associated with Sol Invictus. Christian orthodoxy lent itself to a politically desirable fusion with the official state religion and insofar as it did so, Constantine gave his support to Christian orthodoxy. In 326 BCE, he ordered confiscation of all works that challenged orthodox teachings and in 331 BCE he commissioned new copies of the Bible. In 303 BCE, the Roman emperor Diocletian had destroyed all Christian writings that could be found. So when Constantine commissioned a new Bible, the orthodoxy got an opportunity to revise, edit and rewrite the material as they saw fit and it was then that crucial alterations were made to the New Testament and Jesus started enjoying the new status that has since been current. Of the 5000 extant versions of the NT, none predates the 4th century.

The Nag Hammadi Scrolls, accidentally unearthed by a peasant while digging at Nag Hammadi in Upper Egypt clearly establishes that:
a. Christ did not die on the cross as he was substituted by Simon of Cyrene.

b. Christ married Mary Magdalene and

c. He had a son by this marriage.

The Scrolls are based on documents of 1st century CE or earlier and contained first person accounts of Jesus fleeing Palestine after the Roman conquest. The Gospel of Philip contained in the Scrolls was quite specific on the subject. This also confirms the fact that Jesus never imagined in his wildest dreams that a religion would come up in his name. This also applies to Buddha who would never have imagined that some later followers would establish a religion in his name. Both were essentially teachers and reformers.

Catholicism:
After Constantine the New Testament was used and Roman Catholic faith took roots. They elected a Pope who was the head and grace is conveyed to members through its ceremonies and rights, unlike in Protestantism where the personal experience of grace is emphasized.

Samaritanism:
Samaritans descended from the northern tribe of Israel. In 724 BCE, Assyrians conquered Samaria, deported most of its Israelites and replaced them with tribes from the east. They intermarried with the remaining Jews, with some adopting their beliefs but continuing to worship their own gods.

Shintoism:
It is the animistic religion of Japan, meaning the 'way of the gods' (shin tao). Their shrines are dedicated to rivers, mountains, trees, and other natural objects. They believe that their first emperor Jimaru, in 660 BCE, was begotten by the sun goddess Ameterasu-o-mi-kami. Buddhist teachings got amalgamated in the 8th century. The four affirmations of the faith are- importance of family, love of nature, physical cleanliness and Matsuri or the honour due to gods.

Sikhism:
The first guru was Nanak Devji (1469-1539). He was a Hindu and lived at a time of Moghul oppression. He decided to protect Hindus by forming a group who were to wear a turban, a kirpan (knife), not shave the head or beard and ordered every family to offer their eldest son to this group for protecting Hindu women and others. This was really not a religion. Nanakji, when 30 years, disappeared for 3 days and when he reappeared, says 'There is no Hindu, no Muslim'. He said organized religions were corrupt and rituals and pilgrimages were a waste of time. He was opposed to caste systems and after enough life times of meditation and virtuous activity one can escape the birth cycle and permanently enter the realm of god. The *Guru Granth Saheb* was in the verse form. Then the Amritsar Golden Temple was built. Guru Gobind Singh was the tenth and final Guru, who created a military fraternity, Khalsa the pure, for protecting the people.

## Some religious Systems

Syncretism:
Belief systems that fuse rituals, practices, and doctrines of more than one religion are Syncretic. Gnosticism, Manichaeaism, Bahaiism are examples. The Theosophical Society is another. The Unity Church of Kansas draws from New Thought, Hinduism, Buddhism, Theosophy and the Rosicrucians.

Tantrism:
It refers to ritual practices of Hindus and Buddhists and Jains and even some South Asian versions of Islam. Sir John Woodroffe (1865-1936) wrote- 'It is a fundamental error to regard the Vedanta as simply a speculative metaphysic… its super-sensual teachings can be established with certainty by the practice of its methods'.

Tao te Ching:
Lao Tzu (300 BCE) taught the way of effortless action of freeing ourselves from desire and shining and surrendering to the Eternal Flow.

'Stand before it- there is no beginning.
Follow it and there is no end.
Stay with the Tao, move with the present,
Knowing the ancient beginning is the essence of the Tao'.
Do nothing (*wu wei*) and you will be able to do what you should.

The Church of Scientology:
In the 21st century, the Church of Scientology has emerged as a Major focus on the controversy on new religions and the rise of pluralism in the west. Initially it appeared in 1950. Ron Hubbard is considered as the father of Scientology. Dianetics is the nature of the entity which views the images of the mind. Survival is the starting point of Scientology ethics. Actions that benefit the greatest good to the greatest number are good. It is not much different from the ethics of the Hindus and Buddhists. The basic principle of existence is survival.

So far we have considered some of the religious systems of the world though it is not a complete one. Most of what has been given here are from the book by Goldwag though the present writer has added a few additional information to make it comprehensive. The major religions will however be studied separately to arrive at the conclusive part of our dissertation.

## References:
1. –Isms and –ologies- Arthur Goldwag, Vintage Books by Random House.
2. The Church of Scientology- J. Gordon Melton, Signature Books.

# CHAPTER 14
# ETHICS

Aristotle's Nichomachean Ethics is an important precursor to western philosophy and ethics. We will now study the salient aspects in the text as also the ethics of other major religions. The ancient Hindu tradition is the precursor to all the religions of the world. In India itself, Jainism, Buddhism, Saivism, Sikhism and other variants came up essentially reflecting the core ideas of Vedanta and ethics. Buddhism led to Zen, Taoism, Shintoism and other systems. Abraham went from Urs of the Chaldees with his followers to Egypt and Canaan, carrying with him the Hindu principles that eventually led to the establishment of Judaism and other Abrahamic religions. All of them speak the same truth but with different voices. Some of the salient features of these religions are discussed here below followed by Aristotle's views on ethics.

Morality is social behaviour and ethics is the reason that justifies such morality. Ethics is a set of rules that describe acceptable social behaviour and is a value system. Every religion has its own ethics as morality differs from place to place or country to country. There are at least three attitudes to religion. These are exclusivist, inclusivist and pluralist. For the exclusivist, one religion is correct and true; others are false. The inclusivist considers that other religions do have real value though his religion is correct and true. The pluralist considers all religions as correct and true and all of them lead to the same One God, called differently by the many. The first category typifies Islam and Christianity and perhaps Judaism. The second category typifies the present approach of Christianity and others. The third is typical of Hindu tradition, Buddhism, and Taoism. They are all rooted in the Hindu tradition.

Politics is the science that studies the supreme good for men. While it is desirable to secure what is good in the case of an individual, to do so in the case of a people or a state is something finer and more sublime. People have been destroyed before now by their money and others by their courage; so we must be satisfied with a broad outline of the truth. Things are known in two senses; known to us and known absolutely. Hesiod says:
That man is best who sees the truth himself;
Good too is he who listens to wise counsel;

But who is neither wise himself nor willing
To ponder wisdom is not worth a straw.

The three types of life are: life of enjoyment, the political and the contemplative. The utter servility of the masses comes out in their preference for a bovine existence with its horde mentality. Honour is felt to depend more on those who confer them than on him who receives it. The good is something proper to its possessor and not easily taken from him. Goodness is superior to honour. Wealth is not the good we are seeking, because it serves only as a means; that is, for getting something else. Plato used the word 'auto', self, to designate the form or essential nature of anything. Even considered in isolation, intelligence and sight and some pleasures and honours might be classed as good in themselves.

What is the good for man? It must be the ultimate end or object of human life: something that is in itself completely satisfying. Happiness fits this description. The good is that for the sake of which everything else is done- health in medicine, victory in strategy, a building in architecture and so on. Happiness is found to be something perfect and self-sufficient, being the end to which our actions are directed. Happiness is a virtuous activity of the soul. One swallow does not make a summer; neither does one day. Neither can make a man blessed and happy. Just acts give pleasure to a lover of justice, and virtuous conduct to a lover of virtue. So happiness is the best, the finest, the most pleasurable thing of all. Happiness seems to require prosperity too; which is why some identify it with good fortune, although others identify it with virtue. The end of political science is the highest good. We are able to define the happy man as 'one who is active in accordance with complete virtue, and who is adequately furnished with external goods, and that not for some unspecified period but throughout a complete life'. Happiness is precious and perfect, for, everything else we do we do for its sake. The first principle and cause of what is good is precious and divine.

The soul is part rational and part irrational. Of the irrational soul, one part is common i.e., vegetative, the cause of nutrition and growth. The rational element of principle in the soul urges men in the right direction and encourages taking the best course. Virtue is also divided into similar differentiation; some are intellectual and others are moral; wisdom and understanding and prudence are intellectual, liberality and temperance are moral virtues. Moral virtues like crafts are acquired by practise and habituation. As a cardinal rule, right conduct is incompatible with excess or deficiency in feelings and actions. Virtue is human excellence. This is confirmed by the doctrine of the mean. Virtue, then, is a mean condition, inasmuch as it aims at hitting the mean. Excess and deficiency fall under evil, and the mean state under good. 'For men are bad in countless ways, but good in only one'. So virtue is a purposive disposition, lying in a mean that is relative to us and determined by a rational principle, and by that which a prudent man would use to determine it. It is purposive as being a deliberately cultivated and exercised state of the appetitive faculty; and the mean is determined not merely by a general principle but by application to particular circumstances by a man of good character and intelligence.

In the field of fear and confidence, the mean is courage. Three practical rules for good conduct are:

1. Avoid the extreme. Calypso says, 'far from this surf and surge, keep thou thy ship'. One extreme is always more erroneous than the other. So choose the lesser of the evils.
2. Notice the errors into which we are liable to fall because of our different natural tendencies.
3. To guard against pleasure and pleasant things, because we are not impartial judges of pleasure.

By this way we can have the best chance of hitting the mean. Moral responsibility consists of two virtues- voluntary and involuntary. When performed under compulsion or through ignorance, it is involuntary. Acting through ignorance and in ignorance are different things. The voluntary act is known to the agent himself who knows the circumstances of his action. Moral conduct implies choice as distinguished from desire, temper, wish and opinion. Desire is concerned with only practicable means to an end. Choice is voluntary but not everything chosen is voluntary. Choice implies a rational principle and thought. It also suggests something chosen before other things. Choice involves deliberation 'which happens for the most part, where the result is obscure and the right course is not clearly defined. It is about means, not ends.

The object of wish is in one sense good, in another, the apparent good. Nobody blames those that are naturally ugly, but we do blame those who become so through lack of exercise and care for their appearance. Virtuous actions are under our control and hence voluntary. We fear all evil-disgrace, poverty, sickness, death, unfriendliness and so on- some like disgrace must be feared by honourable men that are otherwise courageous. The man who faces or fears or feels confident about the right things for the right reason and in the right way and at the right time is courageous. The rash

man is a pretender and boaster to courage. Confidence is the mark of optimism. Courage is a mean state. Five dispositions that resemble courage are:
1. Civic courage.
2. Experience of risk.
3. Spirit or matter.
4. Sanguineness or optimism, and
5. Ignorance.

Courage implies the presence of pain. The more completely a man possesses virtue, and the happier he is, the more he will be distressed at the thought of death.

Pleasures are of the soul or the body. Love of learning, music etc., are of the soul and sport and other physical pleasures are of the body. The grossest are of taste and touch. The temperate man holds a mean position with regard to pleasure. He also desires the right things in the right way and at the right time.

Liberality is the best virtue as it consists in giving to the right people. He does not consider his own interest but he is neither acquisitive nor retentive of money and is ready to part with it. Fortune is criticized for it is the people who deserve wealth most that haven't it least. Prodigality implies excess but it is better than illiberality which is deficiency and meanness.

Magnificence or munificence is a special kind of liberality for, the magnificent man is liberal but the liberal man is not necessarily magnificent. (ex: giving with a view to publicity or name due to selfishness). Magnificence in achievement is excellence on a good scale. Magnanimous people are concerned with honour but the pusillanimous falls short in comparison with his own merit and with the claim of the magnanimous man. The conceited man goes too far in comparison with his own merit, but does not exceed the magnanimous man. But the magnanimous man who thinks little even of honour is thought to be supercilious. He takes great risk, and in the face of danger is unsparing of his life. He is disposed to confer benefits, but is hesitant to accept them. He does not nurse resentment as it is beneath his dignity to remember things against others. He is not excitable, takes nothing seriously and is not highly strung. The pusillanimous errs through deficiency and is conceited. He deprives himself of the advantages he deserves and perhaps not knows his quality.

The right disposition towards anger is like patience; excess is irascibility. Amiable people are obsequious; they make themselves pleasant to others, avoid causing annoyance. The opposite are surly or quarrelsome. The intermediate state resembles friendliness.

# Ethics

Truth is praiseworthy and falsehood is reprehensible. The truthful man never exaggerates, and would rather make an understatement. Ironical people employ understatement and are attractive in character because their aim is not profit, but avoidance of ostentation. The intermediate position has the property of tact. Modesty is not a virtue but is good only as a curb of youthful indiscretion. It is a feeling rather than a state.

Just people perform just acts and are balanced. They wish for what is just. They are lawful or fair or equitable. Unjust means the opposite. Justice is a complete virtue. 'In justice is summed up the whole of virtue' goes the saying. Particular justice is either distributive or rectificatory. Distributive justice employs geometric proportion as in allocating shares of property, money etc. The rectificatory justice remedies an inequitable division between two parties by means of an arithmetical progression. Although justice is not the same as reciprocity, proportional reciprocation is the basis of all fair exchange. Injustice is a vice that exhibits both excess and deficiency. Deeds done on ignorance are mistakes. If it is done due to malice, it is unjust and wicked. Mistakes in ignorance and due to ignorance are pardonable. To be just is not easy as it pre-supposes a virtuous moral state. Equity is a rectification of law in so far as the law is defective on account of generality.

Intellectual Virtues:
Plato adopted the doctrine of Empedocles that says 'like is cognized by likes'. Both kinds of intellect aim at truth, but the calculative faculty aims at truth as rightly desired by the exercise of choice. Action represents praxis and Aristotle means by this purposive action.

The five modes of thought or mind by which truth is reached are: art, science, prudence, wisdom, and intuition. Art is a productive state that is truly reasoned while non-art is falsely reasoned, though a productive state. Prudence is practical wisdom. There is an excellence in art but no such thing in prudence. If prudence, science and wisdom are not considered, what remains is intuition. Wisdom must be the most finished form of knowledge. Wisdom is intuition and scientific knowledge and is most precious. Prudence studies particular goods but wisdom, universal truth. Political sciences are species of prudence. Resourcefulness is correct deliberation.

The act of learning is understanding, when one exercises scientific knowledge. So too is exercising the faculty of opinion for judging another person's affairs within the scope of prudence. The act of judging is really, understanding the issue. A correct judgment is equitable as it arrives at the truth. All the five faculties lead to mature judgment and intelligence. While these states are considered natural gifts, wisdom is not. Wisdom is a product of experience. Wisdom produces happiness like health does. Virtue ensures the correctness of the end we aim and prudence is a means for it.

Cleverness is praiseworthy if it is noble. If it is ignoble it becomes unscrupulous. One cannot be prudent without being good. Prudence is related to natural virtue. If one acquires intelligence, he becomes outstanding in conduct and his disposition does not just resemble virtue, but is virtue itself. The right principle in moral conduct is prudence. Socrates thought that virtues are principles but they imply a principle. One cannot be good without prudence or prudent without moral goodness. A man of prudence can be considered to possess all virtues.

Incontinence and softness is effeminacy. Continence and endurance are states identical with virtue. Socrates thought that nobody acts consciously against what is best, they do it because of ignorance. This is contrary to facts. What is the manner of ignorance? Nothing is more potent than knowledge but people do act what they believe to be a better course.

Emotional people can have fits of anger or sexual craving and these produce physical changes. Incontinent people are in a similar state. Continence and incontinence are concerned only with the same sort of things like licentiousness and temperance. Incontinence of desire is more disgraceful than that of temper. They are related to bodily desires or pleasures. The two forms of incontinence are impetuosity and weakness. One cannot be prudent and incontinent at the same time as prudence is morally good. Knowing what is right and doing it right calls for prudence. Both continence and incontinence are abnormal. It is easier to alter one's habits than one's nature. Practice long pursued becomes nature.

Some pleasures are good but most are bad. So it cannot be the supreme good. To choose what is pleasing is different from pleasure. Some pleasures are disgraceful and are to be censured and some are harmful as they may be bad for health. Pleasure is not an end but a process. Pleasure derived from contemplation and learning is good and may also be the supreme good. A happy life is a pleasant life. Pleasure is therefore a constituent of happiness. It is pursued by animals and humans and so in some sense it is the supreme good.

Everything contains the divine by nature. Pleasure drives out pain. They are intense. Pleasure not accompanied by pain does not admit of excess. Friendship is a kind of virtue and necessary for living. It holds communities together and lawgivers attach more importance to it than justice. Friendliness is justice itself. Good men and friends are the same.

# Ethics

Only what is lovable is loved and that is good, pleasant or useful. Three kinds of friendship can be found. Friendship based on utility, on pleasure, and on goodness. The last is perfect both in duration and other respects. The other kinds are inferior and less enduring. Affection resembles a feeling, but friendship is a state. Caring and sharing are qualities of friendship of good men. One cannot have too many friends. Friendship between unequals is also there, like between father and son, or superior man and his protégé. In friendship loving is more important than being loved. It is more in giving than in receiving affection. Loving is the distinctive virtue of friends. Friendship is based on communion within a community- the state of sharing feelings and thoughts, the feeling of being part of something.

There are three types of constitution viz., monarchy, aristocracy and temocracy. The last refers to a nominal democracy where people who wield power are most corrupt and distribute resources without regard to merit. A good democracy of course is ideal. In any of these, unwritten law and written law are two types of justice. The former is by custom and past experience. But in autocracy such laws are ineffective as an individual dictates the law.

Bad men are full of regrets and are not even amicably disposed towards themselves because they have no lovable quality. So one ought to avoid wickedness and try to be of good character. Concord is also a friendly feeling. This is found among good men because they are in accord with themselves and with one another, having broadly the same outlook.

Benefactors are more loving than beneficiaries; it is human nature. Nothing that a son can do is a due return for what he has received; so that he is permanently in his father's debt. Pure benevolence cannot be adequately repaid; the beneficiary must make the best return that he can. It is more important to repay benefits than to make spontaneous presents to one's close friends. Our feelings towards our friends reflect our feelings toward ourselves. A friend is one who effects the good of another for the sake of that other; he is one who wishes for the preservation of his friend for the friend's sake- the same as a mother towards her children; a friend spends all his time with another and chooses the same things as he does; he also shares his friend's joys and sorrows. The good man extends towards his friend the same relation that he has toward himself. In the extreme form, friendship approximates to self-love. Loving is an active experience, while being loved is a passive one. So love and friendly feelings are attributes of those who take the leading part in the action. The good man acts from a fine motive and for the sake of a friend, neglects his own interest. Euripides said, 'two friends, one soul'. The man is his best friend and ought to love himself best so that he can love others recognizing the essential nature in all as being the same.

## Pleasure and Happiness

For Eudoxus, pleasure is the supreme good. What is desirable is good. It is more desirable with the addition of intelligence than without it. Good activities and happiness are not qualities. Pleasure is a process of becoming since development is not a transformation from any one thing to another, but everything resolved into that from which it came. Where pleasure is the generation of something, pain is the destruction of that something. The pleasures of learning have no antecedent pains. Wealth is desirable, but not as the price of treason, and health is desirable, but not if it involves indiscriminate eating. Sight, hearing, memory, knowledge, and kinds of excellence are desirable even if not accompanied by pleasure. Pleasure is not a process as it is in time. Pleasure is instantaneous and so it is a whole. Pleasures are diverse- sight is superior to touch, hearing and smell to taste, in purity; and intellectual pleasures are superior to sensuous ones. Only the good man's pleasures are real and truly human.

One cannot live alone and friends are necessary for happiness. Happiness is a kind of activity; it is clearly developed and is not a piece of property. A friend is the second self. A happy man needs virtuous friends. Strong friendship is felt only towards a few. Friends are true in good and bad fortune. A true friend is one who would not like to trouble you with his misfortunes. But it is necessary for you to visit him during such time without waiting to be invited. The doing of fine and good actions are to be chosen for themselves. It is different from amusement. Play to work harder, as the saying goes. Amusement is a form of relaxation that helps one to exert continuously. So the harder activity is superior to and more conducive to happiness. It is also a contemplative activity as contemplation is the highest thing in us, and what it apprehends are the highest things. The wise man can practise contemplation by himself and it is also a source of pleasure for the soul. Since happiness implies leisure, it must be an intellectual, not a practical activity. Happiness is complete and so life on this plane is near the divine element in human nature. Since it is too high for human attainment, only men of virtue can live such a life and this divine element is superior to the complete being. The best and the most pleasant life is that of the intellect. Moral activity is secondary happiness. The view that happiness is a form of contemplation is correct. It is the wise man that possesses these qualities in the highest degree. Therefore he is dearest to the gods. Goodness can only be induced in a suitably reeptive person. People become good by nature, by habit or by instruction or by all of it. One that objects to what is base and appreciates what is noble is virtuous.

Education in goodness is best undertaken by the state by enacting laws with Incentives and punishment. Otherwise it can be supplied by the parent as the instructions by the father have as much force as legislation. The student of ethics must apply himself to politics. Aristotle's thought can be traced as underlying those of Plato and this view suits an intellectual state better.

Aristotle in the Middle Ages

After the death of Theophrastus, disciple of Aristotle, peripatetic interest in ethics declined. Ariston of Ceos, became the head of Lyceum (c. 225 BCE). Boethicus (480-524 BCE) was the last important Roman writer on Greek philosophy. In the east, Asparius (100 BCE) made a commentary on Ethics. In the 3rd century, Porphyry, student of Plotinus, wrote a commentary that was known to the Arabs. Themistius (317-388 BCE) expounded the Peripatetic teaching in Constantinople. Peripatetic logic followed the conquering Arabs across North Africa and reentered Europe via Spain. Avicenna, the Arab philosopher, wrote non-logical works *On the Soul*, *On the Heavens* etc. in the twelfth century. These were translated into Latin at Toledo. He died in 1174 BCE. The Arab scholar Averrios (1126-98) completed his translation of the Ethics. The Oxford scholar Robert Grosseteste, Bishop of Lincoln, studied Greek and gathered a group of Hellenists for translating Greek authors. These produced Latin translations (1246-7). They were used by the Dominicans, Albertus Magnus and his pupil Thomas Aquinas (1225-74). By 1300, all surviving works of Aristotle were available in Latin. To Bacon, Aristotle was a fount of wisdom. To Dante, he was a maestro. Prof. D.J. Allen in his Philosophy of Aristotle concluded-"One lesson of our age is that barbarism persists under surface, and the virtues of civilized life are less deeply rooted than used to be supposed. The world is not too richly endowed with examples of perseverance and subtlety in analysis, of moderation and sanity in the study of human affairs. It will be a great loss if the thinker who, above all others displays all these qualities, is ever totally forgotten".

## Reference:
1. The Nichomachean Ethics- Aristotle, Penguin Classics.
2. Ethics of World Religions- Arnold D Hunt, Marie T Crotty and Robert B Crotty, Greenhaven Press, San Diego.

# CHAPTER 15
# ATHEIST SPIRITUALITY

Humanity is one; both religion and irreligion are part of it; neither is sufficient by themselves. Spirituality is far too important a matter to be left to fundamentalists. The struggle is to separate the Church and the State and establish universal tolerance of one another. Erudition and quarrels of experts can wait; freedom of thought cannot.

Can we do without religion? Does god exist? Can there be an atheist spirituality? These are the questions to be answered. Andre Comte Sponville, in his book, has come up with a good exposition on the subject except in respect of atheism. He asserts that he is a confirmed atheist and not an agnostic as he believes there is no god. The fact is that this makes atheism another religion which is what he is fighting against. Agnosticism neither accepts nor denies god. It does not matter either way. But one must live today. And this is what Sponville concludes saying that the past and future are immaterial; past is dead and the future is unknown and only the present is the continuous, infinite awareness, of Being or silence. Though he contradicts himself thus, his exposition is quite illuminating. Let us study it.

God, if he exists, is transcendent and perfect. No religion is perfect or transcendent. The questions that religions raise are sociological and existential. The eastern systems cannot be called religions but a mixture of spirituality, ethics and philosophy. They have to do less with faith than with meditation. Buddha, Lao Tsu and Confucius did not identify with any deity. Sponville does mention the Vedas and Upanishads but has not gone into them seriously lest he would have realized that they refer to no god but to a single Brahman and its manifestation severally as the world or universe. Brahman is in all and all that Is, is nothing but Brahman. Jainism, Buddhism et al are but a derivation from this idea of Sanatana Dharma. Eugene Burnouf said 'an ethics without god and an atheism without nature'. All theisms are religions but all religions are not theistic. Stig Dagerman, the Swedish novelist said, 'our need for consolation is impossible to satisfy'. So is our need for love and protection.

'Death is nothing' for Epicurus; as long as we are living, death does not exist. Mourning for the loss of a kin only reinforces atheism. But Sponville fails to see that even if god exists, it is not his work to see that man suffers or grieves for someone's death. If one is born one has to die also and that is the law of nature because all biological organisms (of which man is one) have to meet their end sooner or later. Again, we are responsible for our actions and their consequences. How can god be responsible for it? Religions bind people of a community together. Religion means to 'bind'. Relegere means contemplation, to reread. To commune is to share; communion and fidelity are important in religion. This is what leads to culture in a society. The sense of belonging and cohesion go hand in hand. All communion is not religion.

Mind is memory according to St. Augustine. There is no such thing as society without education, civilization without transmission, communion without fidelity. When faith is lost, fidelity remains. Renouncing a god does not mean renouncing the moral, cultural, and spiritual values that have been formulated in his name. Fidelity involves values and hence responsibility. Ethics should prevail, with or without religion. Fundamentalists, Obscurantists and terrorists 'fight for their servitude as if it were their salvation' (Spinoza). The period of Plato, Confucius, Buddha and Lao Tsu was called the Axial Age by Karl Jaspers. A society can do without religion but not without communion and fidelity.

Montaigne mentioned Socrates more often than Abraham and Lucretius more often than Jesus. Spinoza said that the only law 'is justice and charity- do good and live in joy'. A Jew said that 'god does not exist but we are his chosen people'! Two Rabbis, after long discussions, concluded that god does not exist. One of them went on to perform his morning ritual prayers. When asked by the other, he replied 'what does god have to do with it?' An African proverb says, 'when you don't know where you are going, it is important to remember where you come from'. When a Frenchman wanted to convert to Buddhism, the Dalai Lama quipped, 'why Buddhism? In France you have got Christianity'.

As Kant said, 'either morals are autonomous or they do not exist'. Alain (Emile Auguste Charier) had this to say: 'Ethics means knowing that we are spirit and thus have certain obligations…Ethics is neither more nor less a sense of dignity'. Post-modernity is modernity without the enlightenment according to Regis Debray. And again, 'the fact that a judgment is false is not an objection against that judgment' as per Nietzsche. His attitude is more like a dead end. Without truth there can be no knowledge and hence no progress is possible. Kant, following Montaigne and Horace, said 'dare to know, dare to use your intelligence, dare to distinguish the possibly true from the false'. Montaigne had said that 'there is nothing as beautiful and legitimate as to play the duty of man well and properly'. This is humanism of a high order. Tragic wisdom is the wisdom of happiness and finitude, happiness and impermanence, happiness and despair. The trap of hope is such that it prevents you from experiencing today hoping for tomorrow's happiness. If we want only what we do not have, we can never have what we want. Human nature is portrayed in a song by Nat King Cole-

When it is hot we want it cold, and,
When it is cold we want it hot,
Always wanting what is not.

The very hope that impels you to pursue it cuts off our happiness. 'Instead of living, we hope to live, forever preparing for happiness' as per Montaigne. Only the despairing can be happy says the Samkhya, 'for hope is the greatest torture, and despair the greatest joy. Spinoza puts it differently saying 'there is no hope without fear and no fear without hope'. Serenity is the absence of hope and fear. It frees the present moment from action, knowledge and joy; truth sets us free, not hope. It is love that lets us live, not hope. If there is no hope there is no disappointment. People who desire only what is or what depends on them, who are content to love and to will, cannot be weary or embittered. The opposite of nihilism is love and courage.

The Good Samaritan was neither Jewish nor Christian and Jesus wanted others to follow him or imitate him, not a priest or a Levite. The value of human beings has nothing to do with whether or not they believe in god or life after death or in a religion. On these issues we know nothing at all. Believers and non-believers are separated only by what they do not know. The real worth of people is measured neither by faith nor hope but by the amount of love, compassion and justice of which they are capable.

St. Paul explained the three theological virtues- faith, hope and charity. Of these charity is the greatest. Without love (charity) no gift of language or prophesy would be anything. He said that 'charity never faileth'. Faith and hope could eventually fail but not love, said St. Augustine. So we do not need faith or hope, but only love will remain. Hope and faith refer to the future that is not known but love is charity that is perfect, here and now. The present is the kingdom of heaven. If we are already in the kingdom, we are already saved. Death cannot then take away anything from us. The present is infinite and that is immortality. Thomas Aquinas later said, 'in Christ there was perfect charity but there was neither faith nor hope'. Love is at once divine and more human than either faith or hope. The mind knows no fatherland, nor does humanity. Jesus said, 'render unto Caeser the things that are Caeser's'. And this clearly refers to the need for the separation of the State and Church. We must mention here that Jesus did not create the Church nor did he want a religion in his name. The same goes for Buddha. Both were reformers with infinite love who wanted to change their societies to better ones. Jesus himself never took himself to be god or the son of god. It is his followers that did.

# Vedic Tradition and World Religions

No science can tell us how to live and die, but this is no reason to be indifferent to how we live and die. When Einstein was asked if he believed in god, he wanted to know what the questioner meant by the word god and then 'I will tell you if I believe in him'. Agnosticism implies tolerance and open mindedness; and atheism, a closed mind. Philosophy means thinking beyond the knowable. Metaphysics means thinking as far as possible. Protagoras said, 'of the gods, I can say nothing- neither that they are or they are not, nor what they are. Too many things prevent me from knowing; firstly, the vagueness of the question and secondly, the brevity of human life'.

God could be a spirit, or *apeiron* (infinite) of Anaximander, fire of Heraclitus, impersonal being of Parmenides, the Tao of Lao Tsu, or even the substance of Spinoza. We may add to these, the Brahman of the Hindus. Cicero, Voltaire and many other thinkers have believed in an intelligent creator (intelligent design and so on). The debate on this vis-avis Darwin's theory continues to this day, each attacking the other. Contemplation in silence is preferable to belief in god as it cannot be proved. 'The truth is at the bottom of the abyss' as averred by Democritus and the abyss is bottomless. Leibniz asks: if god is there, whence evil? If he does not exist, whence good?' Sponville gets carried away by his atheism just like Richard Dawkins. They consider that if god exists, there cannot be suffering and evil. This is passing the buck. We must be responsible for our actions. Newton's third law and the law of karma are clear on this point. Where does god come into all this? There are many weak and mediocre beings. Human beings are not automatons and quality is always scarce while quantity is aplenty. Montaigne remarked: 'they want to break away from themselves and escape from the man. That is madness; instead of turning into angels, they turn into beasts; instead of raising themselves, they lower themselves. These transcendental humors frighten me, like lofty and inaccessible places'. Pascal said in favour of agnostics, 'if you win, you win all; if you lose, you lose nothing'. Sponville does not like this as he is a staunch atheist. Dogmatism and terrorism are mutually reinforcing. This is a double offence against intelligence and freedom. Religion and irreligion are a right. Both must be protected by ensuring that they are not imposed through force.

A spirit is a thing that loves and cares. We do believe strongly that religion and religiousness (or spirituality) are different. The former is divisive and the latter unifying. God does not play a part in this at all. Nature is serene and so is spirituality. As Wittgenstein puts it- 'There is indeed the inexpressible; it shows itself; it is the mystical…mysticism wonders not how the world is but that the world is'. As Simone Weil says, 'love and prayer are merely the highest form of attention'. That is the silence of contemplation. As J.Krishnamurthy the late mystic, often used to say, 'meditation is the silence of thought. That is the freedom from the known'. While we can conceive of the infinite, we have no experience of it. We live within the unfathomable. Marcus Aurelius quoted Plato and said that human life is not something great and so there is nothing awesome in death. The word 'tranquillity' is not tranquillity but a concept; it is an experience. Eastern seers have had this experience and that is what has given us the Upanishads.

Romaine Rolland calls the 'oceanic feeling', 'a sense of indissoluble union with the great All, and of belonging to the universal' just as a wave belongs to the ocean. When you feel one with all, you do not need a god. Richard Jeffries states: 'Eternity is here and now. I am within it. It is all around me in the brightness of the sun...like a butterfly floating on the light permeated air. Nothing is still to come; everything is already here, immortal life now'. In *The Stranger* (*L'etranger*), Albert Camus writes: '...emptied of hope, as I stood there staring at the night sky filled with signs and stars, I opened myself up to the tender indifference of the universe for the first time. Feeling it so like myself, so fraternal at long lost I realized that I had been happy, and still was'. Such experiences are found among writers and philosophers like what Spinoza stated, 'we sense and experience that we are eternal. We can see like the Indian seers of yore that the body is not eternal but its essence- the spirit, soul or the Self- is eternal'. Lao Tsu said, 'the Tao that can be expressed is not the Tao of all time'. These quotes signify the same idea of the Vedanta where we find that if you can describe Brahman, it is not Brahman. It is indescribable (*anirvachaniya* in Sanskrit). The Being is at once a mystery and a fact. As Wittgenstein puts it- 'For an answer which cannot be expressed, the question too cannot be expressed...The solution to the problem of life is seen in the vanishing of the problem'. Nothingness clings to us because we cling to it. 'We do not live, we hope to live', according to Pascal. Being and doing is plenitude. Sine you are what you are (dynamic, joyful, and, serene), you lack nothing and this is plenitude. What fulfils you then is not a particular state of being but being itself. When you have everything, you have been freed from possessions itself and this is what verges on spirituality.

When you free yourself of the feeling of the soul and the body, between I and me, between the doer and the deed, there is simply the silence- the I or the Self. All that remains is action, the body in action. As Wittgenstein puts it, 'all experience is of the world and has no need of a subject'. This is the *anatman* of Buddha. When you are absorbed in an activity, can you feel any self at all, no the separation has disappeared, as mentioned by Prajnanapad. Anybody familiar with the Vedanta of the Hindus that is millennia old will know what has been stated above. The oceanic feeling of Romaine Rolland and Freud is the Advaita of the Hindus that is non-duality. *Ekameva advitiyam* says the Hindu scriptures meaning there is one only without a second. This is Spinoza's unity of substance. It is a matter of being one with All (The All is the

Brahman). It is silence or the suspension of speech or *alogos* of Epicurus and *aphasia* of Phyrrus. Parmenides puts it succinctly thus: 'it neither was nor shall be, because it IS'. And this is the 'eternal present' of St. Augustine. The present only exists and that is serenity. The Greek's *ataraxia* signifies this serenity or tranquillity which is nothing but living in the present. 'Good and evil do not exist in nature' according to Spinoza and nothing exists outside of nature. Chuang Tsu said, 'the perfect man is without a self, the inspired man is without works; the saintly man leaves no name behind him'. Beauty is infinity represented in a finite way, says Friedrich Von Schelling. Acceptance or acquiescence is very akin to love. Spirituality is true freedom. If we free ourselves of the past, we are truly freed because past is the only cause of the future.

Where is the need for dogma when you can see? Where is the need for hope when everything is present? Where is the need to wait for eternity when we live in it? Why do you need religion when you are already saved? As long as you distinguish between *samsara* and nirvana, you are in *samsara* according to Nagarjuna. The Brahman of the Hindus, limitlessness of Anaximander, becoming of Heraclitus, Tao of Lao Tse, Nature of Lucretius and Spinoza, silence or the present of J. Krishnamurthy all refer to the One without a second. As Spinoza said, 'Beautitude is not the prize of virtue, it is virtue itself'. The Absolute is not the end of the road but the road itself.

Again as Spinoza would say, 'not because things are good that we desire them; we judge them to be good because we desire them' we do not love because something is valuable. Our love confers value upon what we love. Ethics can lead to but not replace spirituality. And spirituality can lead to but not replace ethics. Love helps us live and truth sets us free. The Eternal Tradition of the Hindus says '*satyam vada, dharmam chara*' or speak the truth and walk the path of dharma or virtue. And this is the idea borrowed by the Greeks some 2600 years ago that became the basis for their philosophy which in turn laid the foundation for western philosophy. At that point of time there were the Taxila, Vikramshila, Nalanda and Nagarjuna universities in India where students from Greece, Egypt, China and other countries studied and thus spread the message of Vedanta in forms compatible with their respective societies and their languages. In fact, sciences like mathematics, logic, astronomy and others spread from India in this way. For much of what has been given here, the author acknowledges his debt to Andre Comte Sponville.

## References:
1. The Little Book of Atheist Spiritualities- Andre Comte Sponville-, Viking.
2. Science, Philosophy and Religion- Ramakrishnan Srinivasan, Citadel.

# CHAPTER 16
# ANCIENT CIVILIZATIONS

Hindu Civilization:

The words Hindu and Dravidian are misnomers but have come to stay and hence we shall retain them for convenience. The word Hindu represents all the people living to the east of the Sindhu River (Indus) for the Persians and Arabs. In Persian Sindhu is pronounced as Hindu. Similarly, the word Dravidian is derived from Dramila or Tamil, the language of the native people of India. In fact it is the oldest language in the world as it has existed since 15000 BCE or earlier in four different types starting with hieroglyphic to the present square letters. The whole of India was peopled by these Dravidians right up to Kashmir. Phallus worship was the earliest in India since at least 15000 BCE. This is represented by a Linga and this Shiva worship has continued since. Saivism is the name given to their religion and Kashmir Saivism is very well known besides Tamil Saivism with thousands of Shiva temples not only in India but in Thailand, and other Far Eastern countries like Cambodia and Indonesia. This was because Tamil Chola kings had conquered these areas with the famous Angkor Vat, Borobudur and other temples that eventually became Buddhist in later years. Mohenjo-Daro/Harappa areas had thrown up seals with the figure of Shiva and other deities.

The Aryan Invasion theory planted by the British has since been proved to be a hoax by archaeologists and scientists. The Rishis of the Rig Veda numbering at least four hundred and perhaps more than thousand had landed in the high plateau of Tibet some seven thousand years or more before now. There is reason to think that they are extra terrestrials as per research by Elliot Scott, Daniken and others. This was probably because they represented a very high level of intelligence with the Vedas and Upanishads that have been the main influence for Greek philosophy. These Rishis moved with their forbears through the Hindu Kush to the Sindhu River basin and down to the East, and South of India when the River Saraswati dried up around 1900 BCE. They integrated well with the Tamil society and groups of them moved all over the world settling and civilizing those areas. During 1500 BCE and after, India had two well known universities at Taxila and Nalanda besides Vikramashila and

Nagarjuna and scholars from China, Egypt, Greece and elsewhere came to study in these universities. This was how there was diffusion of Indian philosophy to Greece and other areas. More details can be found in the research work of this author titled *History of Ancient India*.

Here we shall elucidate briefly the principles of Sanatana Dharma or the Eternal Tradition that formed the basis for religious practices in India and from which religions like Jainism, Buddhism, and Sikhism came up. Essentially it was a way of life that called for truthful and virtuous living. The Upanishads propounded the basic philosophy of the Hindus. It stated that everything in this world is divine and is represented by the Universal Energy or Consciousness, Brahman. That is the only reality. All that exists in this universe is but a manifestation of that Brahman. Brahman is infinite, without a beginning or end. Another chapter gives more details in this matter. Anyone studying the philosophy of the Greeks from Thales onwards could perceive the influence of these Hindu practises on them.

The native Dravidians and the forbears of the Rishis, the Brahmins lived in the Tamil country that extended about four hundred miles below the present Cape Comorin in the South. This was the Kumari Continent where Rivers Pahruli and Kumari with the Mt Meru were located but the entire area was submerged in four geological convulsions between 9000 BCE and 2000 BCE. The first Tamil Sangam was headquartered on the banks of Pahruli at *Then* Madurai (*then*=south). The second Sangam moved to Kapadapuram on the banks of Kumari River and when this was also submerged it moved to the present location. Details on this submerged Continent can be found in the *Bhavishya Puranam*. This was shifted over a period of six thousand years to the present Madurai where the third Sangam functions to this day. Max Muller has given extensive details on the Hindu culture and philosophy.

The humans reached Europe- Crimea and the Black Sea- about 10,000 BCE. According to archaeologists, around 6000 BCE, two civilizations existed- Egypt in the north and Tigris-Euphrates in the present southern Iraq. About half a million people settled in both where huge temples and palaces were erected for kings, priests and aristocrats with common people living in small houses made of sun-dried bricks or tents. The forces of change in both societies were external except for the Pharaoh Akhenaten (1330 BCE) attempting to create a monotheistic religion akin to Judaism and eliminate the power of the priests. This was reversed after his death. This is the scenario given by Cantor. Apparently he was not aware of the ancient Indian civilization that has existed since much before the Floods. But since the Indians were highly civilized and technologically advanced, they were adventurous and many groups travelled widely settling in the Middle East, Egypt, Greece, Europe, the Americas and the Far East.

They were a seafaring people who had conquered many areas in the southeast and Far East. These were the Tamils wrongly called Dravidians by western scholars.

Around 1100 BCE, Egypt was invaded and ruled by a 'sea people' from west Asia but effective power returned to the native dynasty. Cantor is referring to a settlement by Indians in the area and it was not an invasion. These settlers helped to civilize people, consecrated the Pyramids and built cities and monuments. Sumerians, Chaldeans, Assyrians and Babylonians did invade Egypt some time or other but they were the branches of Kshatriya kings that had established these states. By the first century BCE, Egypt was absorbed into the expanding Roman Empire until Moslem Arabs took over in the seventh century of the Current Era. Monarchy was considered divine with its aristocrats and slaves forming their society. The Iraqis did compile law codes (Hammurabi) which helped in the life of the masses. He had stories of the Great Flood and creation stories. Such Flood did occur and this could have influenced the Hebrew Bible which was designed in Spain around 1000 BCE. The final text completed around 300-250 BCE corresponds with the former and discovered in the caves of the Dead Sea. After the Babylonians exiled the Jews to Iraq, these communities lived there till 1948. When Persians conquered Iraq in 500 BCE, Jews were invited to resettle in Judea. God's covenant with the Jews became the main theme of Hebrew Bible.

Athens in Greece became the dominant source of literature and intellectual pursuits between 425-350 BCE. It was a successful democratic republic. The Greeks picked up the alphabets from another sea people, the Phoenicians. Incidentally the name Phoenician was derived from the Indian word Pani denoting the nomadic singing group of people in India, who were well known seafaring settlers in Asia. The Greeks gained knowledge of philosophy, mathematics and science besides astronomy from India where many Greek scholars used to attend the ancient universities of Nalanda and Taxila. The diffusion of such knowledge was from India and western philosophy, derived from the Greek owed its origins to Indian philosophy. The Athenian ruling class was bisexual and pedophilic. More details can be obtained from the book by this author titled *Science, Philosophy and Religion* published by Citadel, Calcutta in 2008.

## Four Worldviews:

The Greeks:

Hebrew Bible, Philosophies of Plato, Aristotle, the Hellenistic or Alexandrian literature written in Greek or Hebrew gave the worldviews forming the foundations of western civilization. Most Greeks (not Thucydides) thought that history moved in circles, repeating itself infinitely. But Jews thought otherwise with each event being singular proceeding along a straight line and this influenced European thinking. Plato's idea of philosopher kings has been a great contribution to society. For him, there was One Big Idea from which everything else is derived. He defined reality as that which is permanent and unchanging. These were only ideas. Anything material deteriorates and decays. Without an idea there would have been no invention like a ship or a chariot. When reason has purified ideas to the utmost, a flight of the soul or a mystical experience allows the human mind to know the idea of the good, 'the source of all things right and beautiful' or god the creator and redeemer. This divides everything into soul and matter, which are joined at birth. Inquiry allows the soul to recover pure knowledge of ideas. At death, the soul and body are disconnected and the soul flies back to god.

Centuries after Plato, in 37 CE, after the death of Christ, the former's teachings were re-written as Christ's teachings as Platonic philosophy. Aristotle, the principal student of Plato, wrote further on the subject, that are literally copied in Christian doctrines. If Plato leads to Christianity, Aristotle looks to modern science. For him, physics showed that ultimately there has to be a first cause, an unmoved mover, which is god. In ethics, he said that selfishness and self-sacrifice do not work for most people. So he looked for the golden mean also, good behaviour is a habitual pattern or slow and steady conditioning.

The Alexandrian scientist Galen proposed a view called alternative medicine that is now the rage. Diet, exercise regimen and herbal medicines combined with good hygiene controls the four temperaments and keep the human body in balance. Ancient Ayurveda from India that talks similarly could have influenced Galen's theory. Hellenistic culture talked of world citizenship.

Romans:

The Roman Empire endured until the Turkish conquest in 1435 CE. The Roman society was mostly equitable and involved plebeians equally in the government though the aristocracy was the main ruler. They built a huge army and treated the soldiers well by giving them land and wealth. It was a multi-cultural society as the people from the conquered states also settled down in Rome and were given citizenship. The Carthagians, the Greeks, the Mediterraneans and others all became a mélange of cultures integrating into Roman society. By far the most stable emperor was Augustus Caesar, the adopted son of Julius Caesar that saw two centuries of stable and peaceful Rome and the largest empire in the world. Their legal system became the standard in England, Europe and USA with local adaptations. The Roman Empire was a religious cauldron and a sexual paradise.

# Ancient Civilizations

## The Classical Heritage:

Matthew Arnold believed that the western civilization was a confluence of the Hebraic and the Classical streams and the Romans were mere imitators of the Greeks in all intellectual matters. But we now know that Romans did make contributions to the classical heritage handed down from antiquity. The Roman culture was logo-centric or focused on the written word. Communication was through stone inscriptions and writing on paper. The educational system foreshadowed in the Hellenistic societies during the second century BCE was improved, systematized and extended the crucial opportunity to the whole of the Roman population. They were more known for art and literary excellence than for science. They excelled in poetry and generally avoided tragedies. Virgil, Horace, Ovid and others wrote under the Emperor's patronage. Roman philosophy embraced the Stoics, and Marcus Aurelius, the 2nd century emperor, made contributions in his *Meditations*. It is a kind of Platonism in which one does his best with what he can control and refine and let the rest go. Cicero, the first century orator, was its principal disseminator. As a lawyer, his oral pleading became the feature of Anglo-American Common Law.

The classical heritage prevented the rich oral cultures of the ancient Mediterranean from surviving in later times. Another deficiency was the lack of social conscience regarding slavery, poverty, disease, and cruelty endured by more than half of the 50 million people. The classical heritage represented a narrow and insensitive social political theory reinforcing a miserably class ridden and technologically stagnant society. By 400 CE, Christianity had also been put through this narrow logo-centric culture and its cruel class ridden manifestations.

## The Christians:

The Synoptic (connected) Gospels of the New Testament may have been taken from a common source written by a writer known only as 'Q', a contemporary of Joshua of Nazareth or Jesus. John the Baptist, the preacher, had predicted the coming of one greater than him and Jesus fulfilled this prophesy. But John ran foul of King Herod, who subsequently decapitated him. Pilate considered Jesus as the 'king of the Jews' and so a subversive, crucified him. Under Simon Peter, the small Christian sect remained loyal to the Torah, but considered Jesus as someone special. Saul of Tarsus or St. Paul, the Jewish Rabbi, set about transforming the beliefs and practices of Christians. He was impressed by the later chapters of the Book of Isiah (written around 500 BCE) in Baghdad). He came from Asia Minor where Jesus was considered a re-born Saviour. He died around 66 CE, four years before the Jewish rebellion against Rome that led to the destruction of the Temple and exile of Jews from Jerusalem. The religion of Mithraism was very popular at that time. Christianity developed an intense rivalry with Judaism, considered as a minority belief and hence the strong anti-Semitsm of Christianity by 200 CE.

Constantine favoured Christians and got the New Testament written. He was a sun worshipper who was not baptized till the time of his death. Theodosius I, after him, banned Paganism in 393 CE and the majority had already become Christian. But Paganism reformed itself with Plotinus's Neo-Platonism conjuring a single deity as the spiritual fountain of life that fructifies the world. By 390 CE, Roman Paganism was as close to Christianity in its monotheism. When the Roman state was dissolved in the Latin speaking world around 458 CE, the Pope replaced the emperor as the political leader of the Eternal City. By the end of the fourth century, St. Augustine, St. Ambrose, and St. Jerome shaped Christian doctrine, ritual and literature. St. Augustine, following St. Paul, considered history as the struggle between heavenly and earthly cities, but only god before the Last Judgment knows the membership roles. Human nature is sinful and corrupt and only those who have received grace can be saved for eternal life.

The Manichaeans or Gnostics postulated that there were two gods- the Christian god of goodness and an evil anti-god of darkness. That is why there was evil in the world. Jesus' preaching of love and equality was democratic but by 400 CE, the bishops and theologians had drained this egalitarian strain out of the Church.

Decline of the Ancient World:

The Visigoths, a mixture of German and Scandinavian people living along the Danube basin overran the Romans in 378 CE at the Battle of Adrianople by killing the emperor and decimating the army. By 410 CE, a second attack took Rome itself and sacked the Eternal City. This was known as the barbarian invasions. By the mid-fifth century, the Latin speaking empire had disintegrated and successive Mongolian and Germanic kingdoms were established in its place. The heavily populated Greek speaking people of Constantinople survived in a shrunken form until 1453 CE.

The fall of the Roman Empire could be attributed to a number of causes. These include the following:

1. Shrinking of the population by 25% between 250 and 450 CE that caused the reduction in the tax base and shortage of soldiers.
2. The population shrank due to smallpox, bubonic plague and venereal disease.
3. It was a slave society. The slaves did not reproduce and so its population diminished with the ending of imperial conquests in the first century. So the size of the working population steadily declined.

4. The slave population did improve productivity but inhibited the industrial revolution that could have increased productivity and compensated for the reduction in slaves. This was pointed out by Franz Oertel, the German economic historian.
5. The cultural cause was due to the logocentric culture rooted in written text. This engendered a conservative frame of mind hostile to military and technological innovation.

## The Cities:

Jerusalem:
The covenant led to Abraham's offering his son Isaac for sacrifice and Yahweh was pleased. God is said to have given Canaan to Abraham and this myth was the foundation myth of Jewish history. The Philistines, the sea-people, invaded Canaan in the ninth century BCE and thus emerged kingship among Israelites. The first king Saul and his sons fell to the Philistines. And David took the kingship. He defeated the Philistines and moved the capital to Jerusalem. Jews incidentally, learned iron making and the alphabet from the Philistines. David had a boisterous sexual behaviour and in one of his unions was born Solomon who also enjoyed many wives. The Bible raised the two to divine levels, but Solomon had a relish for Gentile women. During the period of turbulence, Jewish religious practices changed partly due to external threats and partly due to the conditions within Israel itself. From the tenth to the eighth century BCE, worship at other shrines was there as also inter-marriage with foreigners and Yahweh was fused with local deities.

In the mid-eighth century BCE, the prophets Amos and Hosea foretold the destruction of Israel. Amos asserted that the demands of Yahweh were moral and spiritual. He spoke against the oppression of the poor by the rich and attacked the ritualistic practices of Israel. Hosea explicitly named the Assyrians as the instrument by which Yahweh would destroy Israel if it did not repent. In southern Judea, these waverings were echoed by the prophet Isaiah, who identified the sin of Israel as the rebellion against Yahweh. Micah, like Amos, called for an end to chronic social grievances. The destruction of the northern kingdom of Israel by the Assyrians under Sargon I in 721 BCE made the prophet's demands more insistent in the south. The Book of Isaiah has a text that seems to mock at fasting- 'Is such a fast I desire a day for men to starve their bodies? Is it bowing the head like a bulrush and lying in sack cloth and ashes? ... No, unlock the fetters of wickedness, and untie the cords of the yoke, to let the oppressed go free'. Here Isaiah is saying that religious praxis must be fulfilled by the spirit of justice. Law fulfilled by justice is the Jewish way. Some Hebrew members went beyond cooperation with Assyrians and worshipped their divinities. In the seventh century BCE, prophet Jeremiah predicted that Solomon's Temple will be destroyed because of the forsaking of the singular worship of Yahweh. Josiah (639-609 BCE), brought reforms in response and aimed to centralize all worship in the Temple of Jerusalem. The shrines in the mountains were destroyed and their priests were made subordinate to the priests of the Temple. Ritual magic accompanying action was stopped. The Book of Deuteronomy was given legitimacy by Josiah. After this, Israel depended on the observance of law of the Torah.

The hopes of the exiled Jews were answered in 539 BCE when Persians took the city of Babylon and established control over the empire. The Jews were allowed to return to Jerusalem and to rebuild the Temple. Under the Persian king Darius I, the new Temple was consecrated in 515 BCE but only under the Persian Governor Nehemiah in the mid-fifth century, real reconstruction was carried out and religious law enforced.

The Hellenistic Era saw conflicts between the priesthood and the issue of whether the Jewish culture be preserved despite growing absorption into the Hellenistic world. Jews were given a privileged position next only to the Greek and Macedonian conquerors. The Greek language was adopted and converts observed the law except for circumcision. The Hellenizing influence in Jerusalem led to cooperation with foreign monarchies and adoption of a Greek lifestyle. In 168 BCE, Antiochus IV Epiphanis, the Seleucid ruler of Syria came and polluted the Temple. The old shrines were converted to the worship of Hellenistic gods. By 166 BCE, open revolt started. The rebels headed by Maccabeus ultimately gained independence lasting till the Roman conquest in 63 BCE. The symbol of Maccabean rule was the menorah, the seven branched candelabra. The Maccabean kings played politics with the Syrian empire to keep their independence.

The Romans under Pompey established hegemony in 63 BCE and though the Jews were allowed their religious life, conflicts were common between the two groups of interpreters of the law, the Sadducees and Pharisees, the aristocrats and the commoners. The former dominated the Sanhedrin, the Jewish High Court in Jerusalem. The Pharisees were eager to supplement the law with their oral tradition and rabbinical interpretation and were liberal and progressive. The middle class Pharisees were teachers and scribes and not priests. They both accepted foreign rule as a necessary evil. The Essenes withdrew from the Jewish community altogether and established themselves at Qumran in the Dead Sea. Their library was later recovered as the Dead Sea Scrolls from caves.

## Ancient Civilizations

In the first millennium BCE, the demotic experience of the diaspora (after the Babylonian exile), led to communal Synagogue worship of an immaterial god with belief in personal immortality and resurrection of the dead that had filtered into Judaism in the 2/3 centuries before the Common Era. Hellenistic Judaism resembles the liberal and reformed Judaism of today. Mainstream Judaism today does not involve magic unlike the religion of the Mediterranean including Christianity. Prayer and religious conduct were the only forms of communication with the divine. In 1960, Yehezkel Kaufman of the Hebrew University confirmed Max Weber's view thus: 'The religious idea of the Bible…is that of a supreme God who stands over every cosmic law, every destiny and every compulsion, unborn, uncreated…A God who does not fight against the deities or power of impurity; who does not sacrifice, predict, prophesy, and practice witchcraft; who does not sin and needs no atonement; a God who does not celebrate the festivals of his life. A free divine will that transcends all this- characteristic of Biblical religion and makes it different from all other religions on this earth'. Of course, this assertion is wrong since this concept of God has been literally lifted from the Hindu concept of the Infinite Brahman.

The Jewish position changed to absolute monotheism by 200 BCE from a nebular position earlier. The Jew rationalized a disaster by saying that it is his fault. He acted badly and Yahweh was chastising him. Theodicy or the justification of the ways of god to man had a long workout in Jewish history.

For the Pagan cultures of the ancient Mediterranean, the time was always now. The Jews also stressed on the community as no man is an island. The action of the individual impacts the community. The Jewish culture was at once liberating and compulsively confining at the same time. The Ecclesiastes states that everything is set for a time- a time to be born and a time to die; a time for loving and a time for suffering. The Book of Isaiah talks of the sufferings of the Jews for mankind's redemption- the Torah separated the Jews from the Goyims, the other people on earth, by insisting on circumcision of all males, and by mandating forced rest on the Sabbath every week. The way of the Torah is constant devotion to God.

Jews excluded women from priesthood, but many Pagan religions including Roman, had priestesses playing an important role. Orthodox Jews even today thank God that they were not born as women. In the first millennium BCE, there were priestesses in Israel as was common in the Near East. The Book of J, the lone narrative of the Pentateuch was probably written by a royal princess as it accords with feminine mentality. Women are segregated in Synagogues and divorce is given only to men and not to women. Pharisiac Judaism however, insists that descent comes through the mother. After 200 BCE, they quietly accepted the Near Eastern belief in personal immortality and rebirth. This was more of a concession to the masses. In the Book of Daniel, it says: 'Many of those who sleep in the dust of the earth will awake, some to everlasting life and some to reproach of eternal abhorrence' (160 BCE). The Bible however, does not separate the soul and the body and considers it as an integrated being.

The severe demands it made on the adherents led to alternative forms of Judaism being sought within the homeland. Though Jewish views of the life of Abraham to King Saul are treated as history, there is no basis for this. Their history is not glorious at all or happy. But from this, emerged a culture of mainstream Judaism around which subsequent history develops. Conversion of Gentiles to Judaism was mild and haphazard. Over time, observant Jews became an extremely endogamous group, marrying within a limited circle. In origin, the Jews were a mere sectarian sub-group among the Canaanites but in time, they became a distinct race, an ethnic group.

Athens:
Ancient Judaism and Athenian culture join as the mainstream of western civilization. In reality, the Athenian experience is different from that of the Jews. The silver deposits of Mt. Laurium made Athens a wealthy state. Themistocles persuaded the *polis* in a large navy with this wealth around 500 BCE. Persian incursions were regular from 440 BCE but in 449 BCE, Persia and Athens concluded the Truce of Callias.

Athenians were simple people and lived an unadorned life. Their dwellings indicated this. Their slaves, who made up 25% of the population, were well treated and could hardly be distinguished from free men. Men got together without their women and had only courtesans (hetaerae). Bisexuality also reduced the role of wives in social affairs. Education was very important in Athens. It functioned as a true democracy with more people participating in governance. Justice was free from public influence and private interests. Pericles was the greatest leader of Athens from 443 to 429 BCE when he died. In his famous 'funeral oration', he said: 'We cultivate refinement without extravagance and knowledge without effeminacy; wealth, we employ more for use than show, and place the real disgrace of poverty not in owing to the fact but in declining the struggle against it…Our ordinary citizens are still fair judges of public matters; for, unlike any other nation, regarding him who takes no part in these duties not as unambitious but as useless, we Athenians are able to judge all events even if we cannot originate them, and instead of looking on discussions as a stumbling block in the way of action, we think it an indispensable preliminary to any wise action at all…'.

In an unstable balance of power, Sparta controlled the land while Athens controlled the seas. Between 446-431 BCE, the two sides aligned themselves and Greece was no longer composed of 1500 small communities. A plague destroyed a large part of Athenians in 429 BCE including Pericles, who was the mastermind behind Athenian policy. Athenian religion must be seen from its origins in the religious traditions of the Dark Ages (1100-800 BCE) and attempts at institutionalization in the succeeding periods. Just as Mycenaean civilization shared the influence of pre-Greek, Indo-Europeans and Minoan cultural forms, so the gods of the classical Greek Pantheon were drawn from the same cultures. Zeus was like the Indo-European sky-god, Cretan Bull worship and pre-Greek cults. Worship of the Mother Goddess was common. Religious development included gradual absorption of practices and beliefs of the family and locality and adoption of the more rational versions of gods as presented by Homer and by Hesiod in his Theogony (account of god's origins).

Northerners brought Apollo to Delphi, where he established his oracle and then shared it with Dionysius. The god spoke through a priestess, who in a trance, answered questions asked by officials from Greek cities. Significantly this was an established practice of ancient Tamils that has remained to this day. In this, a priest or priestess invoked the god Kartikeya or even Shiva and danced continuously till in a trance the deity spoke through them in answering questions. Zeus not only exercised his thunderbolt at certain decisive moments but also dispensed good and evil fortune to each man at birth. If punishment was not visited upon man who insulted the gods, it would surely strike his progeny. But for unknowing offences, there was remedy from the gods. Hesiod's Theogony was Greek but shows some near-eastern influences.

The Greek view of man was reflected in the art and architecture of classical Greece. Greek temples had the steps of the base providing the foundation for the columns, fluted and topped with a capital, upon which vested a raised roof; inside the temple was the room in which the image of the god or goddess was kept. All temples were mostly rectangular in shape. The Erechtheum in the Acropolis was an exception. The style of the columns was varied starting with Doric Capitals as in Parthenon, but later with Ionic and Corinthian Capitals. The frieze above the columns was decorated with scenes depicting actions of gods and men, as was the space in the triangle formed by the roof. Pottery in the Dark Ages had geometric figures and later, due to Near Eastern influence, paintings of the background of the vase with complicated and realistic representations were made. Human figured sculpture was the greatest innovation. Here again the reference to Near Eastern is obviously Hindu as such paintings and sculpture were common and can be seen even today in temples of India.

Greek tragedies of Aeschylus in the 5th century BCE (*Prometheus Bound*), Sophocles and his *Ajax, Oedipus Rex*, Euripides' *Hippolytus* were all notable. Intellectuals travelled all over the world to explore and thus history started being written.

Hecataeus' *Histories* is an example. Herodotus, his successor, was considered the 'Father of History'. He considered all versions of a story, even that of opponents, as relevant. Thucydides explained history in terms of events and human motivations and actions. Thales, the philosopher scientist, rejected myth and with others, tried to find the basic substance out of which all other materials were formed. Thales thought it was water but others, air, fire or earth. Pythagoras founded the mystical sect, which believed in reincarnation and reduced reality to special units that could be understood logically and mathematically. The point, the line, and the place, were the constituents of reality.

For Heraclitus, change was the result of external motion acting according to reason (*logos*) in the universe. Parmenides extended this idea to assert that there were two separate realities- the way of truth which was external to human experience and grasped due to reason and the way of seeming or appearance which could be perceived by the senses but was a false way. This is equivalent to the Hindu statement of a rope being perceived as a snake and the truth being revealed with light that it is a rope after all. Zeno continued the Parmenides tradition of the unity of the universe by showing plurality must be limited since 'things may be just as many as they are, no more, no less. If there is plurality, the infinite number of things, for there will always be other things between the things that are, and get others between those others'. He showed that motion and change are impossible making reality immutable and at least theoretically rationally accessible to human comprehension. Other writers posited ultimate plurality. Empedocles held that the four elements were moved by love and strife. Pericles's teacher, Anaxagorus, went further and held that creation came from an infinite number of seeds containing all the elements in their diversity. Ultimately, Leucippus and Democritus combined the idea of basic material with the Pythagorean idea that reality is composed of geometrical units. They held that all things were made up of indivisible atoms and combination of these led to differences in nature. The combinations were ordered by a divine mind or were the result of chance.

In this abstract thought, Homeric and anthropomorphic gods had no place in the system. These abstract thoughts were outside the Greek educational system. Hippocratic medicine was the exception as the others had no use for society. A new group called the Sophists, offered teaching for a price and they were more interested in winning an argument by rhetoric. Hence the word sophistry came about. Aristophanes, the writer of comedy combined the two groups and made even Socrates an atheist and a sophist, which he was not. For Socrates, the world must be ordered to fulfil some moral end. He asserted that a man would not commit an act that he felt to be wrong. Evil conduct was the result of ignorance. Plato, a student of Socrates, made him the major speaker in his dialogues and as A. N. Whitehead said, 'all of western philosophy is but a series of footnotes to Plato'. In his last work *The Laws*, he put forward the best possible state with a view to put it into practice. In *The Republic*, he puts forward Socrates as saying that the human soul had a three-part nature comprising, wisdom, honour and appetite. A good democracy was not also immune to appetite. The ideal state should be governed by wisdom. Wisdom consisted of the ability to perceive the good. Knowledge involved the ultimate reality in the universe- the world of pure ideas. Reality was not contained in transitory things but in eternal forms that are outside of time and space. What exists is an imperfect reflection of its ideal form. They are but 'shadows' on the walls of a cave compared to the real, transcendent and eternal. This can only be experienced mystically by 'a flight of the soul'. This knowledge is what separates the wise man from the rest of mankind. This is the closest that Plato has come to the Hindu experience of *atmajnana* or Self Realisation.

Plato's student, Aristotle, deviated from his teacher by saying reality can be perceived by the senses. He decided that the best form of government was a mixture of the three forms- monarchy, oligarchy and democracy or the rule of one, few and the many. The goal of the state and individual was human happiness. He was for moderation as excess of pleasure results in pain. The perfect Unmoved Mover that set the universe in motion while remaining unchanged was both the originator and its justification.

These Greeks were the foundation for western culture because they were the first thinkers. (Apparently Cantor was unaware of the Ancient Hindu thinkers and their Upanishads. But in the rest of the world, Greeks and Chinese were the initial thinkers). Though Hebrew and Christian cultures tried to challenge them, they could never eradicate the Greek heritage. 'Know thyself' was the prime injunction of Greek thought, borrowed from the Upanishads of the Hindus. Plato held that the soul is temporarily held within the 'earthly frame' of the body, but it comes originally from the divine and to the divine- the very Being, the intangible essence-it will return if properly nurtured. Aristotle reflects the same idea- 'mortals should think like mortals but we should achieve immortality…Man finds the life of reason best, since in it he finds his true nature'. Aeschylus asserts that 'wisdom comes alone through suffering'. Man must not overreach himself. This becomes the central Greek view that has influenced western Christian thought.

Rome:
First century Rome had a million people, Alexandria 750,000, Athens and Marseilles 300,000 each and by 400 CE, Constantinople had 500,000. After the fall of the Roman Empire, Rome had only 100,000 people. In 1500 CE, Paris had 200,000 and London

100,000. No European city had a population of a million until 1820 CE. Cities needed water and sanitation. Garbage and excrement accumulated in the streets, and animals wandered freely and thievery was rampant. There was no public transportation.

The Parthenon of Gods in Athens was plundered by Lord Elgin and the statuary is in the British Museum. Lord Byron denounced the 'Elgin Marbles' as pillage. The word 'Elginism' then came to be coined for plunder in India and elsewhere.

The four reasons for the god-intoxication of the masses are:
1. Hydraulic despotism made the masses obey and work hard.
2. Shortness of life.
3. The education was literary that wrote about god but little about nature and economy.
4. Platonism was the dominant philosophy, which had theological speculation built into its programme.

With the decline of Phoenicians maritime control that included Carthage, the latter took its place and ruled without opposition. The Etruscans, who learned from the Greeks while fighting them, established dominion over most of Italy. They made Rome, a group of villages in the hills of Rome, a city. By 500 BCE, the Latin tribes of Rome got rid of the Etruscan monarchy and over the next two centuries, fashioned the Roman Republic. The power of the tribal assembly grew over the years and by 287 BCE, its decisions made binding law for Romans even without Senate ratification.

Roman religion centred in temples that incorporated various Latin, Etruscan and Greek religious ideas. Janus became the guardian of the gate through which the army passed and was closed in peacetime. Vesta, the goddess of the hearth, was honoured in temples where vestal virgins guarded the eternal fire. Mars, an agricultural god, now became the god of war. At the heart of Roman beliefs was devotion to one's family with worship of ancestors becoming an integral part of family life. This devotion to the family called for unquestionable devotion to the commonwealth of Rome that was the *res republica* or 'common public thing'. More than thirty tribal political groups surrounded the young Roman state. In 280 BCE, the southern Italian Greek cities invited Phyrrus of Epirus to lead an army against Rome. Though the able general won a few battles, his losses were great, and he left Rome in virtual control of the whole Peninsula. (Hence the words, 'Phyrric victory' meaning 'win the battle and lose the war' came to be in vogue).

In 264 BCE, Carthage took to war against Rome and their enmity continued till 146 BCE, when Carthage city itself was destroyed. They had fought three exhausting wars.

# Ancient Civilizations

The Punic wars (so called because of the Phoenicians who settled in Carthage) resulted in Rome developing powerful army and navy. In the second Punic war, Hannibal's brother was defeated and decapitated and the third war was the invasion of North Africa when Hannibal returned to defend Carthage, was defeated at the battle of Zama and forced to surrender. In the war against the Macedonians in 171-167 BCE, they were defeated by the Roman army. It was then divided into four states under Roman control. Rome became a formidable power and was hated in the Hellenistic world.

Romans had assimilated Greek culture and the Near East contact resulted in corruption of morals. Greek was the literary language of the age and its philosophy dominated the Roman educated class. Lucretius the greatest philosopher of the Roman Republic, adopted Greek Epicurianism in his Latin poem *On the Nature of Things*. Through his atomist view of the universe, he hoped to free man from the fetters of superstitious belief. But Stoicism had greater appeal that permitted man to rise above limitations by acceptance of trial and effort, and persevere in the face of difficulties. It was Cicero who held their respect. Cicero's ideal became the basis of European humanism. The poet Catullus (84-54 BCE) presented a counterbalance to Cicero's views of idealism, public mindedness and optimism. Catullus had both pessimism and individualism in his poems:

'The sun can set and the sun can rise again,
But as for us mortals,
When once our little day is done,
There is but one eternal night for sleeping'.

Greek law, based on equity did not demand a study of precedents and documentary evidence as did Roman law which depended on custom and tradition in addition to equity. Julius Caesar in his writings, tells us much about his views on the job in his 'Commentaries' (of the conquest of Gaul). Plautus followed Aristophanes in his slapstick that was followed by Rabelais and Shakespeare. Terence followed Menander for his new Comedy. These were more subtle than the bawdy works of Plautus. Cato the elder (234-149 BCE) represented the anti-imperial and even xenophobic strain in Rome. Polybius had the opposite impulse in Roman life. He was a Greek who wrote Roman history. He evolved the concept of humanitus- brotherhood of all men- an important legacy from Rome's conquest of the Mediterranean world. Conquest put a great strain on Rome to digest all they had swallowed.

**References:**
1. Antiquity- the Civilization of the Ancient World- Norman F. Cantor, Harper Collins'
2. Vedic Tradition- Ramakrishnan Srinivasan, Bhavan's Book University Series, 2000.
3. Science, Philosophy, and Religion-Ramakrishnan Srinivasan, Citadel, 2008.
4. Hindu America- Lal, Chaman, New York, 1951

# CHAPTER 17

# THE PROBLEM OF RELIGIONS

There are five warning signs of corruption in a religion and these are absolute truth claims, blind obedience, establishing the ideal time, end justifying means and declaration of holy war. These corruptions are the cause of all world conflicts. In fact more than a billion people have been killed in the name of religion in the Americas (both north and south), Europe, Asia, Africa, Australia and other places. There need to be reforms in religions if they have to survive in the future.

All religions preach acts of love, self-sacrifice, and service to others. In fact these three require no religion. It is sadly true that more wars have been waged, more people killed and more evil perpetrated in the name of religion than by any other institutional force in human history. We cannot have a quarrel with Islam but only with some of the followers and their wrong or negative interpretation of the religion. When devout adherents of religions claim their vision as the 'true' way and everything else is false, problems arise. This applies to all faiths. Many of the interactions between and among the various descendents of Abraham represent many of the most dangerous flashpoints on the planet. For these religions, a strong missionary impulse is central that have advocated narrow exclusivism.

All religions claim revelation. If these revelations are contrary to each other, all of them cannot be taken as revelation and only one could be the true revelation if at all. Since the oldest revelation is in the Hindu Tradition, those other revelations can be considered valid to the extent that they do not contradict the Hindu revelation. The Vedas are said to be beginning-less (*anaadi*) because they are considered as the breath of Brahman, the Infinite Universal Consciousness. What we would notice in this book is that the Hindu Tradition is what is reflected in all other religions. This needs to be studied carefully before any conclusions are reached. What is required is a common set of beliefs that are benign and non-destructive and that can help people live peacefully as one family. All humans owe their origins to a common source and that is why the Hindus call the entire human race as *Vasudeiva kutumbakam* or the family of Vasudeva or the infinite Brahman. Religions are presently divisive and if they could be reformed to form common minimum principles, humanity may yet survive.

# Vedic Tradition and World Religions

One way suggested by this author is for people to practise their religions in their homes or places of worship and outside of these, religions should have no place in human interaction and all people should move as brothers and sisters. This is because religion is something personal and need not interfere with human interaction. It is spirituality or religiousness rather than any religion that is important. This requires virtuous living as all religions commonly proclaim. There is only one Supreme power, call it what you may- Brahman, Atman, Allah, Consciousness or God. As the Hindus say- *ekam sat vipra bahuda vadanti* or the Truth is one but called differently by the many. Spirituality is independent of any religion. It helps to connect the individual with the world outside and with the infinite, considering all as equal. Since the source of the three Abrahamic religions- Judaism, Christianity, and Islam are basically very similar one cannot see why there should be any conflict at all between them. If we understand that what makes one person walk or talk is the same for all living beings, there will not be any conflict. This power is variously called the Brahman, Atman, soul and so on without which no life is possible.

It is for this objective that Prof Kimbal and many others including this author, have taken it upon themselves to effect a common approach for coexistence among different religious followers. This author has studied the various religions of the world from ancient to modern and has tried to find the common denominators in them so that they could be the basis for universal peace. Of course this also requires universal education without which superstition and blind faith will only rule. The purpose of religion is to regulate a community with ethical and moral value systems so that the community is protected. In 1 CE, the population of the world was about 250,000 according to Aldous Huxley. People in different areas were hunter gatherers and civilization and culture developed later on in a gradual way. Groups of people in different areas were keen to protect themselves from invaders and for this they needed certain rules to unite them. That is why worship of nature led to the concept of god or a higher power ruling everybody came up. It started with the idea of good being rewarded and evil being punished. Religions must have originated in this way.

There is no reason at all for human conflict if the main teachings of Jesus, Mohammad, Buddha or the Hindus are collected together and a new universal religion established, if at all necessary, so that mankind can all live as brothers and sisters as indeed they are since the soul is common to all. One of the major causes for religious discord in recent times is the disparity in wealth. While the rich have become richer, the poor have become poorer. So, clearly economics plays an important part in this process. The world economies should try to address this issue in a concerted way so that such discord goes away. Human greed is a definite contributor for such discord. Of course

## The Problem of Religions

many explanations can be given for this but the bottom line is the assurance of a minimum standard of living for all humanity. After this, if the rich become richer it may not be an issue. Education of all people should be available at no cost or minimum cost at least to the high school level. This will also help in the control of population growth.

The basic question an educated person will ask is this- who is a Christian? Protestant, Catholic, Mormon or the scores of other denominations? Or again, who is a Moslem? Shia, Sunni, Bahai, or other groups? Obviously all of them cannot claim to belong to the same Christian or Moslem religion. If there are no differences between them, why are there so many different churches or mosques? Also each one cannot claim to be the true Christian or Moslem. This issue too needs to be addressed among the respective religious heads. If there is only one Christian or Moslem faith the problems are reduced. Shias and Sunnis kill each other in Iraq, Pakistan and elsewhere. While discussing such matters, one should not get emotionally involved as the problem is universal and needs a solution.

It is not whether religion is the problem or not. Religions may continue to give succour to some people because the majority is not adequately educated and therefore need this succour. But what is needed is to keep religion confined within one's home or place of worship and otherwise live with people in the outside world without religion interfering with their intercourse. The horde mentality is common to man and this can only be corrected by universal education and providing the means for a decent standard of living to all. The rich, be it the nation or the individual, has to play a pro-active role in this. The greed for wealth should be balanced with a will to share and care with the less fortunate, not necessarily by giving aid but by starting free schools, offering scholarships and other means of providing a better life for all.

The Koran affirms that all humans are accountable to god on the last Day of Judgment. Hebrew and Christian Gospels also affirm this. The problem is that both Islam and Christianity developed into a civilizational system with many dimensions. Different schools and sectarian groups in various parts of the world have effectively diluted their appeal causing clashes and discords. The Sufis are the most benign of the groups but their number is small. They draw attention to the inner meaning of religions and in particular, Islam. The same applies to the Christian sectarian divisions and the schisms among the followers. It is clear that these sects have been formed for promoting individual or group interest at the cost of other groups or the interest of the common people. Mohammad's nephew Ali's followers broke away to form the Shia group, who do not owe allegiance to the Caliphate. Again in the treatment of women, much has been said. If we look at the dress code, we can understand that in the desert conditions where there are sand storms, the full body coverage is necessitated for all men and women. This is not a religious requirement but has been made as one. Similarly Mohammad allowing four wives was due to the much fewer males available due to wars. Where the gender ratio is even, the justification for many wives will be at the cost of other men. Islam actually recommends only one wife otherwise. All these can change if there is universal modern education to one and all.

The law of causation of the Hindus suggests that good will beget good and evil will beget evil. One has to face the consequences of one's action. That is why people are advised to do good and lead a virtuous life. Truth is only one and hence everyone has to live with this truth. Religion is a lived reality. The lines separating Hindus and Buddhists or Jews, Christians, and Moslems frequently turn out to be poorly defined and are flexible. The cosmic struggle between good and evil, god and the devil, Ahura Mazda and Ahriman, angels and demons, heaven and hell are all reflected in religions in one way or another. They became important features of these religions. Clear linkages can be found between traditions that cannot always be explained by the geographical proximity or movement of peoples.

All the three Abrahamic religions consider the Israel/Palestine region to be their Holy land because of the events associated with biblical characters and the Prophet Mohammad. Jews believe Jerusalem to be their religious centre as it was established by King David 3000 years ago. They revere the Temple Mount, the site of the Temple that was destroyed by Babylonians in 587 BCE and again by the Roman army in 70 CE. Christians incorporate the sacred stories of the Hebrew Bible besides considering Jerusalem sacred due to the Passion Narration, the Gospel accounts of Jesus' final week, Crucifixion and Resurrection on Easter Sunday morning.

Moslems also recognize Biblical figures and stories as part of God's revelation through prophets and messengers. Jerusalem is their third sacred city as they believe that Mohammad was transported miraculously to Jerusalem, where he prayed with the prophets of old at Masjid al Aqsa and a few feet away from there, Mohammad ascended into heaven for a vision of Paradise. The Dome of the Rock marks this site. Jews believe this site to be the Mt. Mo'nah, where Abraham was preparing to sacrifice his son. The stories among the descendents of Abraham show the three religions as similar and the differences rather discrete. They are based on the foundational affirmations of the same god. There are also common characterisation between these religions that share the same basic teachings. They all distinguish between the religious and the profane. Hindus, Buddhists, Shinto and Native American religions have their parallel sacred stories. All the traditions have the key stages of human life (birth, coming of age, initiation, marriage and death) with similar rituals. The life-

# The Problem of Religions

cycle rituals are different but definable. They all have a saviour figure that will usher in a new age, either here or in a heavenly realm. In the Bhagwad Gita, it is stated that when the society is corrupted with violation of accepted customs and anarchy prevails, god will reincarnate again and again to re-establish dharma. This idea is talked about differently by other religions. One religion is not the same from one century to another or from one continent to the other or from one town to another. This is because interpretations differ from people to people. This diversity exists within a religious community and also within each member of that community. This is true of all religions.

By the same token, all religions cannot be taken as equally valid. Those that have stood the test of time have worked for those that embraced them we need freedom of religion and also freedom from religion that others may impose on those who differ. Abraham Herschel, while speaking on 'no religion is an island' said- 'the history of Christianity contains considerably more violence and destruction than that of most other religions. Church history also exposes repeatedly the gap between the ideal exemplified in the teachings of Jesus and the way Christians have lived and actually behaved. Gandhi believed in the words of Jesus and thought that many Christians and the Christian civilization contradicted Jesus' teachings. The rigid exclusivism embodied in the view that "Christianity is the only truth" is the foundation for a tribalism that will not serve us in the 21st century. Parallel positions can be found in Islam and to a lesser extent in other major religions. ...we are all involved with one another. Spiritual betrayal on the part of one of us affects the faith of all of us...the religions of the world are no more self-sufficient, no more independent, and no more isolated than individuals or nations...'.

Many view religion as a dangerous anachronism. The case of Galileo and Bruno and many others showcases the Christian intolerance to science. Huston Smith in his *Why religions Matter* says- 'The religious sense recognizes intrinsically that the ultimate questions human beings ask- what is the meaning of existence? Why are there pain and death? Why, in the end, is life worth living? What does reality consist of and what is its object?- are the defining essence of our humanity. These questions are the determining substance of what makes human beings human...the conviction that the questions have answers never wavers, and this keeps us from giving up on them'.

At the heart of the religious orientation and quest, human beings find meaning and hope. In their origins and core teachings, religions may be noble, but how they develop almost invariably falls short of the ideal. The propensity towards evil in the Gospel starts with Cain murdering his brother Abel. Moses lashes out and kills an Egyptian. King David's lust for a married woman makes him send her husband to certain death in battle. The apostle Paul confesses his struggle to overcome selfish and sinful behaviour to do what is right. He says-'I can will what is right, but I cannot do it. For I do not do the good I want, but the evil I do not want is what I do' (Romans 7:18b-19). Mob mentality and group dynamics can fragment individual consciousness. Pontius Pilate could not find anything wrong with Jesus but the mob cried out 'crucify him' and he acquiesced. The Mailai mob in Vietnam is another such instance. Such behaviour is powerful and blind religious bigotry is akin to nationalism. They are sometimes intertwined.

When questioned about the greatest commandment, Jesus said -'Love your god the Lord with all your heart and soul and with all your mind. The second commandment is to love your neighbour as yourself'. All religions say the same thing. When group behaviour towards others is violent and destructive, the religion is corrupted and reform is needed. When religions remain true to their authentic sources, it is dismantling its corruptions. The main problem with many such religions is the claim of absolute truth. If the claim of one religion is taken as valid for absolute truth, it would mean that the other religions are not true. Obviously all of them cannot be true unless they are talking of the same truth; in which case there is no need for so many religions in the first place. Religious truths are never inflexible and exclusive in nature. They are rather based on ethical living than anything else. Corrupt religious truths lack this liberating awareness. The genuine questions that arise in the mind are: why was Jesus' self- sacrifice necessary? Why do the four Gospels differ significantly in the recounting of this sacred story? What happened on Good Friday and subsequent days? What was accomplished and how? Does everyone benefit or only the ones god has chosen? The basic truths in religion include presuppositions and require interpretations. Anything that requires interpretation cannot be an absolute truth. All the religions say 'do not kill'. This does not require interpretation. But when a rider is added to it, it becomes subject to interpretation. The most heinous crime in Islam is 'shirk' (associating something with god). God is one and alone. There is no question of association with god when every living being has god in him without which one cannot talk or walk or live. If you say the eyes see and the ears hear, the dead body has both but can neither see nor hear because the 'life' is gone from it. He or she becomes it. So these sense objects are animated by the presence of the soul that departs at death. This is called consciousness, soul, atman and so on by different people but signifying the life principle in all living beings. This is the essence of Hindu teaching that is common to all religions. That is why the Hindu says that god is within all beings and that the whole universe is a small part or manifestation of the Infinite Brahman. Brahman is pure energy and nothing is real outside of this Brahman.

# The Problem of Religions

Christians associate Jesus, a human being with god or as the son of god. They are not the same. Then they have the doctrine of the Trinity. Moslems also have differed in the interpretation of the Koran, the Hadith and the opinions of their legal scholars. Such divisions lead to fragmentation within the religions. Christianity now includes thousands of officially recognized churches worldwide with their own denominations. Differences in interpretations of truth have distorted them. The problem arises when zealous adherents elevate the teachings in their tradidions to the level of absolute truths. It is then that the religion becomes corrupt leading to violent extremism. The Christian extremism is exemplified by Michael Griffin, an anti-abortionist, who killed Dr David Gunn outside an abortion clinic in Pensacola, Florida on March 10, 1993. Later Rev. Paul Hill justified this and killed Dr John Britton and his companion James Barrett at the same clinic on July 29, 1994. They are part of the organization, Army of God, a Christian extremist group. They strung together few of the sayings in the Bible (Psalm, Jeremiah etc.) to justify their beliefs. The sixth commandment 'you shall not murder' has no meaning for them. They break this commandment to murder those considered guilty of murder (abortion).

The Abrahamic religions describe god as omnipotent, omniscient, and omnipresent. If so, ask some, why does he not know and prevent evil? This cannot be divine justice as some people make out. It makes a mockery of civil society with its laws. There cannot be a god for one group and another for another group. If god is omnipresent, it has to be one for all, irrespective of religions. No religion can claim god to be its property to the exclusion of other religions as it defeats the purpose for which the god concept was created. In reality, god as a concept may be at best a convenient way in the path to spirituality. That is all.

Islamic understanding that Allah is the god that Christianity and Judaism also worship then it is good if they bury their differences and live in peace with each other. But in reality they are always in conflict. God has spoken through many prophets and messengers for the benefit of mankind. If the god of Christianity or Islam or Judaism is the only ones, then does it mean that there was no god before these religions came into being? If there is to be a god he must have existed for ever and must be the same for all. He created the universe and its diversity and hence common to all humanity. Some Christian groups like the Southern Baptist Convention made derogatory remarks about Islam and other religions. Bailey Smith, their then president, announced that god does not hear prayers of the Jews. According to him, prayers not uttered in the name of Jesus simply cannot get through to god. How did god hear the prayer of Abraham, Moses and David? Peter the apostle, admitted that his understanding of god was quite narrow. It is the lack of such understanding that generates negative and dogmatic men to create divisions and conflicts in the world.

Abuse of sacred texts can be found everywhere. Nichiren, the founder of a school in Japan, thought that Lotus Sutra was the only genuine sacred text of Buddhism. He claimed that anyone who killed a slanderer of Dharma will not suffer karma's consequences. This is against Buddhist teachings. Shakespeare had said that 'even the devil can quote scriptures for his purpose'. The Koran makes it clear that the faithful who die 'striving in the way of god' go immediately to Pradise. This has been taken up by Al Quida, Hizbullah and other groups to recruit poor, illiterate young boys to train as suicide bombers and these poor children believe that they are going to heaven by blowing themselves to death! Interpretation of many provisions in the Koran like 2:190-91, are made for killing. While interpreting other provisions in the Koran, like in the Hadith (against any form of suicide) alternative interpretations too should be considered. Truth claims based on selective readings of texts lead to corruption in religions. Judaism is a non-proselytising religion and such problems are fewer.

Koran is in Arabic and should be read in it. That too the original text should be the authority. Translations are but interpretations and hence could be dangerous. Jews however, have a long history of critical inquiry on the Torah and its truth claims. Robert Aller in his The Art of Biblical Narrative, states that 'narrative literature, was conceived as a process, requiring continual revision- both in the ordinary sense and in the etymological sense of seeing again- continual suspension of judgment, weighing of multiple possibilities, brooding over gaps in information provided'. The misuse of sacred texts in many forms should not obscure the fact that the texts have been a source of strength, inspiration and guidance for people in many cultures for more than three millennia. Unlike faithful Hindus, Buddhists, Taoists, Jews or Shintoists, Christians and Moslems are expected to carry the good news and the call to faith. They agree that their faiths have a missionary mandate. But cultural imperialism and military power have destroyed any witness to god's love and mercy. This missionary related abuse has been witnessed all over Europe, Africa, the Americas and other areas. Franciscans believe that cultural conversion is a prelude to religious conversion. These people could benefit from the words of Jesus-'do unto others what you would have them do unto you; for this is the law of the prophets' (Matthew 7:12). And the Koran also has the message-'There can be no compulsion in matters of religion'. Both religions emphasize that the love of god is manifest in the ways people relate to others and that they are accountable on the Day of Judgment.

Blind obedience to religious dogma is one of the problems that has been at the back of terrorism these days. The case of Asahara Shoko who started a movement

## The Problem of Religions

in Japan trained his followers to release nerve gas in sixteen central Tokyo subway stations, killing twelve people and injuring more than five thousand. His sect Aum Shinrikyo had about ten thousand followers in Japan and about 30,000 in Russia. His teachings called for blind obedience. At this point, religion becomes evil. All religions have numbers of sects within them. Asahara wanted to create a utopia called Shambala, using Shiva as his god. This was mischievous since Shiva stood as the Creator, preserver and destroyer and pervaded the entire universe according to Hindus. He is equated with Brahman. Similar was the case with James Warren Jones of Indiana. While he was a Christian of the Pentacostal sect, he branched off from his own People's Temple in which blind obedience was called for. In the jungles of Guyana, 914 bloated corpses were sprawled in a clearing, a case of mass suicide of this sect by receiving a deadly potion (November 18, 1978). All this is due to a false interpretation of religious texts. The main reason that drives such people is illiteracy of poor peasants who fall prey to such sects. Such people become slaves to religious doctrines that are the interpretations of some sect leaders. In fact, illiteracy is the single major cause for such atrocities in the world.

The seventeenth century figures Nathan of Gaza and Shabbutai Zevi started a movement by turning inside out some Jewish teachings. Zevi was later arrested in Constantinople and given the option of death or conversion to Islam and he chose the latter. Similar people are found in the Shia sect, the Assassins, who terrorized Syria and Persia in the 11th to 13th centuries. This group also spread its wings in Europe. Christian sermons in support of slavery or apartheid were equally dangerous. The problem arises when questions are disallowed by these sects. Authentic religions always encourage questions and reflections at all levels.

Classical Hinduism (the oldest in the world) includes a world affirming and world renouncing approach at the same time. Correctly understood, this refers to the *varnashrama dharma* which gives four stages for a man's life- childhood, as a student, householder who brings up a family, *vanaprastha* that calls for relinquishing household duties to the son and spending time in contemplation in the old age. The fourth stage is optional- *sannyasa* or asceticism and this is optional as it requires rigorous austerities and practice. This is a structured system in which a person passes through the stages of education, family life, and after settling the children, leaves home to contemplate in a secluded place for spiritual upliftment and final release.

David Koresh and his Branch Davidians in the nineties, Marshall Applewhite and his Heaven's Gate are all similar where Armageddon and the end of the world concept resulted in the conflagration and death of scores of men and children. The latter, a group of 39 men and women willingly 'exited their bodies' in March 1997. In all this the apocalyptic teaching was involved, with disaster waiting to happen. 'Religious traditions teach that ultimate meaning is both connected to and transends physical existence in this world'. The law of karma for the Hindus and Buddhists and the Day of Judgment for the Abrahamic religions are pointers to the scientific truth that action and reaction are equal and opposite (Newton's third law of motion).

Hindus insist on individual emancipation by *sadhana*. Buddha also told his followers in his final advice- 'Do not accept what you hear by report, do not accept tradition, do not accept any statement because it is found in our books, nor because it is in accord with your belief, nor because it is the saying of your teacher…Be ye lamps unto yourselves…Those who, either now or after I am dead, shall rely upon themselves only and not look for assistance to anyone besides themselves, it is they who shall reach the very topmost height'.

It would be we find the practice of terrorism among the Jews too. On January 26, 1984, two Jewish extremists were confronted by Palestinian guards near the Dome of the Rock and Al Aqsa Mosque, carrying bags of explosives. This thwarted a detailed plan to blow up Islamic buildings. The two men were arrested. This later revealed an extensive underground movement within Israel that had plans for an Israeli pilot to steal a military jet and bomb the Dome. Ehuda Etzion was convicted in 1995 and sentenced to 20 years in prison. He had admitted to the plan. So far there have been twelve efforts to destroy the Dome and the Mosque or to wound or kill Moslem worshippers at the site, considered sacred by Jews and Moslems alike. It envisioned the rebuilding of the Jewish Temple on the site that Moslems call Haram-ash-Sharif (noble sanctuary), where Islamic structures occupied. Both Jewish and Christian groups visualize a day when the third Jewish Temple will rise again from the sacred Temple Mount. This hope is connected with some passages in the Bible associated with the messianic cage and will signal the coming of the Messiah. This is related to the second coming of Christ, a cataclysmic battle at Armageddon and a thousand year reign of peace. Such a vision also exists in Islam after the Day of Judgment. The three religions expect the coming of Christ but with separate agendas. The American peace efforts are also clouded by the conflagration anticipated by Christians and Jews. Even the Sermon on the Mount of Jesus seems to fall on deaf ears; 'Blessed are the peacemakers for they shall be called the children of God' (Matthew 5:9).

By a quirk of fate, the United States has encouraged many dictators who became their enemies later on. Saddam Hussein, Gaddafi, Zia and others are examples. They are still supporting the Wahabis and we do not know when this will change. Real democracy has not been seen in any Moslem country though Mohammad was in its favour and against monarchy. The western image of Islam as unsophisticated and anti-intellectual was faulty. During the Dark Ages, Muslims led the world in many areas of science from Spain to India. But a division within the Islamic sects led to their decline from the 16-20$^{th}$ centuries. Moslem rule was occasionally benevolent but mostly troubled by internal strife and ruthless dictators. Human rights issues are quite common in these states. Political reform has been mostly non-existent. While the vast majority of Moslems reject violent extremism, mostly the populace shares the frustrations that fuel the movements such as Al Qaida. There is no definite vision of how an Islamic state is to be established. The rapaciousness of dictators is legendary. Civil war in Algeria is another example. If a state is tied to a particular religious tradition, it will relegate some of its citizens to second or third class status. Israel and Pakistan are examples.

In the United States, Christian groups making up the new religious right are committed to change laws and government structures in the light of Biblical ideals. They work against abortion, homosexuality and gun control and for prayer in schools, capital punishment and so on, on the basis of family values. Efforts by Pat Robertson and others have been rapid with sophistication. Where all this will lead to, is not clear now. 'Beware of people and groups whose political blueprint is based on a mandate from heaven that depends on human beings to implement' says Kimball.

The holocaust of Nazis was not due to Christian belief, (though tacitly supported by the Pope), but the product of a long and deplorable history of Christian behaviour towards the Jews. Jesus and his disciples were Jews and Paul was a zealous Jew who saw the Christian movement as a threat before he had a dramatic experience of conversion near Damascus. After Constantine, many Christian leaders like John Chrysostom, Bishop of Antioch, defined Christian identity in sharp contrast to the Jews and the vitriolic incrimination of Jews led directly to attacks on Synagogues. Beginning with the Crusades (for which a pope has apologized), brutal assaults on Jews and their communities occurred systematically throughout Europe and the Nazi Holocaust was only the natural culmination of this. This is a definite black spot on Christians that cannot be erased. Jesus' teachings by Hillel are an authentic guide to religion. We need to build on this balance in the world. In Tunisia (98% Moslem) and Iran, women have equal opportunity in education and public life. Many women are elected to the Majlis in Iran. In fact the western countries are lagging behind in this respect. But practices such as female genital mutilation, honour killings, not allowing male fighters and paramedics in girl's schools during fire etc., are obnoxious and they need to reform such practices. Saudi Arabia is the worst offender in gender discrimination but the United States continues to prop up that regime. The war in Yugoslavia saw atrocities like organized rape, looting, arson, forced expulsions and so on.

Jesus, Buddha and Mohammad were always available for their followers for clarifications on issues bothering them. But despite the Vatican, Catholic priests have been indulging in paedophilic activities for the past three decades or more and in recent times the Vatican paid $ 168 billion as compensation in a settlement in the United States. Such sexual abuse is still common in India. The treatment of scientists and others as heretics and burning them in the stakes during the fourth century and after is well known. In 1492, King Ferdinand and Queen Isabella of Spain decreed that the Jews had four months to convert or leave the country. About 40,000 Jews fled and the others converted. This was part of the Inquisition that continued in France and elsewhere. The Joan of Arc case is still fresh in our memory. By the 19th century, the Inquisition died out but its office existed till 1965, when Pope Paul VI changed the institution to the office of the Congregation for the Doctrine of the Faith. In October 1998, Pope John Paul II ordered a secret scrutiny of the Inquisition in the Vatican archives.

In most cases, the end was dictated by the few zealots and the means used were justified later on. When Jesus was challenged on picking heads of wheat to heal, he replied aptly-'The Sabbath was made for humankind and not humankind for the Sabbath'. He meant that the means are more important than the ends. Mohammad did a lot for the status of women and their rights like forbidding female infanticide and the need to provide for widows, orphans, the poor and the needy. Gandhi showed that non-violence can achieve great results as was shown in South Africa and India and did not allow the goals to be in conflict with the means.

The Abrahamic religions that claim that peace is at the heart of their faiths are the ones that cause such deaths. Jesus had said that 'all who take the sword will perish by the sword'. This is proving to be true even today. Paul talked of love and reconciliation but this fell on deaf ears. Before the 4th century, Christians seldom took to war as it was incompatible with Christianity and life was sacred to them. Their god prohibited killing even in a just cause. Their 'weapons were prayer, justice and suffering'. But since the time of Constantine, wars and killings in the name of religion were common. The Dark Ages were a chaotic era in which religious views were intertwined with military campaigns against Visigoths, Vandals, Franks, Saxons, Norse, Slavs, Berbers and others. Saxons were converted by force and Charlemagne fought against 'Pagans and infidels' with Papal blessing. Even the clergy engaged in battle.

## The Problem of Religions

Jihad literally means 'striving in the way of god'. It is only a small minority that talks of the 'holy war' as jihad. Peace can only be established if authentic religions followed the path laid out by their Prophets. More importantly conversions should be stopped and it should at best be voluntary. Also, religion should be a personal matter and so kept as such. The common values of all religions should be followed. Some of these are:

- Do not kill.
- Be compassionate.
- Be charitable.
- Be truthful.
- Live a life of virtue.
- Care and share.
- Lead a moral life.
- Be kind to animals.
- Love all beings.

These can be found in all religions we have studied in this book. If a common universal religion cannot be worked out under the aegis of the United Nations, countries should at least pledge to live without conflict and work towards the betterment of their citizens. The most important action that will stem the rot is to make education compulsory and free until the high school level in all countries.

Albert Einstein made a relevant point-'The significant problems we face cannot be solved at the same level of thinking we were at when we created them'. This is because civilization has progressed technologically since the Dark Ages and we need to think anew by making such changes as may be necessary in our beliefs. Since everyone agrees that there is only one god, people must be allowed to reach that god in their own chosen ways. Huston Smith wrote: 'The reality that excites and fulfills the Soul's longing is god by whatsoever name. Because the human mind cannot come within light years of comprehending god's nature, we do well to follow Rainer Marie Rilke's suggestion that we think of god as a direction rather than an object'. While faith and hope are basic to humans, love is by far the highest quality that each being is also born with. Once we learn to share our love with others the world will surely become a better place.

Hindu, Buddhist and Jewish traditions are long established non-exclusivist approaches to religious diversity. Corruption in these religions is more an exception than a rule and arise more due to reactions to excesses from other religions. Hindu and Buddhist traditions are pluralistic, the latter being more of an offshoot of the former.

The Koran says 'believe in the One God and his messages. Jesus, the son of Mary is only a messenger of God'. 'O people of the Book, let us come to a common word between us and you, that we worship none but God, and that we associate nothing with Him, and that none of us take others for lords apart from God' (3:64).

Christian exclusivism is a major problem that the Church should address. The Book of Job and Paul's Apostle to the Romans, readily concede that no one knows the mind of God. Only inclusivist position by the Church, recognizing the activity of God in all religious traditions will give a solution. While most of the religions have taken their basic teachings from the Hindu scriptures, especially the Upanishads, the pluralist quality of the teachings has not been taken by them. The various religious traditions are but 'different responses to the one divine reality', according to John Hick. Similar sentiments can be seen from Wilfred Cantwell Smith, Diana Eck and other pluralists. But all religious leaders and governments must work together and answer 'what is to be done' by a pro-active engagement to see all humanity as a family and as sons and daughters of the One God. The Hindus talk of this as *Vasudeiva kutumbakam* or the family of God.

## References:
1. When Religion becomes Evil- Charles Kimball, Harper Collins
2. The God Delusion- Richard Dawkins.
3. Science, Philosophy and Religion- Ramakrishnan Srinivasan, Citadel.
4. Why I am Not a Christian- Bertrand Russell, Allen and Unwin.
5. War and Peace in the World's religions- John Ferguson.
6. Why Religion Matters- Huston Smith.

# CHAPTER 18

# INTELLIGENT DESIGN VS CREATIONISM

This is easily one of the most debated subjects among scientists and scholars in recent times. This debate between the theory of Intelligent Design and Creationism has been going on for more than two centuries. Evolutionists decry both and say ID is modified creationism, in which god makes a presence. Richard Dawkins, with his theory of Atheism, is a vocal speaker for the denial of a creator god and Daniel Dennett is another supporter of Dawkins. The point most of these scientists and scholars miss is that there is no dispute at all if they look at available evidence. Let us look at some of this.

All their arguments are based on the Big Bang theory which is said to have created our universe. But scientific evidence points to the existence of other universes (multi-verse) and ours is only one among them. So the Big Bang is not a one off spontaneous event but rather an event that goes on all the time repeatedly in cycles. Galaxies and stars are known to collide with each other and among themselves, creating newer galaxies or stars. The universe or the multi-verses seem to be expanding all the time and distances are mind-boggling, making one think in terms of their physical reality itself. We know about infinity. If space is infinite as it appears to be, what is beyond space is a question that cannot be answered at all. So the tautological question remains as there cannot be an answer. As Socrates has said, 'The wisest know how little they know', we can only admire what we cannot know as Goethe famously said. Both the ID proponents and the evolutionists should learn to accept what cannot be known at this point of time and at the present state of scientific inquiry.

Another point made by an author who is a member of the Christian clergy, is that which refers to the Christian religion. He quotes Einstein-'Science without religion is lame and religion without science is blind'. Here, what religion signifies is not the Christian, Judaic, Islamic or other religions but spirituality. This should be clear from Einstein's another statement, 'The finest emotion of which we are capable is the mystic emotion. Herein lies the germ of all art and all true sciences. Anyone to whom this feeling is alien, who is no longer capable of wonderment and lives in a state of fear is a dead man. To know that what is impenetrable for us really exists and manifests itself as the highest wisdom and the most radiant beauty, whose gross forms are alone intelligible to our poor faculties- this knowledge, this feeling- that is the core of the true religious sentiment. In this sense, and in this sense alone, I rank myself among profoundly religious men'.

We have seen from Heisenberg's uncertainty principle or Godel's theorem, that nothing can be a certainty as it changes the moment we care to observe it. The cat experiment is a typical example. We can modify the statements of Kant and Descartes and say-'I am and because of it, the world exists'. So existence itself is a subject decided by our being alive. Consequently, organized religions have no place in civilized society except as a personal faith. Religiousness or spirituality is however important as Einstein has emphasized. But this is referring to a life of virtue, mutual respect and so on as the Hindu tradition and the Greeks have repeatedly affirmed.

One important fact has not been considered by Carlisle in his long book. He refers often to Greek philosophy and how it has influenced Christianity. But, Greek philosophy itself owes its origin to Hindu philosophy. Details on this subject are found in other chapters of the present book. The British campaign of disinformation by introducing the fictitious Aryan Invasion theory was specially aimed at covering up the ideas of original Hindu Seers by making it a product of white Aryans, whereas Aryans are clearly native to India. This matter has been dealt with in detail by this author in his book *History of Ancient India* the 2nd edition of which has now beeen published by SriSri Publications and available globally. So, let us look at the Hindu position on the subject under study.

The Nasadiya Sukta the Creation Hymn in the Rig Veda, the oldest extant text in the world that has come to us by a long line of oral tradition, states that in the beginning there was nothing and all was dark. To quote:

नासदासींनोसदासीत्तदानीं नासीद्रजो नो व्योमापरो यत् ।
किमावरीव: कुहकस्यशर्मन्नभ: किमासीद्गहनं गभीरम् ॥१॥

Then even nothingness was not, nor existence,
There was no air then, nor the heavens beyond it.
What covered it? Where was it? In whose keeping
Was there then cosmic water, in depths unfathomed?

न मृत्युरासीदमृतं न तर्हि न रात्र्या।आन्ह।आसीत् परकेत: ।
आनीदवातं स्वधया तदेकं तस्मादद्धान्यन्नपर: कचिनास ॥२॥

Then there was neither death nor immortality
Nor was there then the torch of night and day.

## Intelligent Design Vs Creationism

The One breathed windlessly and self-sustaining.
There was that One then, and there was no other.

तम॒ आ॒सी᳐त्तम॑सा गू॒ळ्हमग्रे॑ प्रके॒तं स॑लि॒लं सर्व॑मा॒ इदम् ।
तु॒च्छ्येना᳐भ्वपि॑हितं॒ यदासी᳐त्तप॑स॒स्तन्म॑हि॒ना जा॑यतैकम् ॥३॥

At first there was only darkness wrapped in darkness.
All this was only unillumined water.
That One which came to be, enclosed in nothing,
Arose at last, born of the power of heat.

काम॒स्तदग्रे॒ सम॑वर्त॒ताधि॒ मन॑सो॒ रेतः॑ प्रथ॒मं यदासी᳐त् ।
स॒तोबन्धु॒मस॑ति॒ निर॑विन्द॒न् हृ॒दि प्र॒तीष्या॑ क॒वयो॑ मनी॒षा ॥४॥

In the beginning desire descended on it -
That was the primal seed, born of the mind.
The sages who have searched their hearts with wisdom
Know that which is, is kin to that which is not.

ति॒र॒श्चीनो॒ वित॑तो र॒श्मिरे॑षाम॒धः स्वि॑दासी॒ ३ दुपरि॑ स्विदासी᳐त् ।
रे॒तो॒धा आ॑स॒न्महि॒मान॑ आसन्त्स्व॒धा आ॒वस्ता᳐त्प्रय॑तिः प॒रस्ता᳐त् ॥५॥

And they have stretched their cord across the void,
And know what was above, and what below.
Seminal powers made fertile mighty forces.
Below was strength, and over it was impulse.

को अ॒द्धा वे॑द॒ क इ॒ह प्र वो॑चत् कुत॒ आजा॑ता॒ कुत॑ इ॒यं विसृ॑ष्टिः ।
अ॒र्वाग्दे॒वा अ॒स्य वि॒सर्ज॑ने॒नाथा॒ को वे॑द॒ यत॑ आब॒भूव ॥६॥

But, after all, who knows, and who can say
Whence it all came, and how creation happened?
The gods themselves are later than creation,
So who knows truly whence it has arisen?

इ॒यं विसृ॑ष्टि॒र्यत॑ आब॒भूव॒ यदि॑ वा द॒धे यदि॑ वा॒ न ।
यो अ॒स्याध्य॑क्षः पर॒मे व्यो॑म॒न्त्सो अ॒ङ्ग वे॑द॒ यदि॑ वा॒ न वेद॑ ॥७॥

Whence all creation had its origin,
He, whether he fashioned it or whether He did not,
He, who surveys it all from highest heaven,
He knows - or maybe even He does not know.

They did not say anything about other universes since they did not have the scientific tools to know about multi-verses. So they made the best speculation they could imagine. Later on the Upanishads clarified this matter as follows: The only existing matter is energy and everything else is illusory. The universe that we see with its stars and galaxies, living and non-living beings, is but a manifestation of this Universal Energy or Brahman. Life being cyclical like the universe itself, life and the universe end with their merging with the Brahman and a new universe is created. This idea is the closest that comes to the latest astronomical evidence on multi-verses. Stars are being created all the time while other stars are burning out and swallowed by the black holes. The same thing is happening with the universes. They are being created anew while older ones disappear, perhaps into other universes. Einstein's formula on energy, $E=mc2$ suggests the same idea that everything is energy and life and matter are but manifestations of this energy.

This is the philosophy of the Upanishads that has been borrowed by the Greek philosophers besides science, mathematics, medicine and other subjects of knowledge and which paved the way for western philosophy and sciences. The numbers, zero, infinity, theorems of Pythagoras, Newton's laws of motion were all contributed by Indian seers more than two thousand years ago and these are documented in this author's book. Many western scientists and scholars like Schopenhauer, Max Muller and others have admitted that the Hindu philosophy (not a religion as is generally understood wrongly) has been the precursor to the Greek and western philosophy and sciences and is the mother of all religions of the world. The lack of understanding of this fact by western scholars is either a deliberate attempt to suppress or hide the truth about Hindu thought or due to ignorance about it. Carlisle's discussion throughout ignores this fact and only elaborates on Christianity versus ID and not about spirituality that Einstein spoke about.

During the last three thousand years, more than a billion people have been killed in the name of religion or due to inter-group rivalry all over the world. Spain's plunder and genocide in South America, the British genocide and plunder in North America, India and South Asia, and Europe are all well documented. The same applies to the genocide and plunder by the Moghuls in India, Europe and Asia. This in itself is reason enough for the disbandment of religions from the world and the establishment of a Universal way of life for all people in the world, where all men and women are equal, and where there are no borders but only a world authority over-seeing law and order and representative administration. This is not a new idea but has been forcefully argued for by no less a person than Bertrand Russell during and after the First World War.

# Intelligent Design Vs Creationism

Victor Hugo in his *Les Miserables* has this to say on the negative aspects of cloisters: 'Cloisters, useful in the early education of modern civilization, have embarrassed its growth and are injurious to its development. So far as institutions with relation to man are concerned, monasteries, which were good in the 10th century, questionable in the 15th, are detestable in the 19th. The leprosy of monasticism has gnawed nearly to a skeleton two wonderful nations, Italy and Spain…The Catholic cloister, properly speaking, is wholly filled with the black radiance of death'.

The concept of god is irrelevant in the world and so no arguments are required in this regard. Evolution is a fact of life but not all of what Darwin said has been proved right. Again, whether Intelligent Design is there or not is irrelevant to our lives in this planet. All such ideas could be taught and discussed openly for academic purposes so that newer facts and ideas could emerge. If someone wants to believe in god, it is his right and others should have no say in this as long as the matter remains personal. Creation and destruction are part of nature and they continue to occur. It is just a question of 'being' and when the being is there to observe phenomena, there is a world and when the being is not there there is nothing. So the whole question becomes metaphysical and hypothetical. At the relative level, we can continue to live and deliberate on all such things, that is all. Jesus was himself a revolutionary thinker who overturned religious norms. He recast the Middle Eastern world's vision of god, defying political, social, cultural and theological beliefs. The Church was established in the name of Jesus but Jesus himself was certainly not aware of it. He was just a teacher and a reformer of society. Any other interpretation of his teachings will be faulty. As Carlisle has asked, if we say evolution is true, how can we know it to be true, given that the mind that understands it is itself a product of evolution? We cannot say they are true or not as it will introduce a standard that transcends it.

For J. B. S. Haldane, an evolutionary biologist and geneticist, the assumption of an evolutionary theory suggests that there would not be enough time for humans to evolve from a common ancestor. Haldane said that for a mammal to evolve, it must receive beneficial genetic substitution and he showed that the rate of beneficial substitution to be one in three hundred generations. If it took ten million years for the common ancestor to evolve into a human being then 1667 substitutions are possible according to ReMine, author of *The Biotic Message*. Evolutionists agree on the substitution theory of Haldane and are troubled that it was difficult for such an evolution in 1667 substitutions for trebling in brain size, fully upright posture, language, speech, hand dexterity, hair distribution, appreciation of music and other such faculties. Haldane's dilemma was allowing micro-evolution but questioning the dynamics of macro-evolution. Thus he questions the evolution from a common ancestor theory.

## Vedic Tradition and World Religions

Michael Behe asks: 'How can the mousetrap know it will be a mousetrap until it is all together? How can an organism know what it will be until it has already happened? How can an organism evolve towards a functional purpose until it knows what that purpose is? Such arguments are used by the protagonists of ID. They argue as to how inorganic substances create organic cells and amino acids, the building block of life. Such arguments are valid for scientific inquiry at best, but not for a discussion on god, or ID or creationism.

In the ultimate analysis, we may have to accept that the existence of the world itself is a product of probability like god playing dice as Einstein had suggested. Godel and Heisenberg have proved that for every affirmation, there are other equally valid counter-affirmations and hence the probability aspect appears credible. In an article in the Scientific American (June 13, 2013), titled *Quantum Weirdness-It is all in Your Mind*, Hans Christian Von Baeyer has come up with a new idea. The Quantum Theory has a new model, Q'Bism, which combines the Quantum and Probability theories that eliminate paradoxes. One of the basic paradoxes of Quantum Theory is the 'wave function'. The new model suggests that the wave function is purely a mathematical tool and is really not existent- rather it is only a subjective mental state according to this Q'Bism (Quantum Bayesianism) model. The wave functions are used to calculate the probability that a particle will have a certain property such as being in a certain place or another. But it is just a probabilistic tool and not something real. It is like mathematicians using surreal numbers to solve real problems. The wave function simply collapses when an observer is suddenly and discontinuously revising his probability assignments based on new information. The traditional Quantum Theory says that the atom's wave function is in a superposition of two states- decayed and not decayed. This is the position in regard to the cat in Heisenberg's cat experiment where the cat is both dead and alive until the observer looks at it. This riddle is avoided by the Q'Bism model where it insists that the wave function is a subjective property of the observer rather than an objective property of the cat in the box. Only when it is observed the reality about the cat is revealed. Probability is like time; we know what it is, until we are asked to define it.

The ID conundrum can be understood if we study the four major interpretations of Quantum Mechanics:
1. The Copenhagen interpretation of Heisenberg and Niels Bohr that states that an observer causes a collapse of the Quantum state into a new state that describes the actual outcome of the experiment.
2. The Guided Field Representation of Einstein and others suggest that the guiding field exerts an action-at-a-distance force, in which physical effects are transmitted instantly over large distances.

3. The Many Worlds interpretation: This posits the existence of multiple universes in which the observer sees the Quantum state splitting the world into two branches, the real world observer in one branch unaware of the other. Thus the universe branches out like a tree into a vast multiverse.
4. Spontaneous Collapse theory: in this collapses are natural and not observer triggered.

The Q'Bism theory of Quantum Mechanics appears to be the nearest to reality. But this is unable to explain complex macroscopic phenomena like the conventional theory does. It therefore needs to build a standard theory. However it offers a new view of the physical reality in which the outcome of an experiment does not exist until the experiment is performed. Christopher Fuchs puts it thus: 'With every measurement set by an experimenter's free will, the world is shaped just a little as it participates in a kind of moment of birth'. This way, the observer becomes an active contributor to the ongoing creation of the universe.

Bertrand Russell writes: 'The argument that are used for the existence of god change their character as time goes on…In modern times they have become less respectable intellectually and more and more affected by a kind of moralizing vagueness'. The argument by design points that everything in the world is made just so that we can manage to live in the world, and if the world was ever so different we could not manage to live in it. Since the time of Darwin, such arguments have become wide off the mark. It is not that their environment was made to be suitable to them, but that they grew to be suitable to it, based on adaptation. There is no evidence of design in it.

If the argument from design can only produce the best that omnipotence has been able to produce in millions of years, it leaves a lot to be desired. With omnipotence, how could the creator produce the Ku Klux Klan, or Osama Bin Laden or the fascists or the Nazis? As per the ordinary laws of science, we know that life on this planet will die out in due course. It is a stage in the decay of the solar system.

As for the moral arguments for the existence of god, we had in the past three intellectual arguments. All three were disposed of by Kant in his Critique of Pure Reason. But he also invented a moral argument that said among other things, that there would be no right or wrong unless god existed. If there is a difference between right and wrong, is it due to god's fiat or is it not? If it is due to god, then for god himself, there is no difference between right and wrong and so it is no more important to say that god is good. If you say god is good, then right and wrong have a meaning that is independent of god's fiat, because god's fiats are good and not bad; or as some Gnostics said, the world was made by the devil when god was not looking. Belief in god is more due to the way people have been brought up with such beliefs and nothing else. Another is the desire for safety and the feeling that a big brother is there who is looking after you.

By far the best explanation of the problem is offered in the Hindu texts. From the creation hymn quoted earlier it would appear that evolution by adaptation is implied in it but once the evolution has resulted in man, he comes under the law of action and reaction. Man has to face the consequences of his action and therefore good must result in good and evil in evil. The theory of karma posits that the results of human action have to be experienced in this life and since all results may not have thus been experienced, it would be carried forward to his next birth. This would seem to explain why one is born as poor or rich, good or evil, and so on. Hindu philosophy also gives a solution for the ending of the birth-death cycle and becoming immortal. This is by doing action without desiring the results of that action or to perform desire-less action, *nishkama karma*. This will mean that the result of such action is not attached to the person and this way he would free himself from the results of his actions and so will not be born again. That is why true ascetics are not born again. This is the subject of Vedanta found in the Upanishads and other scriptural texts. However god has no place in all this as every living being is considered divine in that it has the soul, a manifestation of the infinite Brahman.

Reality has to be found only beyond the pairs of opposites. When we say evolution, it clearly implies a state of involution. The Samkhya theory of evolution implies as much. According to this theory, involution or potential existence prior to creation is necessary for the evolution of the real world. Prakriti, being infinite energy, evolves the manifested objects of the universe continuously for all time to come. It follows therefore that universes are being formed all the time while they are also being absorbed or annihilated, probably in Black Holes. The Bhagwad Gita gives the abode of Krishna as a place that compares with the description of a Black Hole- that anything that passes near it is sucked into it never to be able to come out of it. So reality assumes a state of uncertainty or assumption and nothing more. We can at best accept the concept of universal energy that is infinite and indeterminate. It is cyclical in nature and the process of evolution, the infinite and indeterminate continues even when some souls escape out of the entanglement in Prakriti. Many scholars consider the ancient Samkhya theory of evolution as comparable to Herbert Spencer's biological theories of evolution. As Dr Seal observes, 'The process of evolution consists in the development of the differentiated (*vaisamya*) within the undifferentiated (*samyavastha*) of the determinate (*visesa*) within the indeterminate (*avisesa*) of the coherent within the incoherent'.

# Intelligent Design Vs Creationism

The cosmogony of the Purusa Sukta of the tenth Mandala of Rig Veda is worth considering here. It gives a picture of involution and evolution, where it is stated, 'The thousand-headed, thousand-eyed and thousand-footed Purusa covered the earth on all sides, and stretched ten finger's length (ten stages or planes of consciousness) beyond it. The Purusa was all that is and all that will be, ruling over immortality; he was all that grows by food (matter). Such was his greatness; and the Purusa (Brahman) was greater still; this whole universe is a fourth part of him, three fourths are immortal in the infinite space'. The ten planes of consciousness apparently refer to the ten dimensions of science out of which only four are known to scientists. The other six are described by the ancient Hindus in a formula of the Ganita Sutras of the Atharva Veda. Kapoor's Vedic Geometry mentions the ten dimensions mentioned in the Maheswara Sutra derived from the Pranava Mantra OM. According to this, geometrical reality extends beyond the three dimensions and gravity to higher dimensional spaces in the space-time continuum. The continuum property is expressed as a ratio of content and frame in the formula: $a$ to the power $n$ divided by $2na$ power $n-1$, where $a$ is a parameter and $n$ an integer. This Vedic revelation shows six additional dimensions compacted at three dimensions. These higher dimensions can be reached by yogic practice and these include levitation, Alpha and Beta states and so on.

The monistic view on the theory of evolution is elaborately propounded in the Nasadiya Sukta of the Rig Veda. The three steps of creation in the Vedic hymns stated in modern terms are:
The Highest Absolute.
The bare Self-consciousness, and
The self-projection of this self-consciousness out of sheer delight, thereby giving rise to a world of multiplicity.

According to this, the world is not a purposeless phantasm but it is just the evolution of Brahman. The absolute creates the cosmos out of its own Being and the whole cosmos is a real creation by its force of creative power known as *maya* or *tapas*.

The Taittiriya Upanishad also follows this monistic doctrine of real creation. 'That from which these beings are born, that in which when born they live, and that into which they enter at their death, that is Brahman'. This Brahman is the Atman; thus the infinite becomes the finite making the Atman as the entire universe. The Brahman is both the material cause and the efficient cause of the universe. The progressive revelation of the true nature of reality is seen from matter, life, mind, vijnan and ananda (bliss) that a person attains eventually and becomes immortal. This is the Upanishadic cosmogony. Thus the theory of involution and evolution of the Vedas and Upanishads stands vindicated. In the beginning there was only the transcendental

Brahman who eventually created the worlds or universes. The emergence of matter led to the creation of life (prana). This prana or life is indeed the manifestation of the Universal energy or Brahman. Everything else followed like the sixteen evolutes- Brahma, *prana*, *sraddha*, five subtle matters, five sense organs and the three internal aspects of mind, intellect and ego. Involution and evolution are the dual processes at the cosmic and individual levels. The individual evolution and salvation is realized by philosophic insight or the recognition of the immortality of the soul.

Significantly, the present period is one in which there is an ongoing dialogue on Creationism versus Darwinism. The truth appears to be neither, according to researchers. The evidence of a great but forgotten civilization appears to be overwhelming. Different researchers have presented their arguments in support of the above civilization in the book *Forbidden History*. Valikovsky, a Russian psychoanalyst, gives the psychological impacts of cataclysmic events in his *Mankind in America*. Our mother earth had only 2 or three land masses in the beginning but due to tectonic and cataclysmic events, these landmasses separated into many continents and thousands of islands. We have seen massive water bodies becoming deserts like the Sahara in Africa. (The word Sahara is derived from the Sanskrit sagara or ocean, as it was a large water body once). The Thar Desert in India is another example of a once green area becoming a desert. The same thing happened when the River Saraswati dried up c. 1900 BCE due to overuse of trees for purposes of fire and house building thereby denuding the forests in the area. Similar was the fate of the Kumari continent (Lemuria) south of Cape Comorin that got submerged over a period of 8000 years between 9000 BCE and 2000 BCE due to a number of oceanic convulsions and volcanic activity including Tsunamis. Thus, the earth's geography systematically changed over the millennia. Myths are known to be based on real events and as such we can understand the possibility of human life for more than a million years. The Darwinian concept of man evolving out of ape has been questioned and most scientists even reject this theory. Georgio de Santillana, an MIT professor, suggests that an advanced scientific knowledge had been encoded into ancient myth and star love. Graham Hancock says, 'Once one accepts that mythology may have originated in the waking minds of highly advanced people, then one must start listening to what the myths are saying'. What these myths say is that great catastrophies have struck earth and destroyed advanced civilizations (like our own) and that such destruction is a recurrent feature in the life of earth and may very well happen again.

Darwinism has not been proved yet by the standards of science. It can be proved if the fossil records are searched thoroughly. This could not be done as mentioned by the biologist Stephen Jay Gould: 'All Palaeontologists know that the fossil record contains precious little in the way of intermediate forms; transitions between major groups are characteristically lacking'. Darwin himself called the origin of flowering plants 'an abominable mystery' that is yet to be solved. Gould suggested the theory of 'punctuated equilibrium' to explain the lack of transitional species and the sudden appearance of new ones. Sir Francis Crick of DNA fame, proposed the concept of 'panspermia', the idea that life was brought to earth by an advanced civilization from another planet. This idea is also suggested by Elliott Scott in his *Lost Lemuria*, where he avers that an advanced race descended on earth from another planet (Venus or Mars) to civilize the people- A hint that the Vedic Rishis were those people who spread far and wide to civilize the world population.

Richard Thompson and Michael Cremo in their book *Forbidden Archaeology*, suggest with strong evidence that modern man existed millions of years before his supposed emergence from South Africa some 100,000 years ago. Human footprints were discovered in Texas alongside with dinosaur tracks and stone tools 55 million years old as also advanced civilizations in pre-history with sophisticated maps of unknown antiquity were showcased. That fossil evidence indicating man as far more ancient than current theory allows, and he did not evolve from apes has been suppressed due to its conflict with entrenched belief systems.

The human brain and its complexities, (playing violin or performing calculus, even consciousness) cannot be explained by the 'survival of the fittest' theory. Creationism is a Christian doctrine that is not supported by the Bible itself. The commonsense notion of intelligent design appears credible as it is hard to deny that an inherent intelligence exists within the universe. Darwin does not account for how new species and features originate. Charles Oxnard, the anthropologist observes: 'The conventional notion of human evolution must now be heavily modified or even rejected…new concepts must be explored'.

The catastrophist point of view holds that sudden disruptions in the continuity of planetary life have altered the course of evolution. Extinction of dinosaurs due to meteor impact, changes in climate due to population growth,, tsunamis, massive earthquakes and other geological convulsions have all caused heavy destruction including landmass submergence, extinction of species and other changes in the course of evolution. Carcasses of ancient mammals like mammoths, and Rhinos were found flash-frozen in a 'zone of death' across Siberia and Northern Canada. The stomachs of these mammals contained warm weather plants suggesting that the ground upon which they grazed suddenly shifted from a temperate to an arctic climate. Hapgood and Einstein opine that a sudden freezing of Antartica, which probably was situated 2000 miles farther north than it is now, could have occurred due to crustal displacement. Ancient maps accurately depicting Antartica also support this idea. The book of Hancock and Flem-Aths testify to the existence of a sophisticated prehistoric civilization. This scenario is like what Plato described of the lost continent of Atlantis.

Stone works in Indian temples in Bolivia, Peru, and Egypt reveal technology of a high order and not that of nomadic hunter-gatherers. The city of Tiahuanaco in Bolivia is dated 15000 BCE and its stonework on immense blocks to tolerances of one fiftieth of an inch and transportation of these blocks reveal technical competence far in excess of what we have today. Similar carved rocks of 150 tons or more being raised to heights of 30 metres or more in temples of South India at Tanjore, Madurai and other places as also at Luxor in Egypt also suggest the same thing. Machu-Pichu in Peru, and the Pyramids of Giza are also examples of superior technology. Evidence of settlers from India in Egypt, Europe, the Americas all suggest that technology from ancient India was used in most of these places. Frank Joseph has also showcased such massive stone structures submerged in the Pacific Ocean areas with photographs in his books. Hancock says: 'We are looking at a common influence that touched all of these places, long before recorded history, a remote third party civilization yet to be identified by historians'. This civilization had a language which may be the common source of all world languages and the existence of a common language with advanced knowledge, proliferated among pre-historic peoples. They were also privy to sophisticated knowledge of celestial mechanics that is probably matched only recently with the help of satellites and computers. These people show an extraordinary seafaring capability that is shown to have existed in the remote past. These may be the missing links in human history. All the above clearly point to India as the source of this common language and technology. The Mohenjo-Daro script perfectly matches with the Rongo-Rongo of Easter Islands thousands of miles away from India and nearer South America, as pointed out by Frank Joseph. Two submerged continents that of Kumari (Lemuria) in the Indian Ocean and Atlantis may hold the key for unravelling this mystery.

The Hindu (January 14, 2013) has reported on the Pandyan inscriptions in copper dated 784 CE which describes the geological convulsion some centuries earlier that submerged large areas of the Kumari continent and forced the Tamil Sangam to be shifted to Madurai from Kapadapuram. This was the third Sangam. In earlier such convulsions, the first Sangam (7th century BCE) had to be shifted from *Then* (south) Madurai (400 miles south of Cape Comorin) to Kapadapuram further north for the second Sangam on the banks of the submerged Kumari River. These facts are also to be found in the Bhavishya Purana, one of the eighteen ancient Puranas. The Plate of

## Intelligent Design Vs Creationism

676 CE states that during a Tsunami, the water turns black. This was probably due to volcanic eruptions that caused the Tsunami throwing up lava.

Times of India (January 16, 2013) reported the study by the Max Planck Institute for Evolutionary Anthropology, Leipzig, which suggests that South Indians migrated to Australia 4000 years ago as per genetic studies. The study confirms that Dravidian speaking groups are the best match to be the source populations for this original migration 45,000 years ago.

The extensive cover-up of the findings in respect of an ancient civilization by the established orthodoxy that controlled the academic life worldwide is now being exposed. Some examples:

1. Stone tools from Hueyatlaco (Mexico) are about 20,000 years old which was revised to quarter million years by the use of four different dating methods. But Steen Macintyre and associates who did the study were not only challenged for the dating but were even isolated from academia by the establishment.
2. The Table Mountains of California, where the gold rush took place, threw up hundreds of stone artefacts and human fossils. J.D. Whitney documented the 9-55 million year old fossils but his report has quietly vanished from text books.
3. Miners in South Africa have dug up hundreds of metallic spheres with parallel grooves dated at 3 billion years but the scientific community has so far ignored these findings.
4. George Cantor found during excavation in San Diego, hearths and crude stone tools of the last glacial period, 80-90,000 years old.
5. The massive Temple of Man at Luxor with its obelisk of 400 tons, Hypostyle Hall and the Amun Temple. These are mind boggling. How these massive stones were crafted and erected in a place is beyond our imagination. The Hall is similar to the 1000 pillared halls in the temples of Rameswaram, Madurai, Annamalai etc.

Cremo and Thompson believe that by this massive cover-up, academic science has quietly cooked the books by not just ignoring the massive evidence but by also suppressing it. They started their project to find evidence to corroborate ancient Sanskrit writings of India which relate episodes of human history going back millions of years. What they found was truly amazing. There is actually a massive amount of evidence that has been suppressed. Today, experts that include Paleontologists, keep clear of such evidence of early humans for fear of their career which they want to protect. Many such scientists have lost their positions for coming up with evidence of ancient humans. The failure of science to deal with UFOs, extra sensory perception, consciousness and other such things is a glaring example. Only the Sanskrit texts have answered the principle of consciousness as part of the Universal energy,

Brahman. There appears to be a deliberate attempt on the part of those in control of the world's intellectual life to make us disbelieve and forget the para-normal and related phenomena. This struggle has been going on for centuries.

The conclusion seems to be obvious. The Hindu theory of Yugas postulate that every 432,000 years, there is a renewal of life and such cycles have gone on for millions of years, implying that human life is indeed very old. It is high time that academia in the west and east cooperated for making further studies and exposing the facts as have been suggested by different authors. All this however also indicate the shortcomings in the Darwinian theory of evolution and a new theory needs to be arrived at.

We would conclude this dissertation with a quotation each from the Mother of Auroville and Swami Vivekananda. The Mother of Auroville, Pondicherry, the disciple of Sri Aurobindo, the mystic, said what is relevant today- 'The time of religion is over; we have entered the age of universal spirituality, of spiritual experience in its initial purity'. This would take us to the age of Vedas and Upanishads when there was no religion and only a way of life existed. This is the only hope for mankind. Science and technology have to be coupled with a spiritual change for the accomplishment of the ideal of universal spirituality. The west has long turned its eyes away from earth and the time has now come to heal the division and to unite life and spirit. Swami Vivekananda said in 1897, 'Europe, the centre of manifestation of material energy will crumble into dust within fifty years, if she is not mindful to change her position…and make spirituality the basis of her life. And what will save Europe is the religion of the Upanishads'. Significantly, exactly fifty years later, India got its independence in 1947. He also said that 'we want to lead mankind to the place where there is neither the Vedas, nor the Bible, nor the Koran, yet this has to be done by harmonizing the Vedas, the Bible and the Koran'. Let us hope this vision becomes a reality in the twenty-first century.

## References:
1. Forbidden History- Ed: J. Douglas Kenyon, Bear and Co, 2005
2. Why I Am Not a Christian- Bertrand Russell, Allen and Unwin, London.
3. Understanding Intelligent Design, Idiot's Guide- Christopher Carlisle M.Div. and W. Thomas Smith (Jr), Penguin-Alpha Books.
4. History of Ancient India, 2nd Edition- Ramakrishnan Srinivasan, Sri Sri Publications, Bengaluru, 2015
5. Science, Philosophy and Religion- Ramakrishnan Srinivasan, Citadel, Calcutta.
6. Indian Philosophy Vol. I and II- Dr.S. Radhakrishnan, Allen and Unwin, London.

# CHAPTER 19
# CREATION MYTHS

This chapter on creation myths from different parts of the world has been included in this work as it can at least obliquely connect with the subject of this book, viz: The origins of world religions have a common source in the Vedic Tradition. We have already referred to the creation story contained in the Nasadiya Sukta of the Rig Veda in an earlier chapter. It would therefore be interesting to see the myths of creation from different parts of the world in what follows.

1. The Eskimo myth known in Siberia to Greenland, speaks of a society rather than the universe. A Raven God, who travels from heaven to earth, and to the sea floor, can change forms with its sacred power. Raven instructs people on the ways to live. He creates first man through the pea-vine and other people as well as animals, birds and other beings from clay taken from the earth's creek.

2. Bank's Islands, north of New Hebrides in Melanesia, has Quat as the Solar God. In the beginning, there was light. Quat must discover night. There are twelve sons of Quat Goro the Great Seed, one for each month. His brother's stupidity brought death to the world. Quat travels to the end of the horizon to bring night back and finishes making the world.

3. The Kano people of New Guinea has death (*Sa*), living in darkness before the god Alatangana. Death came first and then god made the solid earth out of the mud. God stole *Sa*'s only daughter after which death takes one of god's children.

4. The Cosmic Egg myth from China from 600 BCE has Phan Ku, the popular god, complete creation through his sacrifice. The sky dome comes from his skull and his body's vermin become humanity. Because humanity was sacred, god was sacred. But by losing this living god, humanity loses its creator and suffers for ever. Thus, the suffering of humanity could be attributed to the loss of god by the people. Inside the hen's egg there was nothing. From it was born Phan Ku, the god who started creation. The sky was considered as the *Yang* or the male principle and the heavy earth was considered as the *Yin* or the female principle. The *Yang* and *Yin* correspond to the *Linga* and *Yoni* of the Hindus, the male and female aspects of creation. It must be noted here that the *Linga* or phallus is the oldest

form of worship in the world going back to more than 5000 years. This has been showcased elsewhere in this book with references from Greek and other authors.

5. The Blackfoot American Indian people have an old man coming from the south creating lives and things as he moves. Woman is the spoiler. She throws a stone, which sinks, thus, people will die and feel sorrow and also feel for one another.
6. The Russian Altaic creation story has Erlik, the Devil as the first man. In other stories, God Ulgen is the first man. He is self created. The eighth man must bring life from God to the first woman. (Krishna was the eighth child).
7. For the Maidu Indians of California, a creature dives into water, washing the old away and creating the new. The power of god creates Ku'ksu, man, who is born after his death.
8. The Fon people of Abomey (Republic of Benin) have Mauru and Lisa as partners, said to be twins. They were the first inhabitants of Dahomey in the twelfth century.
9. The Australian Northern Arauda aborigines have a 'Karora' myth with the bandicoot totem. The world is destroyed in a flood of honey. If creation is not perfect, it must be destroyed.
10. The Krachi people of Togo have an Ananse spider story. Ananse the Trickster has rivalry with the sky god. The weak spider overcomes god. God has power but Ananse succeeds to trick the god into thinking he is a bird and by finding darkness, moon, and sun, he proves that he was equal to god.
11. The Yoruba of Nigeria have a Supreme Being, Olorun, who owns the sky, the creator. The chief god of the Yorubas, Obatala, gives children to people. Olorun hands over the world to Obatala and withdraws.
12. The Babylonian myth is taken from the Enuma Elish. Apsu and Tiamat are ancestors of gods and symbolize the unformed matter of the world. Marduk was the main god. The text was found in Ashurbanipal's library at Nineveh dating back to 668-626 BCE but is traced back to the first Babylonian Dynasty 2050-1750 BCE and the age of Hammurabi, 1900 BCE and even back to the Sumerians who lived before the Babylonians. The first line states, 'When on high the heaven had not been named'. In the beginning there was Apsy the begetter, the fresh oceans saltwater sea. Tiamat was the salt sea waters. They mingled as a single body and soul. They brought Lahmu and Lahamu into being. Then the gods Anshar and Kishar were formed. The god Anu had a son equal to his father Anshar. Ea the god killed Apsu. Ea and Damkina lived in the watery realm called Apsu. (apa- water in Sanskrit). Marduk was the sun of all. The god Anu made the four winds. The gods made Marduk the King of the world. He killed Tiamat in a fight for her evil ways. Marduk created the universe, the sun and the moon and other bodies. He then

created man and said 'man' shall be his name. (This man is Manu and the myth spread from South India that sent people to Sumeria in the third millennium BCE. The Sumerian language is akin to Tamil and the Sumerians were like the Tamils. Please see, *History of Ancient India* by this author for more details).

13. The Quiche Mayas have the Popol Vuh in Guatamala. They were conquered by the Spanish and their religious books were destroyed. They were re-written in Latin by a convert and a copy made in Spanish by Franciso Ximenez. After three flawed creations, a perfect one was made. But it was redone because men will not be perfect as gods. God says 'earth' and it came into being. The earliest authors for this myth were the ancient Indian settlers, the Mesoamericans, 950-1500 BCE. They used the Mayan calendar.

14. The Tahitian and Samoan myth has a golden cosmic egg, the source of all life (Hiranyagarbha or the golden cosmic egg of the Hindus). The Supreme Being, Ta-aroa (unique) existed within the egg acting as the incubator. He created Tu, his companion. They filled the world with gods and the first man was Ti-I whose wife was Hina. The gods started a battle among them and Ta-aroa and Tu cursed them. Hina saved the stars and the seas, rivers and mankind. Ti-I caused the destruction of eternal life inspite of Hina.

15. The Egyptian myth has Ra as god and Afrophis, the dragon. The myth is 3000 years or more old. The sun god Ra travelled the heavens in a boat disappearing in the underworld. Osiris was the moon god and Isis, his sister and the patron goddess. Horus was the son of Osiris and Isis, and the saviour of mankind.

16. The north-eastern Indian tribe Minyong has the myth in which the lesser gods conspired to drive out the Father- Heaven, Melo- producer of darkness and chaos. But the powerful men and animals of the middle realm arrange to bring order enough to permit light and life. Bong and her sister Bomong were born to Sedi who was sad that Melo the sky went away. Bong had a stone that her sister removed from her head and light dazzled and spread. The cock cried ko-ko-ko. Light and heat again came to earth.

17. Hesiod's (8th century BCE) theogony records the evolution of the Greek gods. From chaos (nothing) was created the earth, Tartarus the underworld, and Eros (love). Earth gives birth to heaven and the sea by herself. Then they bring forth the Titans. Kronos, the time, devoured his own children and thus brought an end to all that was begun. Titans were the elder gods, Kronos the most important and Zeus the most fierce. Prometheus was the most famous who stole fire for man, thus placing man above Zeus, and tricked Zeus, making him furious, taking it out on Epimetheus. Zeus punished Prometheus. Pandora is supplied a gift box by

Zeus thus surprising her. She shuts hope in the box as hope will make the world brighter. In another version, the Pandora's box is supposed to have been a source of a lot of trouble
18. The Genesis of the Pentateuch written by Ezra in 397 BCE has Elohim as the greater god. It is a monotheistic religion with one god Yahveh who said 'let there be light' and there was light.

Most of the Greek, Judaic and other myths of the world were based on the Cosmic Egg (Hiranyagarbha) story of the Hindus. The Big Bang is also related to it.

## References:
1. In The Beginning, Creation Stories from around the World- Virginia Hamilton, Harcourt Inc, NY, San Diego, London.
2. History of Ancient India- Ramakrishnan Srinivasan, SriSri Publications, Bengaluru, 2015

# CHAPTER 20

# DESTRUCTION OF LIBRARIES

This chapter has been included to showcase how books and libraries worldwide have been destroyed mainly due to religious fanaticism and for this the well researched book by Fernando Baez was very useful and this author has drawn extensively from his reports in his book *A Universal History of Destruction of Books*. Apart from these destructions of valuable texts that could have given us a better idea of history from ancient times, we also have had geological convulsions like earthquakes, tsunamis, volcanic eruptions both on land and under sea, all of which submerged large areas of continents and in the process also submerging valuable ancient texts. This is particularly true of Lemuria that is known in Indian Puranas as Kumari that was once part of the Indian sub-continent contiguous with the Cape Comerin and extending to about 400 miles in the Indian Ocean that was submerged in four such convulsions between 9000 BCE and 2000 BCE. About this we shall not add more as they have been dealt with in many books including those under reference.

In April 2003, after the US seizure of Baghdad, mobs against Saddam Hussain looted Baghdad Archaeological Museum. Thirty objects of great value disappeared; more than 14,000 lesser pieces were stolen and the gallery was destroyed. On April 14, a million books in the National Library were burned. The National Archive, with more than ten million registries from the Republican and Ottoman periods, was burned. Subsequently the same took place at the libraries of Baghdad University, the Awquaf and scores of university libraries all over the country. In Basra, the Museum of National History was burned along with the Central Public Library, the university and Islamic libraries. In Mosul, manuscript experts removed specific texts from the Museum Library. In Tikrit, the looters walked away with pieces from the museum. Thousands of archaeological sites were left unguarded and illicit transnational trafficking in artefacts took place.

Goethe saw a book burned and said, 'how an inanimate object is punished'. In 1999, the Sarajevo National Library with 1.5 million books including 100,000 manuscripts was bombed out. The civil war in Columbia caused the destruction of several libraries. In Hebrew, Iranian, Greco-Roman and Meso-American worldviews, destruction and creation are the only alternatives the universe believed in. Several annihilation myths are to be found all over the world. 2.5 million Years ago the *homo habilis* led to the *homo sapiens sapiens* and the modern humans. Writing developed a few thousand years ago. So, 99% of human existence is pre—history. 'The book is an extension of memory and imagination', said Jorge Luis Bergen.

In Greece 405 BCE, in an attempt to unify Athenians in the wake of their defeat in the Pelopponesian war, Patrocleides decreed amnesty that mandated the erasure of public records and sanction against those that kept copies of past records. In 356 BCE, Herostratus destroyed the Temple of Artemis at Ephesus, one of the Seven Wonders of the World. In 1992, the National Library of Bosnia with 1.5 million books and 778 manuscripts was destroyed. John Milton had said, 'He who destroys a good book, kills reason itself, kills the image of god as it were in the eye'. Rebecca Knuth considers libricide or destruction of libraries, as equal to genocide or ethnocide. These destroyers are radical dogmatists. Nachman of Bratislava, born 1772, a Jew, said, 'To burn a book is to bring light to the world'. The Jewish mystic Sabbatai Zevi, the 'False Messiah' said that destroying the Holy Scriptures would bring about a new era. In Egypt, the poet Akhenaten, a monotheist, had all the religious books that preceded him, burned in order to impose his own writings on the god Atun. In the 5th century BCE, Athenian democrats burned the book in a bonfire, *On the Gods,* by Protagoras, for impiety. The Spanish Cardinal Jimenez de Cisneros burned the Islamic books in Granada. In 1530, Fray Juan de Zumarraga, creator of the first Mexican Library, burned the Aztec codices. A French librarian burned Hebrew books in 2002.

**The Near East:** In Sumer, Southern Troy (Mesopotamia), at least 10,000 tablets of clay containing ancient texts were destroyed due to floods or other causes. The fourth level excavation of the Temple of Goddess Eanna in Uruk, uncovered tablets dating back to 4100-3300 BCE. The floods in the Tigris/Euphretis Rivers submerged towns and libraries. The Sumerians or the Blackheads (ancient Tamils, the settlers were black) believed in the supernatural origin of books, invented by Nidaba, the Goddess of grain. In the legend of Enmekar (c.2750 BCE), the King of Uruk was punished for not having his deeds written down. In 2800 BCE, the monarchs gave absolute authority to the scribes for preserving books. The Akkadians who conquered Sumer forced the scribes to teach them writing and the same was done by Assyrians, the Persians and the Amorites. So, the same written signs were used for the exposition of most diverse languages. The Ziggurates of Sumer were built with the same clay used for books. The scribes wrote in cuneiform on the heat treated clay tablets by incisions with a bone or reed. When the signa acquired phonetic attributes, they were reduced from 2000 to less than half that number. Around 3300 BCE, the Uruk period, tablets became more elaborate and the first libraries were invented. In Ur, and Adab, the remains of tablets from two libraries active around 2800-2700 BCE were found.

In 1964, Sabatino Moscati, an archaeologist, while excavating near Aleppo in a hill found evidence of the city of Elba. In 1975, thousands of tablets were found in a room used as a library. The first bilingual dictionary in Sumerian and Ebolaite was also found there. The Akkadian King Naramsin had attacked and burned Elba (2254-2218 BCE).

Between 1792-1750 BCE, Hammurabi the sixth in succession looted libraries and brought them to his palace library. The language was ancient Akkadian in cuneiform. His code was also stored. In 689 BCE, Sennacherib's troops razed Babylon. His grandson, Asurbanipal, founded the most famous library in Nineveh, itself devastated in 612 BCE. Thousands of tablets disappeared and most destroyed. From 1842, excavation by the British removed more than 20,000 whole tablets that are now in the British Museum. So far, 30,000 tablets have been discovered containing vast literary texts. 233 libraries existed between 1500-300 BCE. Between 1800-1200 BCE, Hittites had created libraries near Ankara. 10,000 tablets in at least eight languages have been found including legal documents, prayers and so on.

Darius the Great and his successors Xerxes I and Artaxerxes I had thousands of tablets in Persepolis including the Zend Avesta (c. 518). King Vishtaspa ordered two copies of the text. In 331 BCE, Alexander attacked Darius III with 40,000 soldiers and 7000 cavalry. Darius fled and was murdered by his own cohorts; Babylon and Susa surrendered. Alexander, drunk, set fire to the palace at the instance of a Thai courtesan. The treasure of Persepolis was carried away and burnt that includes the Avesta. In 1931-34, 30,000 tablets were found in Elamite the Persian language.

**Egypt:** The first papyrus writing goes back to 2500 BCE, during the fourth Dynasty. The 160 papyrus containing the Canon of Turin during Rameses II (1290-1224 BCE), though damaged, were the first registry of Egyptian Pharaohs and Kings. More than 80 % of Egyptian literature and science has been lost. Rameses II created one of the first papyrus libraries and constructed the Temple for his remains, the Ramesseum, containing a library. Ethiopian Assyrians and Persians looted the place and the books disappeared. In the first century CE, the Temple was taken over by Christians and was made into a church. Akhenetan destroyed most books by burning. His successors erased even his face from the stones and restored from memory many ancient papyrus contents. The House of Life, an antecedent library to that of Alexandria, was located in the Temple to Horus at Edfu. The librarian priests wrote on medicine and magic. On the walls of the library, along with the image of Seshat, goddess of writing

(Saraswati, Hindu goddess of knowledge), 37 titles, the books of magic, knowledge of secrets, forms of the gods and other texts were all stored but they were all destroyed when Christians attacked Egypt's ancient monuments.

**Greece**: Out of hundred odd historians of Greece, only the works of three from the Classical period and a few more from later periods are available in texts. Orpheus' poem with interpretation (4th century BCE) is available only in fragments and 500 years of Greek literature is lost. Felix Jacoby's *Die Fragmente der Griechischen Historiker* contains fragments of 800 or more histories of the Hellenistic period. More than 75% of its literature is lost. Book selling in the market place was common in 400 BCE and was known as Bibliotheken. Out of 120 works of Sophocles only 7 are available. Out of 9 works of Sappho only 2 are available, out of Aristophanes' 40 works (comedies), only 11 survive, and out of 82 tragedies of Euripides only 18 are available. Out of Corinna's 5 texts only a few fragments are available. 101 comedies of Diphilus, 100 of Eupolis and 250 of Alexis are totally lost. The works of pre-Socrates and Sophists exist only in fragments. The great works of Gorgias of Leontini *On Not Being* and *On Nature*, were also lost. The writings of skeptics and stoics exist only in quotations. Zeno's *Republic* exists only in fragments. 500 books of Crisippius were also lost and exist only in fragments.

**The Library of Alexandria:** A number of stories are there on the destruction of this library. Caeser fought against the Egyptian troops of Aquilus and destroyed the palace and 4000 books were burned. Romans were said to have destroyed the library. In another story, an earthquake between 320 and 303 did some damage to Alexandria and another powerful earthquake in 365 brought down numerous buildings and part of Alexandria sank. Another story suggests negligence due to funds being cut off for the library.

**Other Ancient Libraries:** The Pergamum library of King Eumenes was created in the second century BCE. About 300,000 books were collected by Eumenes and copied into Vellum and Pliny confirms this. During the war in Asia Minor, Mark Antony sent 200,000 volumes to Cleopatra for the Serapeum of Alexandria. They all disappeared. The geographer Strabo said that Aristotle was the first collector of books but only fragments of what Aristotle wrote remain. He was the teacher of Alexander and when the latter died, his world changed abruptly. He died in 322 BCE leaving his library to young Theoprastus and when he too died, it was given to the care of Stratus instead of Neleus who was an expert on Aristotle. Neleus transported most of Aristotle's works from Athens to distant lands. He probably sold the books to Alexandrian and other libraries. Sulla destroyed houses in Athens, killed Apelicas hiding in the library and shipped the books to Rome. Lucullus too collected books and sent to Rome.

# Destruction of Libraries

They both opened their libraries to friends. The Emperor Caracalla (188-217), in a fit ordered burning of Aristotle's works because he thought the latter had poisoned Alexander. Similar was the fate of the Ark and the Law of Israelis.

**China:** Qin Shi Huang burnt millions of books and four hundred men of letters were buried alive. In 206 BCE, Huang's Imperial Library itself was burnt down. The Han Dynasty in 207 BCE restored cultural activities. In 311 CE, libraries at Luoyang were sacked by Huns. In 316, the pillage was repeated. Between 907 and 960, destruction of libraries was common. The Kaiteng library was burnt in 975. In 845, Wu Zong ordered destruction of 4600 temples and their libraries.

**Rome and Early Christianity:** Books of Nuna in Rome were burnt in 181 BCE and again in 186 BCE, books were collected and burnt. When Nero was fiddling, 3000 bronze tablets were burnt and Augustus's two libraries were burnt down. The Capitaline library was burnt in 114 CE. In 191 CE, the library of the Temple of Peace was destroyed in a fire and in 100 CE, the Timgad library was burnt. In 263 CE, Goth destroyed the library of Celso in 410 CE, Alaric and his friends or followers sacked Rome and its libraries. In 448 CE, Poephyrry and his books were burnt. Arcadius ordered destruction of books in 398 CE. Theodosius directed a mob to collect books from house to house and destroy them. Hypaties, the first woman scientist and daughter of Ptolomy was killed by a mob, mutilating her body and burning the parts and her books in the library. In 363, Jovinian burnt a huge library in Antioch and 300 books in Greek were all destroyed. Tertullian had said, 'all heresies are instigated by philosophy'. Between the second and sixth centuries, the loss of books in Rome and its territory, was enormous and cannot be estimated.

**Constantinople:** The seventh to ninth centuries saw the burning of the Royal College Library of Byzantium, the palace library and one in the the city, and the destruction of 120,000 books in a fire caused by the usurpation of Basilicas. In 1204 CE, the fourth Crusade sacked libraries and thousands of manuscripts destroying books of Callimachus, Sappho and others. In 1453 CE, the city of Constantinople was sacked by Turkey along with churches, libraries and other monuments.

**Between Monks and Barbarians:** There was a time around the 4th century when not a single library existed in Europe. Marcelinus wrote, 'The libraries are locked up like tombs in perpetuity'. The Vikings destroyed libraries in Ireland, burned buildings and monasteries. The ancient library of York was burnt. In 585, Monte Casino library in Italy was destroyed along with the monastery and its books. During World War II, the Allies bombed monasteries though the books were moved to the Vatican.

**The Islamic World:** Between eleventh and twelfth centuries the libraries of Baghdad were destroyed in the Turkish Invasion, the Zahiria library in Damascus was destroyed in the Crusades, the Royal Library of Isfahan was burnt by Alauddin Ghauri, the library of Bokhara was destroyed by Genghis Khan and the libraries of Daminia were also burnt. In 1256 CE, Hashshasin burnt the Alamut library (200,000 books) and destroyed the library of Medina. The Mongols not only destroyed the libraries of Baghdad but also killed 500,000 people besides executing the Caliph and others. In 1393 CE, Tamarlane, the nephew of Genghis Khan, destroyed the libraries in Syria.

**Misplaced Medieval Fervours:** Almanzor burnt all books in the library of Hakani except the sacred Islamic books in 981 CE. Pope Honorius III sought out the books of Dionysius and burnt them in 862 CE. In 1247 CE, Louis IX ordered the burning of the Talmud and related Hebrew books. In the sixteenth century, 12000 Hebrew texts were burnt in Cremona, Italy and the Roman priests and the Emperor caused the burning of the Talmud and other texts. In 1232 CE, Dominicans destroyed the books of Aristotle in Marseilles. Canon defines heresy as 'a religious error in which a person persists by his own free will and for considerable time, against the truth proclaimed by the church'. If this definition is accepted, the destruction of books may be considered as amounting to heresy. Pope Innocent's Crusades destroyed scientific books and the Gallic books in Paris in the year 1259 CE. The semons of de Bresse were burnt in 1155 CE and in 1328 CE John XXII ordered the burning of books. In 1492 CE, Cisneros ordered the burning of all Korans, Islamic books, and half of Sufi literature. In 1325 CE, the Aztecs founded the city of Mexico and this was destroyed by the Spanish and a new city has come up on the place and it is sinking.

In 1492, Spain reached the New World and the Inquisition had been created in 1478. Spain had suffered seven centuries of war and was totally impoverished (718 Pelagio rebelled against the Moslems). So the New World discovered by Columbus became the salvation as they could plunder hundreds of tons of gold and artefacts from there. This also probably saved Spain from Chaos. Columbus had said that 'with fifty men we can dominate all of them'. The native culture inspired the Spanish but they could subjugate them only by imposing their imperial culture. They plundered everything in Tenochtitlin and other places and systematically killed millions. Reverence turned into theft and plunder or pillage. They annihilated historical foundations. The natives were forced to convert on the threat of death and Spanish was taught to all of them. The Aztecs had documented all their deeds, accounts of years, months and days. Their writing was in glyphs or pictograms representing god Teotl. Bernard Diaz de Castillo said, 'we found the houses of idols and sacrifices…and many books made of their paper which we seized by fraud'. Churches took the place of Aztec Temples,

## Destruction of Libraries

monasteries took the place of the houses of wisdom and mansions displaced ancient palaces. Most of the Aztec codices survived are of colonial origins as the earlier ones were destroyed. Between 1524 CE and 1530 CE, the learned used Latin to write down the most remote chronologies like the Tlatelolco Annals transported to the National Library of Paris. In 1530 CE, Zumarraga made a bonfire of all the writings and idols of the Aztecs. The intention was to erase the past. Mayan paintings were a great loss because they contained their histories as the paintings were burned by Cortez in royal houses, where the archives of the papers were depositaries. All libraries of the Aztecs were thrown into flames.

The Mayans had dominated most of the Mexican states like Yucatan, Tabasco and the Central American countries like Guatamala, El Salvador, Honduras and Belize. They had two calendars- solar of 365 days and lunar of 260 days. Though they were in decline when the Spaniards invaded, their art and writing were completely burnt. A few wise men that were zealous managed to preserve a few that remained through oral recitations of the lost texts. Cisneros had earlier burned all Moslem manuscripts and both were Franciscans. In 1562, in Mani, Yucatan, he burnt 5000 idols and 27 codices of the ancients. Only three Mayan codices have survived mainly because of the secrecy they maintained on their traditions. The fourth king of Aztecs, Itzcoatl (1427-40) also burnt numerous works to erase the past.

**The Renaissance:** Villenas' translation of Virgil and Dante were confiscated on his death and destroyed by the Dominican Barrientos, tutor of Prince Henry. Suleiman I reached Hungary and killed 20,000 European soldiers including King Louis II (1506-26 CE). Suleiman sacked all villages on the Danube and the Corvinus library was destroyed. A few books survived. Savonarola's excesses of Biblioclasty, is well known. He had burnt artefacts, books and everything in Florence including musical instruments while Botticelli watched his works going up in smoke. One year later, the Church tortured Savonarola at the same place and burnt his body. In 1687, Mirandola's library was in flames. Villeneuve, Servetus and others were all famous writers and their works were all burned. Only a few copies have survived. The Anabaptists believed in the separation of the Church and State and their books were all burnt by the Church in 1559 CE. In Pinelli's library, Nostradamus' books were all burnt by the Inquisition who had institutionalized such acts. The Pope Leo X excommunicated Martin Luther and burnt his books. He was alarmed at the success of Protestants. Pope Paul IV, a fanatic, ordered burning of books. The Spanish Inquisition at Lima was bloody as it was in Mexico City.

**England:** Richard de Bury (1281-1345 CE) defender of books saw heplessly the destruction of books in the land of Shakespeare. In 1520 CE, 6000 copies of the New

Testament were burnt. Henry VIII perpetrated the purge of books between the years 1536-40 CE. Thousands of manuscripts were burnt in 1570 CE, John Dee's library was pillaged in 1589 CE and in 1666 CE, a mysterious London fire destroyed many libraries. Wilkins, Thomas Hobbes, John Cleland all found their books burnt and as late as 1960 CE, moral action groups burned copies of books in England and Japan. John Flamsteed, the Royal Astronomer, destroyed his own work because of Newton's machinations. The latter was notorious in plagiarizing the former's calculus. Newton and Edmond Halley published Flamsteed's work '*Historia…*'. The latter petitioned the new king and got 300 copies burnt. Only after his death was it again published. Newton took revenge by not referring to Flamsteed in his principal work *Philosophia… Mathematica*.

**Revolution in France, Spain and Latin America:** Pascal had said, 'Men never do evil in such perfect and acclaimed way as when they do it moved by religious conviction'. Voltaire was arrested for his views, and Diderot's *Pensees* was burned by the order of the Paris Parliament (1746). In 1768, this parliament arrested Marie Suisse and other authors for selling books of Voltaire, d'Holbach and Fontenelle. Their books were all burned. Louis XIV forbade the circulation of Beaumarchais' *Le Mariage de Figaro* and he was arrested and the books were burnt. The Reign of Terror of 1792 CE sent thousands to the guillotine and St. Juste demanded the death of the King, who was then executed in 1793 CE. During the violence, 8000 books were burnt and more than four million destroyed elsewhere. Hundreds of books were burnt in the Place Vendome in 1794 CE when the Abbey of St. Germaine was burnt with 49387 works and 7071 manuscripts. Balzac was not spared either. The Louvre manuscripts and the library lost its books in a fire in the Tuileries in 1871 CE. The Palais Royale was burnt with its books as munitions paper. The Library of Montserrat in Spain with its archives was totally burned by the French troops. By 1825 CE, the Spanish completely destroyed all the books and artefacts in Latin America. Sacking of convents and libraries in Mexico and Caracas in 1817 CE destroyed everything. Besides all this, fires have destroyed countless private and public libraries between the eleventh century and now. Earthquakes and floods have also contributed to this destruction between 1060 CE and 2000 CE.

**The Rise of Fascism:** The Spanish Civil War (1936-39) destroyed books and cultural artefacts as General Franco and his cohorts destroyed hundreds of bookshops and libraries in Spain. The Cathedral of Cueuca with 10,000 books was destroyed as was the 72 tons of books in Barcelona. Private and public libraries were sacked by Franco. Another 28 tons of books were also destroyed at the archives of the Ministry of Education. The Holocaust caused the biblioclast- destruction of millions of books and Jews with them by Hitler and his goons. Goebbels caused the most systematic destruction of books and libraries all over Germany, Poland and so on, and made public bonfires. In 1933 CE, books were brought in trucks from all over and burnt. Helen Keller wrote, 'You may burn my books and the books of the best minds of Europe but the ideas these books contain have passed through millions of channels and will go on'. The Nazis looted Holland in 1940 CE that was unprecedented. The Kloss Library of the Masons, library of the Institute of Social History, and the Rosenthal Library were all destroyed. The archives of the women's movement, the Theosophical Society Library were all burnt. The Chaim Library of Amsterdam was also burnt. The Israeli Seminary of Holland lost all its books as also the Jewish Literary Society. 29,000 deported Jews lost one million books.

In Belgium, the Louvain University Library was burnt twice. In France 723 libraries were seized with about two million books besides a million Jewish books and were destroyed by the Nazi occupation. Between 1940-44 CE, the Jeu de Paume Museum with its collection of 22,000 works was stolen by the Nazis along with the Louvre books and artefacts. The Turgenev Library of Paris was sacked. The same story continued in Austria and Poland. Some 15 million books were lost in Poland and a similar number in other countries. In aerial bombardments of England, it lost many bookshops and libraries and artefacts. The Coventry Library, the Inner Temple, Bristol University, Guildhall and many others saw the same fate. The Prague library and other libraries in Czechoslavia were all burnt. The same story continued in Russia. While withdrawing from France, the Nazis destroyed the Library in Dieppe and the 11,000 volumes at the Douai and Le Havre Librares were sacked. In 1944 CE, the National Library of Paris was destroyed. The Bonn University lost a quarter of its holdings and the libraries of Bremen, Hessische at Damstadt all lost more than a million books. The Stadtbibliotheks of Dresden and Frankfurt lost 300,000 rare books in bombings as was the Greifswald University. Hannover's library lay in ruins in bombings by the Allies. Karlsruhe, Kassel, Kiel, Milan, Naples were all ruined in bombings. Hiroshima and Nagasaki were completely destroyed with all its books and treasures. Other Japanese libraries in Tokyo, Aomori, Miyagi, Oita and Fukuoka were destroyed by incendiary bombs. Cadiz, Spain, Chile, West and central Java, Sulewasi and other places witnessed losses of libraries. In the United States of America, many libraries were burned or lost due to negligence and natural causes. Anthony Cornsteck is remembered as the man who destroyed maximum number of books in American history.

**China and the Soviet Union:** The Chinese set fire to the British Legation in 1900 that also consumed the Han Lin Yuan Library. Between 1935-45 CE the number of

Chinese libraries during the war was huge. The Nankin Library was destroyed with 230,000 books. The Tsinghua National University lost 200,000 books. The libraries of Grand China University, the University of Shanghai and those of many towns were burned. Out of 4041 libraries at least 2500 were destroyed. This extended to Tibet where 6000 monasteries and 100,000 monks were attacked.

Similar things happened during the Russian Revolution when Latvia, Lithuania, Estonia, Romania, Hungary, East Germany and Poland all lost millions of books during the Russian occupation. In East Germany, the Russians confiscated and destroyed five million books.

The story does not end with this. In Sri Lanka, the army destroyed 100,000 books and old manuscripts of the Tamils in Jaffna to erase Tamil culture. The total number of books destroyed thus worldwide during the current era of 2000 years may exceed 500 million besides millions of manuscripts, artefacts, and paintings that could have given us the real history of the world. Strangely, almost all this depredation and destruction could be traced to religious fanaticism. This is more so because most of the world except India, China, Greece and Egypt had no civilization till a couple of centuries before now and only barbarians lived during this period. There cannot be any other explanation for such extensive destruction of culture represented by books, artefacts and manuscripts. Luckily, the world has since woken up to this and this can be evidenced from extensive archaeological excavations, marine expeditions and the like during the past three hundred years. Of course much more needs to be done and even as we write, thousands of researchers are working on ancient manuscripts in India and elsewhere besides studying inscriptions, archaeological finds and such like, trying to find more information on ancient histories of the old world.

## References:
A Universal History of the Destruction of Books- Fernando Baez, Atlas and Co, New York.

# CHAPTER 21
# GREAT DISCOVERIES IN ARCHAEOLOGY

This chapter is not directly related with the subject matter of this book but was added in view of its importance vis-à-vis the development of religious systems in the world. This should throw some light on civilization in the distant past. Apart from the ten discoveries we have presented some of the adventures of archaeologists during the last three hundred years that have enabled us to know about those civilizations and their monuments.

1. **Rosetta Stone:** Napoleon's army was in Egypt in 1799 CE. Pierre Bouchard was getting his workmen to extend the fortification against possible British attack when they found a block three feet long and one foot thick. On it was inscribed in Greek, Egyptian hieroglyphs and Demetic in 196 BCE. This was not a complete find as one part of the stone was not found though broken from the main piece. It dates to the Ptolomaic period in 196 BCE when Ptolomy V Epiphanes ruled Egypt. The text was a Memphis decree giving the details of royal cult, grain inventories and other information. This is not an important message but gave the historians an insight into that period. It was in Basalt stone and hence very hard. Jean Francois Champillion decoded the stone's message with help from Thomas Young. The stone connects ancient Egypt to the Ptolomaic period.
2. **Troy:** In 1870 CE, Turkey, Heinrich Schliemann was in Hisarlik, looking at the area where Troy once stood and now remained buried. His excavation revealed correctly ancient Troy that was destroyed in 1200-1100 BCE, when order became chaos and the Dark Ages fell upon Greece for centuries. In 480 BCE, the Persian Emperor Xerxes set out to conquer Greece after sacrificing 100 cows on this hill of Troy. The Greeks burned Troy. Schliemann collected ceramic pots and other well preserved artefacts and documented them. What Homer said in Iliad was found to be true after all (700 BCE). After his excavation and announcement in 1872 CE, modern archaeology took its roots. Sir Charles Leonard Wolley excavated Urs in 1920 CE and Sir John Marshall did the same in Mohenjo-Daro in India. Other efforts like the Hannibal's Alpine route from classical texts like those of Polybius and Pliny are now history.

3. Twelve strata were excavated that threw up artefacts from 85 BCE to 500 BCE. The stratum I went back to 3000 BCE to the end of Bronze Age around 2200 BCE and possibly earlier to Neolithic times. Troy lay directly on the trade route between east and west. The Trojan War was possibly a trade war to break the monopoly of Troy in this trade. Luxury goods for the west including textiles, gems, and other material were traded by the Greeks for grain, olive oil, wine and so on. Troy offered the seaway between the Black Sea and the Aegean Sea. Specialists in the Hittite culture (1500-1100 BCE) in Anatolia (now Turkey) have found Troy in that ancient language also. Substantial evidence of warfare was found in the artefacts like arrowheads etc.

4. **Nineveh's Assyrian Library:** This was the key to Mesopotamia. Kuyunjik mound outside Mosul was excavated in 1849 CE by Austen Henry Layard, who then found the lost city of Nineveh. The Royal library of Assyrian King Ashurbanipal at Nineveh was found with more than 3000 clay tablets that contained many literary works like the epic of Gilgamesh, Enuma Elish and the Law Code of Hammurabi. In 612 BCE, Nineveh, which was till then the capital of Assyria, was completely destroyed. The cruelty of Assyrian rulers is legendary. The Babylonian ruler Nabopolassar, father of Nebuchadnezzar who had sacked Jerusalem attacked the weakened Assyrian kings and Nineveh was destroyed and burnt. The burning possibly helped in curing the clay tablets of the library and made them hard and so the texts were found in tact. Layard had earlier excavated Nimrud, the Assyrian site in 1845 CE. The Assyrian king Sennacherib's palace was excavated intact. It was 630 feet by 600 feet with eighty rooms. The tablets found were inscribed in cuneiform in which small wooden stylus was pressed into soft clay to make an impression of letters. In a smaller mound, the tomb shrine of Jonah was found. Sennacherib was the son of Sargon and ruled between 705 and 681 BCE. Ashurbanipal collected the archive of Mesopotamian lore leading to the largest collection of texts from all over the state. He had all the material copied that came from Elam, Old Akkad, Old Sumer, Babylon and Susa, especially older texts from temples. These texts included those going back 2500 years to his rule, with copies to boot.

5. The Assyrians preserved their culture as well as those of their ancestors and contemporary neighbours, even those that had to be translated to Assyrian language. Layard's book *Nineveh and its Remains* was very popular. The tablets included another version of Genesis of the Bible, the account of the Flood, older texts like the Sumerian accounts from 2500 BCE and earlier, and the Code of Hammurabi (that echoed in the Law of Moses). One could conclude that the Old Testament was influenced by many older texts. The texts record thousands of

years of Mesopotamian life in the Sumerian, Akkadian and Babylonian cultures. 10000 tablets broken into 26000 fragments give us information on the economies of Mesopotamia. Cuneiform texts from the Ubaid culture (6000 years ago) before Sumer, to Achaeminic Persia (2500 years ago) gave a long pictorial evolution that became cuneiform.

6. **King Tut's Tomb:** Howard Carter was the first to have a glimpse of the 3400 year old tomb of the Egyptian Pharaoh that was not found till then, though the tombs of other kings were found. He was digging many areas since 1918 but eventually got to see the rich tomb. Apart from tons of gold, the boy king's canopic jars, scenes of his family in happier days, gold cobras, four figures of Isis, Nephthys, Selkis and Neith all in gold, faced inwards in the four directions, his royal chariot with gilded wood, ivory, faisance and painted wood and many such artefacts were found. Fine carved alabaster vessels, golden cups, ivory chests (painted) were also found. King Tutankhamun's death was during a civil war in Egypt. Most other tombs had been looted but this was intact as it was not discovered till then. The objects in the tomb tell us about King Akhetnaten's wealth and power though the Theban Priesthood of Amun had destroyed most of the king's city Amurna, and his personal material goods. Tutankhamen was Akhenaten's son by his second wife. Tutankhamen had married his stepmother's daughter, his stepsister.

7. **Machu Pichu:** Hiram Bingham's persistence got him the reward in finding this well protected monument that survived the Spanish plunder of South America. The Inca Emperor Pachacuti built it in 1450 CE using acoustic engineering, till then unheard of. It was built deliberately in isolation on a vertical ridge above white water torrents. It had an intact urban plan with quarters for clans, stone staircases with some having polygonal faces with upto 12 sides and hundreds of agricultural terraces down the vertical slopes. The granite stones touch perfectly without any gap. The proud Incas fiercely guarded their secrets with this Machu Pichu. It has important astronomical markers like the intiwatana (hitching past the sun), sun temple and so on. The Incas had priest relatives called amautas who were poets, architects, astronomers and mathematicians.

8. **Pompeii** (1748, Southern Italy): On August 24th of 79 CE, there was a massive volcanic eruption at Mt. Vesuvius that buried Pompeii. The region was volcanic and its patron goddess was Venus. Flowers and trellises were everywhere. Their paintings show luscious fruits hanging on trees, fish gaping from Pompeian mosaic with the Temple crowning the height of the city above Sarno River. Vesuvius buried not only Pompeii but the nearby Herculaneum city also. The Emperor Titus came down to Compania to see the devastation. The Spanish King Bourbon, Charles III sent many Pompeian sculptures to Spain in 1748. He set

up royal franchises for excavations. Whole buildings with excellent paintings on walls were found in tact. Roman architecture was at its peak. Its art collections are the best examples of Roman art. It was Pliny the Younger who was eye-witness to the eruption and described the event. It was called Plinian eruption.

9. **Dead Sea Scrolls:** the Ruins of Qumran was where the Dead Sea Scrolls were found accidentally by two Bedouin shepherds, young boys, in a cave. Wadi Qumran (dry river bed) was surrounded by cliffs and caves. The scrolls date back to 250 BCE to 1st century CE, providing a perspective on Jewish religious sects of that period. It was also closely connected with Israel's statehood. Rome was destroying Jerusalem around 70 CE. Nero's abuses were unchecked after his teacher Seneca died and his old advisor Burrus also died. Nero was not interested in ruling the state. Queen Boudica stirred up her Britons in the north of Britannia and burned Roman cities. Then Julius Civilis led a revolt in Batavia (Netherlands) and the eastern province of Judea, a powder-keg of the Jews, hated Roman Yoke and rebelled under the Sicarii or zealots. Pliny described the Essenes of Qumran on the rebellion of Jerusalem. He mentions the balsam trade from the area. The Oasis of En Gedi had the balsam secretion from healing saps. The Dead Sea was called Lake Asphaltitis. In 66-70 CE, the Jews wrapped their sacred writings, some, hundreds of years old, along with commentaries by Rabbis and lifted them from Synagogues around Judea and the second Temple itself. They were placed in safe hands, or disguised in merchant carts bound for the desert of Qumran. It was then that the Emperor Titus burnt Jerusalem. Thus the scriptures in sheepskin, suitably wrapped, were placed in the caves of Qumran. More than 1000 such scrolls were found in tact, written in Hebrew, Aramaic and Greek. The oldest were in Hebrew around 600 BCE, later modified into an early form of aramaic Hebrew. The Hebrew alphabets were themselves borrowed from Phoenicians. One document is in copper scroll. Since 1947, the eleven major caves of Qumran have yielded these scrolls 40% of which were in tact in clay jars.

10. The Scrolls have a chequered history between Jordan, Israel and USA. All have now been printed and available and the Scrolls are in the hands of Yale University. The Scrolls include the Torah, Law as in the Genesis and Nevi'im, Prophets as in Isiah, Histories as in Samuel, Writings as in Psalms, almost the whole of Jewish Canon, and at least one book of Isaiah, fully preserved. These Biblical Books were later on adopted as the Old Testament. The Bedouin boys Mohammad and his cousin were responsible for this find.

11. **Thera, Aegean Bronze Age:** Spyridon Marinatos, the archaeologist, was digging with workers near the village Akrotiri. He saw in the trench, held by a worker, a perfectly preserved Minoan Stirrup Vase with a unique decoration of blue on

white, a dolphin motif. He along with his fellow archaeologist Christos Doumas, unearthed a whole city buried by volcanic eruption. The destroyed Minoan fleet was also unearthed. This was probably the Atlantis written by Plato in Timaeus. The original island was mostly submerged by volcanic eruption and earthquakes and now only a small island remains. Thera is easily the most preserved prehistoric site in Europe of the Aegean Civilization. The eruption was in 1620 BCE. Block after block of 2-3 storied houses have been excavated (about 2.5 acres and more was to be dug up later) which are in tact with lovely paintings. Plumbing and drainage systems were all found and the houses well preserved. The frescoes too show the high level of art and civilization. Trade of emery with Egypt is also seen as evidence. Minoan paintings can be seen in Egyptian tombs of Rakhmire and Senmut that show Minoans bringing materials from Crete in vessels with other items like bullheads venerating both religions. Ancient pre-dynastic Egyptian stone vessels (pre- 3000 BCE) made of diorite are found in Crete in the Minoan Age (2100-1500 BCE). Emery from Crete was traded with Egypt. The hardest material after diamond, emery was used in polishing stone in Egyptian tombs.

12. **Olduvai Gorge**, the key to human evolution: Louis and Mary Leakey excavated at Olduvai near two gorges. Mary saw teeth of a hominid and the skull was dated to 1.7 million years. Due to geology and plate tectonics, the African Great Rift Zone is an ideal place for human origins. In 1974, Donald Johnson found 'Lucy', belonging to the Australopithic human family. In 1981, Eugene Dubois found the incomplete human remains of the Java man in Indonesia. Raymond Dart had already found the fossilized Taung baby skull embedded in limestone in 1924. The geology and Rift Zone often includes obsidian for tool making because of volcanic activity. Obsidian is volcanic glass good for cutting and weapons. Basalt is another material. In 1929, Leakey had found a high density of flaked black obsidian tool fragments littered at Kariandusi in Kenya. In 2000, a new female infant was found (Lucy's daughter) in Dikkia, Ethiopia.

13. **Tomb of 10000 warriors, China:** in 1974, farmers were digging a well when they found a treasure of warriors in different poses of martial arts, about 8000 of them, over an area covering 21 sq. miles in the Lishan Hill of the Han Dynasty. This was created by a Qin Dynasty emperor for his tomb. These terracotta figures surrounded the central tomb between the rivers Yangtze and Yellow. This was Lintong near Xian in Shaanxi Province. Zheng Qin (259-210 BCE) was the emperor whose tomb it was. He was known as 'the Tiger of Qin', later known as Qin Shi Huangdi. Huangdi is the generic name for 'emperor'. He was ruthless and brought unity in China. A bronze tablet from 221 BCE says-'In the 26th year of Qin's reign, all the feudal states were merged by his majesty. Civilians are now in peace,

the Huangdi title is claimed for the emperor's great achievement. The ministers Zhuang and Wan are thus instructed to 'standardize and unify measurements which cause confusion'. The tomb mound itself is more than the size of three football fields and a height of 140 feet (14 floors). Liquid mercury was used for replicating rivers of China- because of this full excavation has been impeded. By 206 BCE, after half a century of reign, the empire was broken up. The grand historian Sima Qian (100 BCE) wrote that 700,000 men were transported to the spot, began digging and shaping Mt. Li…Replicas of palaces, scenic towers…as well as rare utensils were brought to fill up the tomb. 30-40000 artefacts were kept in this tomb. Bronze and other metal objects were there. A 30 metre structure with multiple staircases was excavated at the centre of the tomb in 2007.

Let us now look at some of the archaeological expeditions in the world. Nabonidus who succeeded Nebuchadnezzar to the throne in Babylon in 555 BCE ordered excavations of the sites of ruined temples to find out the names of their builders. He found 18 cubits below the pavement, the foundation stone of Naram-Sin, Grandson of Sargon of Akkad, which for 3200 years no king had seen. (This was 1500 years overestimated).

In many Pyramids there were no hieroglyphs and it is conjectured that Egyptians of those times were of a different religion from their countrymen and hence did not have any inscription in hieroglyphs.

Sumerians came in waves from another country entering Mesopotamia in 3500 BCE, displacing a primitive people. Researchers now believe that these were the Dravidian Tamils from India in view of ethnic similarities and in language with the Tamils. They settled in southern Mesopotamia, built canals and reservoirs for irrigation. They filled the sea for extending the land and erected famed cities like Ur, Nippur, Uruk, Lagash and others. They were a sophisticated people but in time they were buried by a swarm of invaders. In 2400 BCE, a Semitic race from the west marched to Sumer under Sargon I and established the Akkadian Empire unifying all Mesopotamia under one rule. One of them, Hammurabi in 1750 BCE, united them once again after the Sumerians regained control, three generations after Sargon I.

Along the Tigris in the north, a new power, Assyria, rose in 1200 BCE. They were the cousins of Babylonians. They achieved complete dominion over Mesopotamia by the 9th century BCE. Babylonians are considered by researchers to be Aryan settlers from India as also were the Assyrians, the descendents of Kshatriya kings of India.

Hammurabi made Babylon his capital of the Mesopotamian Empire that included most of Sumer. Then Assyrians overran the empire after decades of Hammurabi and in 699 BCE, Sennacherib resolved the problem by destroying the city. The cities of Sumer and Babylonia were built with mudbricks as also baked bricks and mostly they used sun-dried mud. The Procession Street of Babylon had murals of lions on the side walls indicating the Indian connection as there were no lions in that area and only India and central Africa had them. The hieroglyphs also were similar to the script of Mohenjo-Daro Harappa.

The Babylonians buried their dead in large jars (adults) and shallow elliptical bowls of pottery (children). This again is similar to the practice of Tamils in ancient India as has been found from excavations at Arikamedu and other areas of the Tamil country. The Bull and lion are standard motifs for them as it was for the Tamils. Similar was the bull's head from the king's grave at Ur. The Old Testament enshrined Ur's name as the birthplace of Abraham. Ur belonged to the pre-Sumerian period. This also suggests migration of the Tamils to Sumeria via Ur and Abraham's move to Egypt and Canaan. The list of kings of Sumer, name a group of mythological kings of antideluvian days and then the dynasties that ruled after the Flood. The first dynasty ruled around 2500 BCE for 250 years. Afterwards, sovereignty passed to other cities like Lagash etc. Then the non-Sumerian, Sargon of Akkad, came and conquered the city-states in 2350 BCE. The third dynasty held sway between 2123-2011 BCE. The founder of the third dynasty was Ur Nammu or Ur Engur. Two short inscriptions on stone in the premises of the Moon Golden Temple records dedications to Ur Nammu, Nannar (god of the city of Ur). Ur Nammu was a builder and built defences around the city of 26 feet height and a rampart of brick of 77' base (3/4ths of a mileX ½ mile area). The Sumerians claimed divine powers and the royal palace fittingly placed within the sacred area under Nannar's protection and its founding marked by the same ritual as that of the Temple.

Before the Spanish invasion of South America, the Indian civilization was of a high order of sophistication both in the south and north. The Incas ruled in Peru, the Aztecs in Upper Mexico (*astika* in Sanskrit meaning the devout became Aztec). These South American cities are thought to belong to a race long anterior to those living at the time of the Spanish conquest. Modern researchers believe them to be the Hindus from India, especially the Brahmin Iyers of South India (Ayer). They had a high culture and civilization. The idols found there during excavations were those of Hindu gods and goddesses Ganesha, Shiva, Durga and others. The wise man of Ebun said, 'In ancient times, our fathers burned the sacred resin-pom- and by the fragrant smoke their prayers were wafted to their god whose home was the sun'. Apparently, these are the fragrant incense sticks used in temples and homes of India even today during prayer offerings.

## Vedic Tradition and World Religions

The Aztecs of Mexico did not know who built their wonderful cities-Tenochtitlon, Tula, Cholula and Teotihualin- or where they came from, what language they spoke or where they had gone. They gave the name Toltec to their forgotten arts and building skills. These people then drifted to Mayan, and other civilizations over time. Their language was Nahautl. Their teachings have a common goal- a personal freedom and belief in the human mind changed to self-love and self-acceptance. There is no absolute right or wrong, good or bad, except in the human mind, and the Santa Claus and gods, they create in their own image. Their wisdom is based on the mastery of awareness, of transformation and of intent. The one leads to the other. Parallels to these could be seen in the Hindu philosophy and way of life. The Toltecs disappeared 200 years before the Aztecs settled in the city of Mexico. Their codices were burned by the Spanish. The Toltecs were said to be the origin of civilization.

In the 8th century, they came from the north and settled in Tula, north of Mexico City. They were experts in the smelting of metal and stone carving was their speciality. Their culture disappeared in the 12th century, probably overran by a second wave of people, the Chichimecas, who also disappeared and Mexico entered a dark age until the Aztecs came to power in the 1300s. They lasted for 200 years until the Spanish invasion for plunder and religious conversion. The word Toltec meant 'master builder' or 'artist'. They built the Pyramids at Teoti'huacan. They had deep spiritual understanding and knowledge of astronomy with systems of government, and agriculture. The great Pyramid of the sun and moon are connected by a mile long Avenue of the Dead, bordered by numerous temple platforms. In 500 CE, it was home to some 200,000 people and they lasted for more than 500 years, longer than its contemporary, Rome. By 700 CE, a great fire burnt most of the buildings.

Quetzalcoatl, the feathered serpent, was their major deity, the god of morning and evening stars. Toltecs brought a culture that changed the fear based on love. As an artist of the spirit, the Toltecs followed no rules, had no belief systems, and no leaders to obey. Happiness was a result of love and acceptance flowing out of him and knows that there is an endless supply of love in him. The universe was filled with light from billions of suns. This light was the messenger that carries the message of creation to the whole universe. This messenger was the 'nagual', and the physical parts of the universe was the 'tonal'. They brought the idea of 'dreaming'. Their objective was to control the mind. This dreaming appears to be the 'maya' of the Hindus that hides reality from us due to ignorance.

The mastery of intent was the mastery of love. The Toltec exploration of his life is like a serpent; waiting for the prey is like a jaguar. Like the jaguar, the eagle also hunts and is prey to no other. That way one becomes the master of intent. The Toltec surrendered his attachment to what he knew and believed. Relinquishing attachments to all concepts about anything and everything in creation is the biggest challenge. He may have desires, only that he has no attachments to the outcome. He knows that everything he believes is the truth and a lie. His favourite song:

Live in the abundance of the universe.
Live with a wide open heart.
Live a spiritual life.
Live in unlimited happiness.
Live as an artist of the spirit.
Live in gratitude for the gifts.
Live in healthy relationships.
Live in love.
Live in truth in relationships.
Live with the child within.
Surrender unto the infinite.

One can easily perceive the Hindu philosophy and way of life in the Toltec's way. In fact researchers have affirmed that the Toltecs, the Aztecs, the Mayans, and the Incas were all Hindu settlers that reached South America after touching California. Hindus have always been peace loving and that is why there have been repeated invasions from the Moghuls, Europeans and the British into India from time immemorial. This was also a reason for their settling in various parts of the world from pre-historic times. Similarly, the South American settlers could not stand up to the powerful Spanish invaders or conquistadors and the latter's onslaught, decimated the local Indians and only those converted natives could survive. This was also because of detachment from the fruits of action and living a life of love and truth like the Hindus.

We shall now study some of the mysteries and monuments of the world:

**The Stonehenge** of Salisbury, England, was used by the Druids, a caste of Celtic priests, 3000-5000 BCE. The monument of stones laid across a circle oriented towards the midsummer solstice sunrise had astronomical ramifications. Druids showed their belief that we incarnated time and time again and that we come from other galaxies, the stones being a symbol of this reality. Recently, another coastal area in England revealed stone formations as in Stonehenge.

**Easter Island** in the Pacific had Moai as their inhabitants. The Moai blocks of stone with inscriptions in Rongo Rongo, a script almost identical with the Mohenjo-Daro script, ranged from 4 feet to 72 feet long and 13 tons to 165 tons in weight. Only 288 of the 887 stones are at their final resting place. The Moais are known as the inhabitants of Rapa Nui. Only 26 wooden tablets with Rongo Rongo inscriptions exist now. Chile has annexed this island that is 2000 miles away and its population is about 3800 today. How these heavy stones were cut and put in place is a mystery like those of the Pyramids or the Tamil Temples.

**Shangrila (Shambala)** is in Tibet in the midst of the Himalayas. Beings from outer space are said to have inhabited this place of peace. Sanskrit is said to have originated here and all the initial Buddhist texts were in this language. A yogi went in search of Shangrila, so the story goes, and met a holy man who initiated him in *kalachakra* which then made its way to Tibet in 1026. Shambala is since known in Tibet. Tibetan texts describe the 'hidden land' in detail. In the centre lay the *kalapa* (*kalabam* in Tamil), the capital and the king's palace. The shambala inhabitants have been using aircraft and cars and shuttle between underground tunnels. They had clairvoyance and moved at great speeds.

**Atlantis**- the Santorini Island of the Greeks is said to be part of the submerged continent of Atlantis as per Plato and this extended into the Caribbean Islands and the Yucatan Peninsula (Plato in Timaeus and Critias). The two have told Socrates about Atlantis and its Pyramids and other mysteries now under the sea. This continent from 50000 years went under the sea during the last glacial period about 12-15000 years ago. They were technologically very advanced but were destroyed because of overuse of resources as is happening in the world now.

1. Dr Ray Brown explored a Pyramid on the sea floor off Bahamas under water and found a huge Pyramid with a crystal at the top. The crystal and metal devices found there were taken to Florida and they suggested amplified energy in them. 2. Dr Mansan Valentine photographed and published roads and buildings found off Bikini Islands where many underwater ruins were found. 3. A huge 11 room Pyramid was found 10000 feet under water in the mid-Atlantic with a large crystal top, reported by Tony Benlk. 4. In 1977, a huge Pyramid was found off Cay Sal in the Bahamas, photographed by the Air Marshall's expedition, about 150 feet underwater. The Pyramid was 650 feet high. The surrounding water was lit by sparkling white water flowing out of the openings and surrounded by green water, instead of black, normally found at such depths. 5. Boris Astuma led a Soviet expedition in which was found a sunken city about 400 miles off Portugal with buildings made of strong concrete and plastics. The remains of streets suggested the use of monorails. 6. Heinrich Schliemann who found the remains of Troy, left a written account of the discovery of a bronze vase with a metal unknown to scientists, in the Priam Treasure. Inside it are glyphs in Phoenician stating that it was from King Chronos of Atlantis. Identical pottery was found in Bolivia.

Like Lemuria, Atlantis went under the sea in three cataclysms between 50000-12000 years ago. 11,500 years ago, dramatic planetary events sank and shifted continents and Sumerian texts give clues to all this. Polar tilts that occur periodically appear to be the cause for this. In fact the North Pole has shifted substantially from its original position according to scientists. Also, like in Lemuria, people lived long lives and were tall (8-12 ') and in Lemuria 5-6 ft. Genesis speaks of giants. Skeletons of men of 8-12 feet have been unearthed by archaeologists. Spanish Conquistadors also spoke of such giants around the Andes. They harnessed gravitation and electro-magnetic forces and used crystals to focus these energies.

Edgar Cayce suggests that Atlanteans possessed atomic power and radioactive forces. It is also believed that Atlantis was populated by extra-terrestrials from Andromeda and probably knew how to harness these forces. Pyramids were the focal points of their civilization. They did not bury their dead but cremated them like the Hindus. Pyramids were used for healing. They used special vehicles like aircraft and missiles for eliminating enemies. This is similar to what is described in ancient Sanskrit texts about different astras or missiles and *Pushpakavimana*.

**Lemuria:** The Lemurians were said to be spiritual and peaceful people. Known as Mu to the west and Kumari to Indians, it was close to Shangrila where Sanskrit came from. The Essenes and Gnostics date back to this period. Wise men ruled the country. They had their religious ceremonies and marriage with one person and the family was the centre of life. All were equal and prosperity was shared by all. Most writings on Mu are in Sanskrit. Their culture lasted for about 15,000 years and partly perished when part of the continent went under the sea in a number of geological convulsions. *Bavishya Puranam* gives details of the seven mountains, rivers and so on. The civilization continues in the Tamil Nadu and in India at large to this day. (For more details, please see *History of Ancient India* by this author).

**Extraterrestrials (ETO):** Metrodorus of Chios said in the 4th century BCE, 'To suppose that earth is the only populated world in infinite space is as absurd as to believe in an entire field sown with millet, only one grain will grow'. Though extraterrestrials visit periodically, the details are deliberately suppressed by western powers.

**The Crystal Skulls:** Mitchell Hodges found in 1924, old crystal skulls that were 5000-36000 years old. It appears that he bid for them in a British auction at Sothebys in 1943. 15 skulls were in the Andes and they were palpably to use for electromagnetic and other purposes. These skulls had kinetic energy and are said to move on their own. Nick Nocarino had these skulls that gave off brilliant prisms of light. They exhibit enormous energy (the Shanara skull) with tremendous healing power. These are probably left by extraterrestrial visitors. In 1938, stone discs were found in China. The Dropa people left these discs with information to be recounted by them. They are like the crystal skulls. 22 Beijing skulls were also found there in the caves. In all 716 discs have been found but not much is known about them due to Chinese secrecy.

**The Ica Stones:** The Icas are the people from the Pampa Colorada in Peru. Javier Cabrera, a physician, collected from an illiterate farmer, stones with images of a fish carved on them. The farmer said that he found them in a cave and later sold many such stones to him and other tourists. These ancient stones are made of andesite, a hard gray to black volcanic rock, covered with oxidation/varnish. His collection depicts pictures of natives doing medical procedures on patients- brain transplants, heart transplants, surgery showing blood vessels, acupuncture and so on- procedures that are only now being used. There are also images of maps showing earth from an aerial view with continent masses as existed 13 million years ago. They also show Atlantis and Lemuria. Many animals like the dinosaur are also there on the stones. A large stone shows the hemispheres of a planet having intelligent life and space travel capacity. Dr Cabrera believed that Pampa Colorada was the alien spaceport that was used with a form of electromagnetic energy to propel their ships. The Pampa has huge iron deposits that may be the cause of electromagnetic activity. 15,000 stones were there, most of which were in Dr Carrera's museum.

**Piri Reis maps** of Charles Hapgood: in 1929, historians found a map on gazelle skin that was drawn in 1513 by Piri Reis, an admiral of the Turkish fleet. He says that he copied and compiled the data from a large number of source maps dating back to the 4th century BCE or earlier. This map clearly shows the northern coastline of Antartica. Only in 4000 BCE or much earlier, it was not covered in ice but since then it is full of ice, miles deep. The map is so accurate but at that point of time they did not have technology for such accuracy in maps. Hapgood suggests that the Minoans and Phoenicians passed on such charts and these were collected and studied at the library of Alexandria. The US airforce has confirmed the accuracy of the map. Only a highly civilized people from outside could have drawn the map as from far above in space only could such clear information could be obtained and at that time, people did not have that technology. Clearly, only aerial surveillance could have helped create such a map. It was probably drawn by a people from the Andromeda galaxy 12,000 years ago and given to the Atlanteans.

In fact, maps have been found from the 14th century showing Greenland in ice, joining of Alaska and Siberia that were since separated. Nazca pictograms have been found in

Peru extending to miles in the shape of birds etc. These could be distinguished from the air only. Ancient people called the Nazca are said to have made these pictograms that abound everywhere including a large human figure in a space suit. This 'Giant of Atacama' stands 390 feet tall and has lines surrounding it like the Nazca. In 1900, Greek divers found a shipwreck off the island of Antikythera at a depth of 150 feet. Apart from pottery and jewellery, they found a huge mechanism dated to 87 BCE. Such a complex mechanism does not exist on earth. Apparently, it is from outside. There are 20 different gears with markings of sun and the moon and the zodiac. The gears turned annually to indicate different positions of the planets.

**Pyramids:** the large stones in pyramids were kept in position using anti-gravity rods from large spaceships, the only possible explanation for such things. As yet, we do not have a mechanism to lift and place such heavy and large stones at elevated places or even for moving on the ground. Many have reported being cured of their illness like migraine, arthritis etc., after visiting the Pyramids. The room below the Sphinx is said to contain the Ark of the Covenant, though so far it has not been found. The Pyramids were not just used as tombs but to show the entire life cycle and reincarnation, if we go by the artefacts found in them. Such pyramids are common throughout the world. The stone lid of a Sarcophagus in a pyramid shows (Mayan King Pacal) a man wearing a space helmet at the control panel.

The pyramids, including the Mayan and Incan ones, show that large pieces of stone weighing many tons in weight are laid precisely that even a pin cannot enter the joints. Clearly, they seem to be the work of extra-terrestrials. Elijah is said to have 'went up to heaven' in a 'chariot of fire'. Such stories abound in Sanskrit and Tamil epics like the Tamil Nayanmars being transported in a blaze of light to heaven described in the *Thevaram*.

**Crop Circles:** These are found all over the world with precise circles appearing overnight in England, South America and other places.

# References:
1. Ten Discoveries that Rewrote History- Patrick Hunt, Archaeologist, Stanford University, Plume, Penguin group.
2. Great Adventures in Archaeology- Robert Silverberg, Bison Books, University of Nebraska Press.
3. Hindu America - Toltec Wisdom Book- Allan Hardman, Adams Media, Ma., Avon.

4. Secrets and Mysteries- Sylvia Browne, Hay House Inc., Read Tracy Press.
5. The Vedas- Paramacharya Sri Chandrasekhara Saraswati, Bharatiya Vidya Bhavan, Mumbai.
6. History of Ancient India- A Reappraisal- Ramakrishnan Srinivasan, 2nd edition, SriSri Publications, Bengaluru, 2015.

# CHAPTER 22
# AFTERWORD

Thus far, we have studied the origins of world religions and how they followed one from the earlier one. Just as nothing comes into being on its own, religions too appeared one after another starting with the most ancient of human traditions, the Hindu Tradition generally known as *sanatana dharma* or the Eternal Tradition in the west. Most researchers are agreed that the oldest object of worship is the Shiva Linga of the Hindus known to the west as Phallus worship. The Linga is shaped in the form of the male and female reproductive organs, the base pedestal being the female and the stone phallus the male. These Lingas have been found all over the world by archaeologists including South America, China, Australia, Europe and other areas. The Rome Museum has many such Lingas unearthed by Spanish archaeologists in the Vatican area in recent years. It is actually a fertility symbol and was part sun and nature worship throughout the world in pre-historic times. Even Emperor Constantine in the 4th century CE was a sun worshipper known at that time as *sol invictus*. Some 2500 years ago, the Greeks were worshipping the phallus as evidenced by mention in the Greek Plays of Aristophanes and others.

In the beginnings of civilization, the world population was very small and scattered over different river systems. People were concerned with the security of their clan and propitiated the sun and moon and for agriculture, the fertility gods. While it will be rather speculative to suggest that extra terrestrials first started human civilization in the world, it is impossible to pinpoint any specific evidence in this regard. In the foregoing chapters we have studied various practices of people in different parts of the world and how religions evolved. In this regard, it would be worth our while to consider some general pointers on the subject.

We have found that all religions have a common denominator of principles and ethical systems. These include commandments like do not kill, love your neighbour, speak the truth, have compassion, do not injure others, and live a virtuous life of kindness, caring and sharing. Some of the conclusions may here be listed for study:

# Vedic Tradition and World Religions

1. A religious ethic may be based on a profound awareness of god as the creator to whom people are accountable. The expressions may vary from one to the other religions.
2. Morality may be the expression of an internal principle of cosmic truth. The Hindu Sanatana Dharma, the code of Manu is linked to a cosmic order. *Rta* in Sanskrit signifies such a cosmic order though it has other connotations like truth, duty, virtue and so on.
3. The main thrust of a religious ethic may be the maintenance, transformation and/or perfecting society.
4. The primary purpose of the moral path, on the other hand, may be the attainment of an individual experience.
5. Religions differ in their view of the resources upon which people can draw to achieve their goals.
6. Religions vary in their adaptability to social change

While these are generalities, we may list a few of the particular commonalities in the development of religions. These are:

1. Safety and survival of the community. For this people chose to pray to nature like the sun and the moon so that they are protected from marauding groups from other areas and to protect their crop.
2. Since they realized that children are born by the union of men and women they chose the organs of reproduction as the gods of fertility and accordingly the phallus with the pedestal came to be venerated.
3. It was the Hindus, the oldest people of the civilized world that came up with this form of worship and this continues to the present day in India.
4. Religion and religious practices thus started around this symbol and developed in different parts of the world.
5. Virtue was the basis of all such religious development that was exemplified by the practice of *sanatana dharma*. This simply postulated that people should be truthful and righteous; not harm others and other such prescriptions. It was clearly a way of life.

Here it is useful to mention the recent excavations in Sri Lanka where a 2 ton weapon (*gadai*), apparently used by Hanuman 6000 years ago and mentioned in the Ramayana, was found that required two cranes to lift from deep under the earth. It is found in an excellent state of preservation without rust or decay and it is so large that Hanuman must have been very huge to have been able to carry it around. There have been many such things found in the world like the placing of a huge stone weighing 150 tonnes or more in place in pyramids and temples as mentioned in earlier chapters of

## Afterword

this book. Apparently such things are incredible but true. Unfortunately the Moguls and Christian missionaries have destroyed thousands of documents and ancient texts besides the Library of Alexandria in the course of their marauding missions in the world. To this should be added the submergence of large areas from continents like Lemuria and Atlantis and consequently we have been left with only scarce evidence on the subject of ancient civilizations.

The west has seen in recent times, a shift from religion to non-religious philosophies that took agnosticism to the centre-stage. Atheism too was spoken of by scientists and others but this had the possibility of becoming a religion like communism. That is why great thinkers like Bertrand Russell, Huxley and others preferred to remain agnostic that neither affirmed god nor denied it. For them human progress was more important and for this the concept of god was found unnecessary. Technological progress was seen to be combined with a virtuous social order for the survival of mankind. Technology poses questions that did not exist in earlier times.

Religions need to be flexible and adapt newer challenges and needs if they are to serve human survival. It need not touch on the Hindu's Self-Realisation or the Buddhist Nirvana or Japanese Satori as they are essentially for the few ascetic souls. Before people evolve to such levels they have first to pass through lower levels of experience. Islam, and to some extent Christianity, however are at their crossroad as rigid rules become incompatible in a technology driven world. Here, we must note that it is only the Eternal Tradition of the Hindus that has said at the end of every invocation or other texts like the Upanishads, 'May all the peoples of the world be peaceful and prosperous' or *sarve janah sukinoh bhavantu*. Also they end with the word 'peace' repeated three times (*Om Shantih, Shantih, Shantih*) in all the texts. No other religion anywhere in the world has such prayers in their holy books.

We conclude this dissertation with the words of Benjamin Franklin who put it succinctly by describing the principles on which the American Dream can fructify:

1. That there is One God who made all things.
2. That He governs the world by His Providence.
3. That He ought to be worshipped with adoration, prayer, and thanks-giving.
4. But that the most acceptable service of God is doing good to men.
5. That the Soul is immortal.
6. And that God will certainly reward virtue and punish vice, either here or hereafter.

He had also listed the virtues that include temperance, silence, resolution, frugality, industry, sincerity, justice, moderation, cleanliness, chastity, and humility. There could not have been a better way of explaining the principles of the Vedic Tradition for people to follow irrespective of their faith. This is what this author has always emphasized- Follow your faith at home or place of worship but at all other places interact with people as brothers and sisters, the way in which Swamy Vivekananda addressed the Chicago Parliament of Religions in 1899 and for which he got a standing ovation from the audience.

## References:
1. History of Ancient India- A reappraisal- Ramakrishnan Srinivasan, 2nd edition, SriSri Publications, Bengaluru, 2015.
2. The Vedas- Acharya Chandrasekhara Saraswati, Bharatiya Vidya Bhavan, Mumbai.
3. Ten Discoveries that Rewrote History- Patrick Hunt, Archaeologist, Stanford University, Plume, Penguin group.
4. Great Adventures in Archaeology- Robert Silverberg, Bison Books, University of Nebraska Press.
5. Science, Philosophy and Religion- Ramakrishnan Srinivasan, Citadel, Calcutta.

The Art of Living

&

The International Association
for Human Values

**Transforming Lives...**

The Founder

## Gurudev Sri Sri Ravi Shankar

Gurudev Sri Sri Ravi Shankar is a universally revered spiritual and humanitarian leader. His vision of a violence-free, stress-free society through the reawakening of human values has inspired millions to broaden their spheres of responsibility and work towards the betterment of the world. Born in 1956 in southern India, Sri Sri was often found deep in meditation as a child. At the age of four, he astonished his teachers by reciting the *Bhagwad Gita,* an ancient Sanskrit scripture. He has always had the unique gift of presenting the deepest truths in the simplest of words.

Sri Sri established the Art of Living, an educational and humanitarian Non-Governmental Organisation that works in special consultative status with the Economic and Social Council (ECOSOC) of the United Nations in 1981. Present in over 155 countries, it formulates and implements lasting solutions to conflicts and issues faced by individuals, communities and nations. In 1997, he founded the International Association for Human Values (IAHV) to foster human values and lead sustainable development projects. Sri Sri has reached out to more than 300 million people worldwide through personal interactions, public events, teachings, Art of Living workshops and humanitarian initiatives. He has brought to the masses ancient practices which were traditionally kept exclusive, and has designed many self development techniques which can easily be integrated into daily life to calm the mind and instill confidence and enthusiasm. One of Sri Sri's most unique offerings to the world is the *Sudarshan Kriya,* a powerful breathing technique that facilitates physical, mental, emotional and social well-being.

Numerous honours have been bestowed upon Sri Sri, including the Order of the Pole Star (the highest state honour in Mongolia), the Peter the Great Award (Russian Federation), the Sant Shri Dnyaneshwara World Peace Prize (India) and the Global Humanitarian Award (USA). Sri Sri has addressed several international forums, including the United Nations Millennium World Peace Summit (2000), the World Economic Forum (2001, 2003) and several parliaments across the globe.

# The Art of Living

## In Service Around The World

The largest volunteer-based network in the world, with a wide range of social, cultural and spiritual activities, the Art of Living has reached out to over 300 million people from all walks of life, since 1982. A non-profit, educational, humanitarian organization, it is committed to creating peace from the level of the individual upwards, and fostering human values within the global community. Currently, the Art of Living service projects and educational programmes are carried out in over 155 countries. The organisation works in special consultative status with the Economic and Social Council (ECOSOC) of the United Nations, participating in a variety of committees and activities related to health and conflict resolution.

### Stress Elimination Programmes

Holistic Development of Body, Mind & Spirit The Art of Living programmes are a combination of the best of ancient wisdom and modern science. They cater to every age group - children, youth, adults and every section of society – rural communities, governments, corporate houses, etc. Emphasizing holistic living and personal self-development, the programmes facilitate the complete blossoming of an individual's full potential. The cornerstone of all our workshops is the Sudarshan Kriya, a unique, potent breathing practice.

- The Art of Living Course - Happiness Program (for 18+ years old)
- The Art of Living Silence Program
- Sahaj Samadhi Meditation
- Divya Samaaj ka Nirmaan (DSN)
- The All Round Training in Excellence (ART Excel)
- The Youth Empowerment Seminar (YES!) (for 15-18 year old)
- The Prison Programme
- Achieving Personal Excellence Program (APEX)
- Sri Sri Yoga www.srisriyoga.in

# International Centres

**INDIA**
21st km, Kanakapura Road Udayapura
Bangalore – 560 082
Karnataka
Telephone : +91 80 67262626/27/28
Email : info@vvmvp.org

**CANADA**
13 Infinity Road
St. Mathieu du Parc
Quebec G0x 1n0
Telephone : +819- 532-3328
Fax : +819-532-2033
Email : artdevivre@artofliving.org

**GERMANY**
Bad Antogast 1
D - 77728 Oppenau.
Telephone : +49 7804-910 923
Fax : +49 7804-910 924
Email : artofliving.germany@t-online.de

www.srisriravishankar.org
www.artofliving.org
www.iahv.org
www.5h.org